SUBMARINER

SUBMARINER

BY
CAPTAIN JOHN COOTE
ROYAL NAVY

W. W. NORTON & COMPANY
NEW YORK · LONDON

To the memory of

CAPTAIN ROBERT BOYD
DSO★, DSC, ROYAL NAVY

– a hard act to follow

Library of Congress Cataloguing in Publication Data

Coote, J. O. (John O.)
   Submariner / by John Coote.—1st American ed.
      p.   cm.
   Includes index.

   1. World War, 1939–45—Naval operations—Submarine.   2. World
War, 1939–45—Naval operations, British.   3. World War, 1939–45—
Personal narratives, British.   4. Coote, J. O. (John O.)
5. Submarine boat captains—Great Britain—Biography.   I. Title.
D784.G7C66   1992   91–25063
940.54′51′0941—dc20   CIP

ISBN: 0–393–03074–1

W. W. Norton & Company, Inc., 500 Fifth Avenue, New York, N.Y. 10110
W. W. Norton & Company, Ltd., 10 Coptic Street, London WC1A 1PU
                  1   2   3   4   5   6   7   8   9   0

CONTENTS

FOREWORD

by Admiral I. J. (Pete) Galantin, USN(Rtd)

In 1940, before the U.S. entered World War II, Commander James Fife, USN, was embarked as an Observer in HMS *Triumph* based on Alexandria, under the command of Lieutenant-Commander 'Sammy' Woods. His mission was to get first-hand experience of British wartime submarine operations that might translate into improved materiel and personnel readiness of our own subs. There was little to learn on the technical side but much to emulate in the skills and daring of Royal Navy submariners. Alas, those qualities were not immediately transferable to a U.S. force whose pre-war mission and training were misdirected.

At any rate, from this experience and the excellent performance of British submarines under his operational control the South-West Pacific, Rear Admiral Fife when he rose to be the Commander, Submarine Force, Atlantic Fleet (COMSUBLANT) seemed to many of us to be anglophile to the point of preferring the British pronunciation "sub-már-in-er" to the American "sub-mar-een-er". As one of his staff, I suggested that we resolve this light-hearted impasse by adopting a new word, "submarinist", denoting a trained, highly skilled master of our arcane speciality.

The Admiral did not like the word, but I think it fits Johnnie Coote. To the qualities of leadership, decisiveness, attention to detail and acceptance of responsibility which are essential to successful submariners, he adds uncommon energy, initiative and innovation, plus a rare gift of expresssion that is enjoyable throughout this lively and fascinating account of submarine duty in war and peace.

My own entry into submarine duty was in 1936 when Commander Scott Umsted, USN, was in charge of our submarine school at New London, Connecticut on the Thames River. In World War I he served in one of our L-class submarines (450 ton displacement) which operated out of Bantry Bay, Ireland. To expand his students' knowledge of submarines beyond the narrow bounds of a hardware-oriented course, he required that we read and report on six books concerning submarines. American writings on the subject were so limited that we had to turn to British and German authors to meet the requirement. We did know that the first use of a submersible in war was in the United States. A Connecticut Yankee, David Bushnell, had built a one-man, hand-propelled submersible which unsuccessfully attacked Admiral Howe's flagship, HMS *Eagle*, at anchor in New York harbor in 1776.

Considering that the United Kingdom now operates both nuclear-powered attack and deterrent (ballistic missile) submarines, and that her navy was first to use nuclear submarines in combat, with consequent great impact on the Falklands War, it is well to recall the precarious origin of her submarine arm.

In the nineteenth century it was Britain's naval policy to avoid introducing new weapons which could make existing armament obsolete. This was especially pertinent to the submarine, for it was quickly recognized as the chief threat to Britain's naval superiority. In 1899 Great Britain, Germany and Russia were willing to abolish submarines, but the U.S. and France were opposed to giving up the weapon that favoured inferior naval powers. Then, after World War I and its evidence of the devastating effect of Germany's unrestricted submarine warfare, when 7 million tons of shipping were lost, the U.S. joined the U.K. in proposing abolition of submarines. Britain even argued that the Versailles Treaty's prohibition of U-boats in the German Navy was a first step toward banishing all submarines. France continued her opposition, but in 1930 Great Britain proposed again that submarines be abolished. However, international agreement could be reached only in specifying rules of war to govern submarine operations, rules that were impractical, unenforceable and finally ignored.

No doubt this persistent disinterest contributed to the fact that, by the outbreak of war in 1939, Britain's submarines were not as technically advanced as those of Germany and the U.S., nor as numerous as they should have been. Yet they performed heroically and effectively in some of the world's most difficult submarine operating areas. The Mediterranean is a particularly uncomfortable area for submarines, as Johnnie Coote's experiences in *Untiring* vividly testify. Not great in extent, the Med's generally calm, clear waters are subdivided into even more confined seas. Numerous nearby air and naval bases concentrated the enemy's anti-submarine surveillance and counter-attack, whilst their minefields made the transit of straits and shallow areas extremely hazardous. Even between patrols in Malta, submarines were not spared bombing.

As with the U.S. submarine force, the U.K. submarines suffered a higher percentage of personnel loss than any other branch of her armed forces. Small wonder that a submariner's life expectancy in the Med was little more than 12 months! Of the 76 subs Britain lost, 45 went down in the Med. The larger U.S. boats, built for long-range operations in the Pacific, would probably have fared even worse.

From the inception in Washington of the British Joint Services Mission, the Royal Navy always detailed an outstanding officer to fill its submarine billet. When Johnnie Coote came to that spot in 1955, I was Head of the Submarine Warfare Branch in the Pentagon. It was a time of great activity, promise and anticipation in our submarine force. *Nautilus* had just commenced operations, and soon her astonishing performance at sea gave evidence, not only of the coming revolution in submarine warfare, but portended a revolutionary change in sea-power itself. We had already created what was in effect the first ICBM by mating the Regulus cruise missile with the submarine *Tunny*. We were well on the way to improving that system with a supersonic Regulus and larger submarines, when its technology was overtaken by the Polaris ballistic missile launched from nuclear-powered submarines. Meanwhile, our hydrodynamic test submarine *Albacore* was proving the ideal hull-form for future attack submarines. Another significant development was the steady progress towards a realistic anti-submarine (ASW) capability for our submarines.

Thus Johnnie Coote could not have come on board at a time of greater significance in the evolution of submarine capabilities. His professional competence, keen observations and engaging personality made him a welcome visitor in submarine wardrooms and shoreside headquarters as well. He happily shared the risks and discomforts of special submarine operations at a time when Soviet reaction to intruders in their territorial waters was predictable. That regime had shown its readiness and ability to shoot down aircraft that inadvertently or otherwise violated its airspace. Fortunately its anti-submarine capability was not so well developed. Should a US or British submarine have failed to return from patrol, who would know from what cause – operational accident or hostile action?

I. J. Galantin
Admiral USN

PREFACE

Most of this book was written as a young Lieutenant forty-five years ago during my end-of-war leave in Cornwall. It was my way of telling my father what had happened to me during his 3½ years as a Japanese prisoner. Whatever the early chapters lack in literary merit may be offset by their immediacy in recalling events so soon after they occurred.

Untiring's war was fought in what had become a military backwater and was of no strategic significance. But that did not lessen the offensive spirit of the consummate seaman and inspiring leader to whose memory I have dedicated this book. Like many other successful submarine captains, he was a hard man to beat at poker or liar dice, always weighing up the odds against him with clinical precision. It was his cool judgement, fortified by the luck which favours the Irish and the brave, which brought our thin, riveted hull safely home with the Jolly Roger flying when it sometimes seemed more likely to end up as another name on the submarine war memorial.

We came back with more than our share of memories of those chilling count-downs between a frigate clattering overhead in firm contact and the moment of her pattern detonating. The only boat I know of which survived a direct hit by a depth-charge was USS *Halibut* in the South Pacific. She was saved by it chancing to explode on her deck-gun. The story of her safe return after being damaged beyond repair is modestly told in his *Take Her Deep* (Algonquin Books, 1987) by the writer of the Foreword to these memoirs. He was one of many American submariners who made my tour on liaison to the USN Submarine Forces so enjoyable.

But for the intervention of my skipper on the stormy 1979 Fastnet Race – Eric Swenson of New York publishers W. W. Norton – I would never have dusted off the 1946 manuscript and updated it. In this I was greatly encouraged by Leo Cooper and Tom Hartman, who gave every appearance of enjoying his role as literary slip-fielder.

No book about submarines can safely be written without drawing on the encyclopaedic knowledge of Gus Britton, the archivist at the Submarine Museum. I am deeply grateful to him as the faithful custodian of our heritage.

JOHN COOTE
Titty Hill Farm
June 1991.

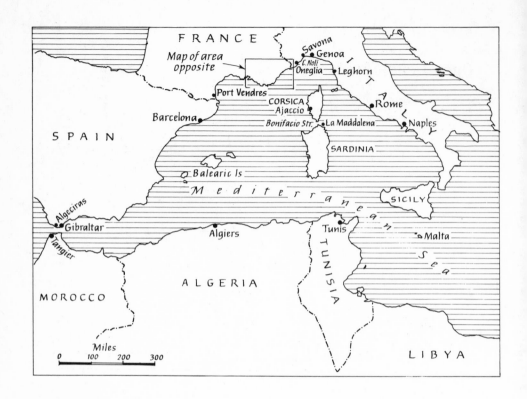

FRANCE

Savona
Genoa
C. Noli
Oneglia
Leghorn

Map of area opposite

Port Vendres

CORSICA
Ajaccio
Bonifacio Str.
La Maddalena

Rome

Naples

Barcelona

SPAIN

SARDINIA

Balearic Is

Mediterranean

SICILY

Algeciras
Gibraltar
Tangier

Algiers

Tunis

Malta

MOROCCO

ALGERIA

TUNISIA

Sea

LIBYA

Miles
0   100   200   300

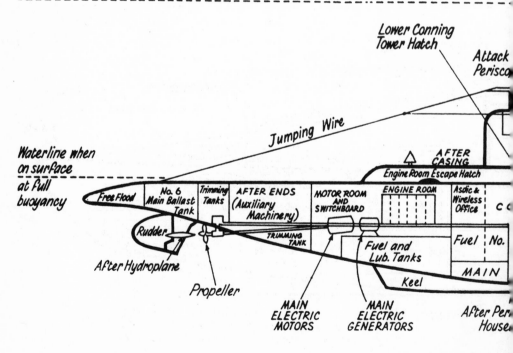

Waterline at periscope depth

Lower Conning
Tower Hatch

Attack
Perisc...

Jumping Wire

AFTER
CASING

Engine Room Escape Hatch

**Waterline when
on surface
at full
buoyancy**

Free Flood

No. 6
Main Ballast
Tank

Trimming
Tanks

AFTER ENDS
(Auxiliary
Machinery)

MOTOR ROOM
AND
SWITCHBOARD

ENGINE ROOM

Asdic &
Wireless
Office

C...

Rudder

TRIMMING
TANK

Fuel and
Lub. Tanks

Fuel

No.

After Hydroplane

Propeller

Keel

MAIN

MAIN
ELECTRIC
MOTORS

MAIN
ELECTRIC
GENERATORS

After Per...
Hous...

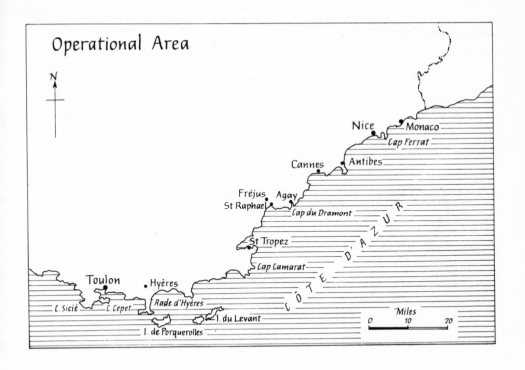

Operational Area

N

Nice • Monaco
Cap Ferrat

Cannes • Antibes

Fréjus • Agay
St Raphael • Cap du Dramont

St Tropez

Cap Camarat

Toulon • Hyères

C. Sicié — C. Cepet — Rade d'Hyères

I. du Levant
I. de Porquerolles

CÔTE D'AZUR

Miles
0   10   20

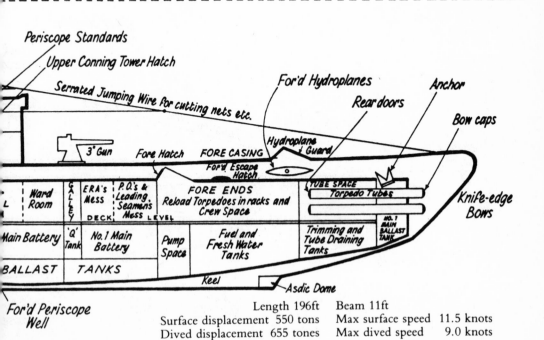

Periscope Standards

Upper Conning Tower Hatch

Serrated Jumping Wire for cutting nets etc.

For'd Hydroplanes

Rear doors

Anchor

Bow caps

3" Gun   Fore Hatch   FORE CASING   Hydroplane Guard

For'd Escape Hatch

Ward Room | GALLEY | ERA's Mess | P.O.'s & Leading Seamens Mess | FORE ENDS Reload Torpedoes in racks and Crew Space | TUBE SPACE Torpedo Tubes

DECK   LEVEL

Knife-edge Bows

Main Battery | 'Q' Tank | No.1 Main Battery | Pump Space | Fuel and Fresh Water Tanks | Trimming and Tube Draining Tanks | NO.1 MAIN BALLAST TANK

BALLAST   TANKS

Keel   Asdic Dome

For'd Periscope Well

Length 196ft   Beam 11ft
Surface displacement 550 tons   Max surface speed 11.5 knots
Dived displacement 655 tones   Max dived speed   9.0 knots

★ 1 ★

DELIVERY TRIP

'Dit-da . . . da-da-dit . . . dit-dit, sir. Changes at 0800.'

Prompted by the helmsman through the voice-pipe, I clacked out the current three-letter identification code on the Aldis lamp towards the unknown challenger, invisible against the opaque background of the Mull of Kintyre. The signalman joined me on the bridge, took over the light and flashed: 'Submarine *Untiring*, bound Holy Loch.' The other ship's light rogered and spelt out: '*Loch Erivale* bound Larne. Maybe we'll see you there. Any luck on your patrol?'

'Ask again in July. We're just starting work-up.'

'Good luck. Dit-da . . . dit-da-dit.'

'AR' meant end of conversation. Bunts, short for bunting-tosser, the signalman, always accented the final dash, as if to hammer home the point. Like 'good*bye*'. Then he clattered down the conning-tower to catnap in a corner well away from the ladder so as to avoid the green ones cascading down the hatch. Approaching a landfall always meant having to dash up and down the conning-tower ladder like a yo-yo to the cry of 'Signalman on the bridge'. If it wasn't for responding to the identification challenge of every passing ship or aircraft, it would be at the whim of the skipper or one of the Officers of the Watch wanting to exchange some in-joke with a chum in one of them.

'Still,' thought Bunts, 'this bastard looks like being better than Nobby Clarke in the old *L23* who prided himself on using biblical quotations when making signals.' After a while he could tap out Deuteronomy on the lamp in his sleep, and the Concordance was more dog-eared than the Signal Book. We had only had three days at sea since leaving the builder's yard on the Tyne, but Bunts had already weighed up the skipper and decided that he was good-oh.

A man of few words, which meant short signals. He had volunteered from the Merchant Navy at the tail-end of the Depression

1

– one of the Hungry Hundred RNR officers who took regular commissions in the Royal Navy for the marriage allowance of five bob a day on top of submarine pay. Serving as a sub-lieutenant in the Royal Navy offered greater security than being the mate in a tramp steamer waiting for a charter from the Baltic Exchange.

At 28, Robert Boyd was the oldest man on board, although Guts Willoughby, the roly-poly Coxswain, looked old enough to be his father – a legacy of unspeakable runs ashore in Kowloon and Wei-Hai-Wei, when he had been the gunlayer in an old 'O'boat and was reputed to have been confined to Rose Cottage for the first time at nineteen. That was the CDA mess, standing for Contracted Diseases Ashore. Two stone heavier and two inches shorter than anyone else on board, one corner of the Chiefs' and P.O.'s mess table had been rounded off to enable him to get his 'chest' past it when turning in on his settee-berth. Now he was the undisputed boss of the lower deck. He was at once Master-at-Arms, ship's doctor, father confessor, took the after planes at Diving Stations and manned the wheel entering and leaving harbour. He enforced the Captain's and First Lieutenant's orders in the uncompromising manner of a bucko mate. Furthermore, he was custodian of the rum, dishing out its daily issue as if it was the dwindling water supply on a life-raft.

The Captain was a most likeable Ulsterman with fair hair and the soft brogue of a native of the Islandmagee, often mistaken for a Canadian. In those days, before 'laid-back' had become part of the language, he was seen as a cool customer. He joined *Untiring* from Malta with a Distinguished Service Cross (DSC) earned as Number One of *Utmost*, the first to complete a full tour of eighteen patrols in the Tenth Flotilla against shrinking odds. The lads reckoned he knew the score and would bring them back with the Jolly Roger flying from the after periscope. As a matter of fact, Bunts was already surreptitiously making one out of the large black flag which he had nicked from the Base signal-tower at Blyth. Later he'd stitch on the white skull and crossbones cut from an officer's pillow-case and wait for the Captain to add solid bars for each enemy ship sunk – red for each warship, white for merchantmen. But those ice-blue seaman's eyes could be relied upon to weigh up the percentages. Not like those crazy Poles who charged their targets with a periscope showing. Nor like stories he heard in the canteen at Blockhouse of a commissioning pep-talk by one Captain who told his Ship's Company that he would prefer a posthumous Victoria Cross to a DSC handed out by the King at Buckingham Palace. He got neither, being lost with all hands on his second patrol. As the signalman, the most Bunts could look for was a mention in despatches and rating up to a Leading Signalman, even if he lasted the whole commission and could pass the exams. So what the hell? But, he admitted to himself, much as he wanted to walk away in one piece, he'd rather do so armed with a few yarns to spin in the pubs around Pompey.

The trip round from the Tyne through the Pentland Firth had been a shambles. When *Untiring* left Blyth at dusk to join her escort for the passage, it was blowing hard from the north-east. Bitterly cold, steep grey seas broke over the forecasing, smashing up against the conning-tower, dousing the inadequately clothed Officer of the Watch and two look-outs before pouring solid down into the control room. *Untiring* was only 550 tons, just 200 feet long and distinctly short on surface buoyancy, so a passage in a gale was just what her totally inexperienced crew did not need. About the only gear properly stowed down below were the four reload Mk. VIII torpedoes firmly held in their racks by steel straps. Just as well, for they weighed over a ton each and all had warheads and pistols fitted. And you could rely on the Coxswain to secure the jars of rum in his store. The fore-ends, just 25 feet long and 12 feet across at their widest point, was home for twenty of the ship's complement of four officers and thirty-two ratings. They shared the space with sacks of vegetables, loaves of bread, tins of shale oil for the torpedoes, seaboots, Ursula suits, Davis Escape gear, sodden once-white submarine sweaters, half-open kitbags, unclaimed personal kit forming the scranbag, partially unlashed hammocks and a pile of balaclavas and stockings knitted by anonymous old ladies in Shropshire – and a heap of greasy wet fenders, spare parts and berthing warps shoved down the torpedo hatch just before sailing. By the time Farne Islands were abeam, the whole lot was awash in an oily goulash, sloshing backwards and forwards across the deck as the boat lurched and shuddered northwards at her best speed of 11 knots. Soon evidence of the young matelots' inability to hold down eight pints of Newcastle brown added to the squalor. And the heads were overflowing.

Notwithstanding the fact that the Flotilla Operations Officer at Blyth had routed her on the surface with a trawler escort as far as the Minches on the West Coast of Scotland, *Untiring* was opened up for diving, ready to drop out of sight if she was threatened by aircraft – friendly or otherwise. No chances could be taken with either, so Bunts was on call to challenge or reply by light. The identification flares at the after-end of the bathtub of a bridge had to be those in force at any given time. Even they didn't guarantee immunity from a keyed-up Wellington pilot dropping out of the low scudding overcast and suddenly seeing his first-ever U-boat right in front of him with Distinguished Service Order (DSO) written all over it. As the submarine and her escort rounded Cape Wrath into relatively sheltered waters next day a queue formed outside the galley at noon.

'What are we on, chef?' asked Titch Bailey, the youngest Ordinary Seaman on board, sent aft from the fore-ends to collect 'dinner' for his mess-mates.

'Roast beef of old England, various veg from my auntie's allotment, roast spuds, RBG and clacker,' said Albert, the two-badge stoker who had volunteered to be cook so as to be out of the watch-bill and pick up a few extra tots from his customers. At home he wasn't even allowed to make toast.

'What's RBG then?'

'Where've you been, son? Never served in a West Country ship before? It's Rich Brahn Gravy, of course. Goes with everything except cornflakes or clacker. For that you have this delicious custard,' he said, ladling leather-skinned ochre sludge all over the pastry. 'Gets your back up a treat, but you're too young to know about such things.'

If only Albert knew, thought Titch, who was love-sick, homesick and seasick – in that order. He would get over the last two, but Bella, his landlady on Tyneside, was for keeps. 'A man-eating nymphomaniac who looks like Betty Grable,' he told Bunts in confidence. Once he had to get out from under her and jump through the window into the garden in the rain, when her husband got back ten minutes early from his night shift at the Yard. 'Threw my kit out after me and it all landed in the compost heap.' Later Bunts met her in the Dog and Partridge and somewhat cooled the envy of the other matelots in the fore-ends.

'More like Bessie Braddock,' he opined. 'Dirty fingernails. Had her hair in curlers. Dressed like a badly lashed-up hammock. You'll have to do better than that, Titch. Besides, she's old enough to be your mum. You know what's the matter with you? You're cunt-struck.'

Titch collected the mess dinners and moved forward to the Petty Officers' mess, the size of a railway sleeping compartment and home for eight senior ratings. There the Coxswain was serving out the rum tot by tot from wicker-covered stone jars.

'Nineteen in the mess. Four under age. Two stopped. That's thirteen tots for your mess, boy,' he said confidently as he slurped the fore-ends' ration of 70-proof Barbados rum into their mess fanny. 'Don't forget, I added three parts of water if Jimmy the One asks you.'

All junior rates were required by King's Regulations and Admiralty Instructions to draw their daily ration of one-eighth of a pint of spirit as watered-down grog. That way it would go sour unless drunk on the spot, so that the daily issue could not be bottled for a future occasion or simply banked as a trade-off for a favour, like procuring a substitute for a duty watch in harbour. But in submarines this particular article in KR and AI, like others, was rarely enforced. The skipper had already let it be known that it was all the same to him if the rum ration was held over during patrol for issue on return to harbour. What with this arrangement and the Coxswain's allowance for spillage – known in the free-masonry of Submarine Coxswains as Swainage – to say nothing of writing off a couple of cracked jars every time a depth-charge landed anywhere in the vicinity, the 'Swain controlled the most valuable commodity on board – even better than blank railway warrants.

Ted Broadbent, the dapper little Chief Engine Room Artificer (ERA), was appointed as Engineer Officer of *Untiring*, for her complement did not allow an officer in that billet. He leant across the mess table with his tot pointed in the direction of the Petty Officer Telegraphist.

'All yours, Sparks. All yours for a couple of B. 182s.'

'What do you know about B. 182s, you ignorant greaser?'

'I know two things about them: one, you're carrying them as spare valves for our wireless transmitter; and, two, I need them for the circuitry of my organ.'

A roar of laughter. The Stoker P.O. choked on his tot at the idea of the Chief ERA electrifying his cock.

'Yours is so small you couldn't even find it, let alone wire it up.'

'Before this commission is over, you'll regret that remark. I refer to the electric organ I am building in my seat-locker. The day we surface after our first depth-charging, we'll have a sing-song, led by me very own organ. But first you've got to come across with the B. 182s. I need them to be able to play chords. Now here's a down-payment. Leave some for my toothache.'

Sparks all but downed the Chief ERA's tot in one, just pulling up somewhere between 'sippers' and 'gulpers', having promised to look into the matter.

Urrrrrrrr . . .

'What the fuck, it's the klaxon,' shouted the Coxswain, jumping out of his mess and charging through the bulkhead door into the Control Room, ready to take over the after-planes on diving.

'Shut main vents. Blow one main ballast,' ordered the unmistakable calm voice of the Captain down the voicepipe. 'Who hit the klaxon push?'

'I may have done, coming down the hatch,' admitted a look-out who'd just been relieved.

'That's why we only execute the order to dive on the second blast of the klaxon,' said the Captain evenly. Then he turned to the look-out: 'Do you know why we do not dive on the first blast of the klaxon, but wait for the second before opening main vents?'

'No sir. It seems to me we'd save a couple of seconds by going down right away.'

'If you'd been with us in *H.43* you'd know the answer to that one.'

H.43 was the 1916-vintage H-boat in which Gus and I and a handful of the crew had served with him for a few months in the anti-submarine training flotilla at Campbeltown before being drafted to the building yard at Tyneside. 'Her electrics were very shaky. One day someone switched on the echo-sounder and a gremlin in the wiring set off the diving klaxon on a long steady note. The watchkeeper on the panel promptly pulled the plug and down we went.'

'What happened to the bridge watchkeepers?'

'Oh, one of them was still hanging on to the periscope standards when we brought her up.'

Early in the morning watch, after an overnight passage through the Western Isles, the horizon ahead started to pale as nautical twilight asserted itself over the Ayrshire coast.

I took bearings on Sanda Island, Rathlin and Ailsa Craig, then brought the boat round to pick up the buoyed channel which would lead *Untiring* to the Cumbraes and Dunoon. A brief increase in the rush of wind being sucked down the conning-tower by the diesel generators told that the intake was being choked by an oilskinned body forcing his way up on to the bridge.

'Control-room, who's coming up the ladder? Have you forgotten that you have to get the Officer of the Watch's permission first?'

'Sorry sir,' said the helmsman.

'It's me,' said the Captain, by now clipped on to the bridge rail. 'But you're right to pull him up on that one. You might just have dived not knowing that I was half-way between the upper and lower lids. It has happened before now. How's it gone during your watch?'

'We've just exchanged challenges with *Loch Erivale* on her way to Larne, and I've altered to 090° as in your Night Orders, sir. She's a lot easier on this course. We nearly got pooped a few times after Skerryvore.'

'I put your fix on the chart before coming up. It's like old times. We are at the crossroads of some of the busiest shipping lanes in the world. When I was an apprentice in the Head Line we always had to tell the Chief Engineer when we sighted Ailsa Craig. To him that meant Clydeside and hame were just around the corner. Then he'd take a swig from the bottle he always carried in his overalls and burst into tears.'

'When do we shut off from diving, sir?'

'Not until we reach the Cumbraes. I know there hasn't been a U-boat attack in these waters since 1940, but you can't be too careful with our birdmen. We're now inside the exercise area used by the Fleet Air Arm from Machrihanish. Just because their pilots wear naval uniforms doesn't mean they know a friendly submarine from the Gosport ferry.'

Two years to the day later, a snorkel-fitted U-boat was to sink an aircraft-carrier right there off the Mull of Kintyre and get away with it.

'I'll take her for a moment. Tell Number One we'll need to muck out down below as best we can before reaching the depot ship. Commander (S) is sure to board us on arrival. I'd hate him to get his shoes covered in puke and rotten cabbage leaves. The worst part is the fore-ends. That's your part-of-ship, so you'd better get the T.I.★ cracking. Also get Number One to draft the on-arrival requirements signal to Captain (S). Don't forget the dental appointment for the Chief ERA. We need him on top line for the work-up.'

Being a small submarine had its advantages. Her surface silhouette was low, which gave her some protection from being jumped at night, whereas a 1,250-ton T-boat on the surface during a calm moonlit night in the Med would be about as conspicuous as a fleet destroyer. *Untiring* was also highly manoeuvrable, surfaced or dived. Since British submarines, unlike any others, fought the War without angled torpedoes, so that the track of each fish on firing was always straight ahead, the ability to slew round and fire from the hip got many a salvo off with a chance, when the clumsier big submarines were left flat-footed as the target slid past the firing-point, or D.A.†

A low silhouette also paid off underwater, presenting a smaller

★ Torpedo Instructor – Petty Officer in charge of the torpedo armament.
† Director Angle – the aim-off needed to put the torpedo on a collision course with the target.

target to enemy. Our smaller ballast tanks could be flooded faster than the big boats. In a trimmed-down state, with ballast tanks already half-full, *Untiring* expected to get under in 20 seconds, which didn't give the bridge watchkeepers time to hang about once the klaxon had gone.

But *Untiring* paid the penalty on the surface, where she was slow and extremely wet, especially prone to being pooped in a following sea. How the standard Type VIIC U-boats maintained patrol on the surface in the North Atlantic in winter, only diving when in close contact with their targets, was the wonder of the British submariners. They were only 20 feet longer than *Untiring* and about 200 tons more displacement, yet they could wind up to 18 knots on the surface – invaluable in running outside the screen of a 10-knot convoy to get ahead for an attack, or for regrouping a wolf-pack.

The Captain mused over these characteristics as the submarine steamed on up the Clyde towards the boom at Dunoon. 'With only 12 knots we'll have only one chance to get off a salvo in a night surface attack and no chance of breaking off a gun action without diving.'

'Suits me,' said Number One, who was the only other officer besides the Captain to have done any war patrols. 'I've had a bellyfull of surfacing for gun action after missing with four fish, then being put down for a bollocking if we didn't get in first strike with the gun.'

Passing Largs, the Captain ordered the boat to be shut down from diving, when all the main vents were cottered shut to prevent being opened by mistake in harbour for that most spectacular of all submarine evolutions: an involuntary dive alongside the depot-ship. All the Captain knew about his boat and her makee-learn crew of young H.O.s* was that they seemed to be in an adequate state of training for a surface passage. The basic drills were understood and could be carried out safely in slow time. The fine tuning, reflex responses, finding the right valves in a darkened compartment and dealing with emergencies instinctively would all have to come together in the next two months of work-up.

The other side of the boom showed the reasons for the gate being kept shut against midget submarine attack. The Tail of the Bank was crowded with the assembly of an obvious troop convoy, probably destined for the Desert via the Cape. *Pasteur* with her vast funnel, *Britannic*, the pride of Liverpool, *Windsor Castle*, *Andes*, the graceful *Empress of Britain* and a dozen others were surrounded by their

---

* Hostilities Only ratings, joined for the duration, mostly conscripted.

escorts, using every available anchor berth between Gourock and Greenock. A Colony Class cruiser flying a Rear Admiral's flag had a swarm of barges and pinnaces from the Escort Group's destroyers and corvettes lying off her quarterdeck ladder.

Probably the convoy briefing is going on, thought the Captain. A couple of Woolworth carriers had their Swordfish and Fulmars ranged on the flight deck. Just about enough to discourage a U-boat making a surface attack, but not worth a prayer against shore-based He 111s or Ju 88s. The next morning the whole armada had vanished, leaving the Tail of the Bank to MacBrayne's paddlewheel ferries and the Clyde puffers.

'*Forth* is calling, Sir,' said Bunts. 'Makes from S3: Welcome to the Third Flotilla. We've been waiting for you. Berth port side aft on *Tantalus*. Request the pleasure of your company to lunch.'

'The old bugger has no need to request the pleasure of my company,' muttered the Captain, who knew Captain (S) in all his moods. 'And I doubt if it'll give me much pleasure, but make back: "Good to be here at last; lunch accepted with pleasure."'

As the casing-party led by the Second Coxswain clambered over the side of the bridge to get breasts and springs ready for going alongside, the Captain had to admit it was good to be here at last, after the frustrations and delays during building. He hoped he was bringing a useful reinforcement to the submarine fleet, but had an uneasy feeling in the pit of his stomach that there might be mechanical as well as personnel bugs to be worked out of *Untiring* before she could give a good account of herself. Vickers Yard at Walker on the Tyne had been pressed into building submarines when its parent yard at Barrow-in-Furness could no longer meet the need to replace heavy losses off Norway and in the Mediterranean which had wiped out almost all the operational boats in the submarine fleet of fifty-two with which the Royal Navy started the War.

To say that the labour force in Tyneside was diluted was an understatement. There was that avoidable but nevertheless fatal battery explosion caused by workmen smoking and using grinders throwing off sparks alongside a ventilation flap marked 'open' when it was shut. This permitted an explosive build-up of hydrogen at the end of a trickle overcharge. It set back our completion date by a month, not helped by a ca'canny (go-slow) by the Geordie workforce whose main preoccupation seemed to be finding enough in their pay packets to punt on the dogs at Gosforth each weekend. Besides, *Untiring* was only the third of a new batch of U-class, involving many modifications, none of them familiar to workmen who were accustomed to building destroyers.

The grapevine alerted *Untiring*'s crew soon after they reported to the Yard that the first boat of the new series, HMS *Vandal*, built at Barrow, had disappeared without trace whilst on independent exercises on the second day of her work-up with the Third Flotilla. She was last seen at dawn by the postman at Loch Ranza at the northern tip of Arran when *Vandal* weighed anchor and proceeded to exercise in an area only four miles square in Kilbrennan Sound at the entrance to Loch Fyne. A passing submarine saw a white smoke candle burning on the surface that afternoon, but thought nothing of it.

To this day no one has found her.

The next boat was *Untamed* which had preceded *Untiring* off the stocks at Tyneside by a month. Offices, girlfriends (or 'parties' as Jack always called them), friendly pubs, boat knowledge, how to get round the Yard for those extras ('rabbits'), clapped-out old pushbikes and the addresses of even cheaper digs were inherited from her. She was our chummy ship, earmarked to end up in the Med together in the Tenth Flotilla. Meanwhile, as *Untiring* cut her generators and slid towards the ample saddle-tanks of *Tantalus*, there was scarcely a man on board who wasn't looking forward to a reunion with his opposite number in *Untamed*. For most they would be the only faces they knew in a whole new world of a depot-ship and sixteen strange submarines, half of them operating off Norway or in the Bay of Biscay and the rest far advanced in their working-up before joining flotillas in the Med or the Far East. *Untiring* would follow them, if she passed the succession of examinations which Captain (S) and his staff had in store for her.

Under the critical eye of Captain (S) and Commander (S) standing at the head of the ladder up to the depot-ship's well-deck, the Captain greased her alongside. A one-bell landing, as American submariners call it: just 'Half-Astern together' then 'Stop' on the engine-room telegraphs to leave the boat precisely alongside the big T-boat, with the periscope standards of the other five boats on the trot all dead in line. No backing and filling, no curses from the motor-room as the operators pushed the big chopper switches in one by one to get the power into the water. The plank was manhandled across to *Tantalus*'s casing, with the Captain first over, followed by Bunts, who doubled as ship's postman and had to get the mail down quick, or else. Or else a kick up the arse from the coxswain and no favours at tot-time. With the Captain safely frog-marched along the depot-ship's promenade deck to the cuddy – Captain's quarters under the quarterdeck – it was time for the lesser members of *Untiring*'s crew to catch up on the gossip from next door, whilst Number One showed Commander (S) quickly through the boat. By now she was about as tidy as a railway station buffet on Saturday night. Still it was an improvement. I spotted a term-mate on *Tantalus*'s bridge.

'Hey, Sandy, where's *Untamed* lying? I've got Peter's old submarine notebook and some other gear he left in the office at the Yard. Besides, he owes me a Pimms.'

Sandy gave a thumbs-down. 'Two days ago. Never surfaced at the end of an A/S exercise off Sanda.'

'Christ,' I thought. 'We passed right by Sanda this morning and there was no one around.'

Had it been fully light we might have seen the four dan-buoys which the escort vessels laid to mark *Untamed*'s resting place in only 164 feet of water, when the hull tapping ceased and the clock told them there was no longer any hope of survivors being found alive.

★ 2 ★

JOB NO. J 6444

'Take the turning down off the main road just by the Royal George pet, and it's the big gates in front of you.'

The tram conductress looked tired and undernourished, but her nonstop Tyneside patter had kept her fares in high spirits all the way down from the city centre. I supposed she lived in one of these rust-red terraced two-up and two-downs in the cobbled streets dropping down to the riverside. She had kept her home going through the Depression, the strikes and now the blitzes. She still scrubbed her front doorstep Persil-white every morning, even in the certain knowledge that the smoke canisters along the pavement would be set off whenever there was a moon and the pall of acrid brown would bring on the baby's cough again. Better that than have Jerry bombers pick out the silver ribbon of the Tyne, as Albert kept telling her before he went away. Silly sod volunteered when he could be knocking back ten pounds a week at the Yard. I wondered how many matelots she had directed to the Yard gates from the tram during the War. That big draft arriving in the late summer of '40 must have told her that the battleship *King George V* was about to commission.

But Jerry never got to hear about it from her, nor from any of her neighbours.

'Be like Dad, keep mum,' said the posters and the Government cartoons at the flicks.

'Second Front Now' walls on either side of the street with broken bottles all along the top led to a pair of massive wrought-iron gates.

'Job number J 6444? That'll be the Submarine Office you want.' The Yard policeman directed me, after noting my shiny new stripes and crumpled uniform. 'Been having a roll in the hay with some Wren, no doubt,' he thought, not knowing about the long night

I'd spent jammed in the corridors of a succession of trains from Gourock to Newcastle Central.

'Submarine Office – Keep Out' it said on the door. Seated at a desk by the window, the Captain was poking irritably at a shaky old office typewriter, surrounded by official OHMS bumph.

'Come aboard to join, Sir', I reported.

'About time, too, Coote. I've had being my own Correspondence Officer. No one else has joined yet and I can't cope with this baby Caxton any longer. Finish off this letter to Captain (S) now and tell me all about *H 43*. Does she still work? Found that Censor stamp yet? Or the missing page in the cypher manual?' The Captain harked back to last winter and handing over his only previous command.

'She looks like going on for ever – so long as she stays above 90 feet. The new management has settled in well. We never did find that Censor stamp but won one from the Padre of the depot ship: we borrowed the missing page from *L 23* for the CB muster, so there won't be any come-back on either count. Your successor, Shaver Swanston, is not the most popular officer in the mess ashore in Campbeltown. He had occasion to throw one of his leather seaboots at me. I ducked, and that was the end of the large ornamental mirror in the ante-room. Gus fell off the plank late one night after mustering the stocks and cooking the Wine Books. He had to go to sea on crutches for a week. In short, everything is pretty much as you left it. They all send their best to you.

'But tell me about J 6444. I don't even know if she's an S-boat or a U-class.'

'She's a "U", due to complete at the end of March. Looks to be on time. She's already launched and will be the next but one to leave the yard.'

'Does she get a name or number?' I asked, since at that time Their Lordships were running short of names for new-construction submarines and were simply calling them by their numbers in the signal pendant list.

'Until I got this Confidential Admiralty Fleet Order last week we were HMS *P 59*: but now all boats are to have names, by command of Winston, who suggested *Tiptoe* and *Tulip* for *T*-boats. We're to be *Untiring*.'

The door flew open at that moment and a scruffy Sub-Lieutenant burst in. His uniform was beyond further repair – a lot of leather patches held together by small bits of the original doeskin.

'For God's sake, Johnnie, don't say you've come to join *Untamed*?'

'No, you're quite safe. I'm *Untiring*.'

Peter Acworth had been in the same Submarine Training Class at

Blyth. Presently two other officers drifted in with whoops of 'beer' and tapped the firkin standing on the filing cabinet, which ruled out any serious work between 1130 and lunch at noon. But the time was not wasted, since the talk was of kingston valves, main motor field regulators, telemotor pumps, HP air compressors, battery ventilation systems and the rest of the submarine jigsaw which each fresh crew had to learn from scratch in the context of their own boat.

Down in our boat the workmen clattered down from their lunch. Over seventy of them – double the size of the crew which would eventually serve in her. They were all working in separate gangs under orders from different bowler-hatted chargemen, without any supervised co-ordination to allow the different jobs to be progressed without getting in each other's way. The smallest compartment in the boat – the tube space, 14 feet long and all but filled by the inboard ends of four torpedo tubes – had three gangs working in it. There were those assembling the firing gear on the tubes, trying to juggle heavy components into nearly inaccessible positions over the tubes with less headroom than any miner would accept. These men were back to back with electricians trying to run cables to the foreplane housing indicators. In their turn they were walking all over a gang fitting the Asdic oscillator into a small trim tank. Sitting on the deck just outside the tube space, there was an old man studying form in Course Jottings in the *Sporting Pink* through a magnifying glass.

'Try "Go Slow" in the 2.30 at Wetherby,' the Captain suggested, 'and double it with the 10–1 I'll give you if we leave the Yard on time. What else do you do, with respect?'

The old man didn't look up. He hawked and shook the newspaper for a better view of the small print. 'Well, if you were to ask me nicely, I'd tell you that. And if you would shift the firing gear gang, the electricians and the Asdic fitters from the fucking tube space, I'll get on with my job in there. Meanwhile perhaps you'll kindly bugger off and get on with whatever you're paid to do except get in the way.'

Back in the office the Captain put me on to the job of sorting out the heap of correspondence and store-notes. Spares and portable fixtures for the submarine arriving bit by bit from sub-contractors all over the country were unpacked and locked in a lay-apart store till they were needed. Like collecting a Meccano set in the wrong order. The complex Naval Storekeeping procedure was reduced to destroying half the notes, signing the remainder and returning them to their originators. Meanwhile the Stoker Petty Officer was already there unpacking crates, sorting out and checking the gear. The idea was that 18 months later he could produce at five minutes' notice a Washer I.R. Pattern 6431A from the depths of a bilge in the submarine.

My place behind the typewriter was soon taken by Gus King, the navigator. He had been an Actuary – 'actually' – in peacetime and was handy when it came to working out the Laws of Probability at poker dice. Beyond that, his love of classical music, lugubrious appearance, introspective manner and studied courtesy were at odds with his new way of life. But the sailors respected him as they would a Benedictine friar who unaccountably wandered into their messdeck.

Our First Lieutenant, Don Wilson, the Australian unknown quantity, appeared, a heavily built sheep farmer with a Player's Navy Cut beard and hands like briar roots.

'The troops have arrived and they're just going to come in one by one to meet the officers.'

That explained the awful racket coming from the next-door room. The ship's company of thirty ratings had come up from Blockhouse the night before and were getting to know one another whilst awaiting further orders. This consisted largely of swopping lies about their relationships with barmaids in Pompey, interspersed by lurid claims of knee-tremblers in the corridors of the train on the way up during the night.

'Got it in as we went through York.'

The first one to come in was, naturally, the Coxswain. Chief Petty Officer Willoughby had a face like someone who'd gone the distance with Popeye and was ready for more. He shook hands with Number One who ran through the set questions.

'What was your last submarine, Willoughby?'

'You mean before *H 43*, sir?' What a twat, he thought, my papers have been here for days. The next question will be to ask if I have a family. But he retained himself. '*Clyde*, sir. I was in her for three years and five months. With Commander Perkins and then Lootenant-Commander Parker-Bailey. Gunlayer and then Second Cox'n.'

The Coxswain then introduced the remainder of the Ship's Company.

'Petty Officer Sims, sir.'

A wiry little Torpedo Gunner's Mate wearing a Distinguished Service Medal (DSM) stood before Number One.

'How do you do, T.I.?' Torpedo Gunner's Mates were called by the initials of their old rating of Torpedo Instructor, usually contracted to 'I'. 'What was your last submarine?'

'This is my first, sir.'

His accent placed his home nearby on the banks of the Tyne – a Geordie.

'Volunteer?'

'Not me, sir, luffed in at HMS *Vernon* while doing the Torpedo Gunner's Mate's course.' So, for openers we had to live with an unwilling conscript in charge of our main armament.

'You see, sir, I was a destroyer rating. My job was to sink U-boats, not to serve in the buggers.'

His service documents bore this out. His DSM had been won in an Escort Group in the Atlantic, whilst previously he had been promoted in the field for some mad escapade ashore with a landing party at Narvik. There had to be misgivings about him. Geordies, natives of Tyneside, are slow to make up their minds, but when they do, nothing will shift their prejudices.

'Broadbent, the Chief Engine Room Artificer, sir.'

No problems here. A sharp, bald-headed little man of unimpeachable professional antecedents. Forget the fact that he played the cornet. Maybe Gus could help here.

One by one they were put through the hoop. The overriding impression was of a bunch of kids concealing their bewilderment behind a braggadocio they'd picked up in the canteen at Fort Blockhouse. Over half were conscripts. Only four, including the Coxswain and the Chief ERA, had ever done a war patrol. All but three were Hostilities Only ratings.

'Now, lads,' Number One swung into his collective pep-talk after the formalities were over. 'To many of you, the idea of serving in submarines is not one which crossed your minds a few months ago. I am authorized to tell you that anyone who has been drafted into submarines and wants to revert to General Service has a perfect right to do so after 90 days. All you have to do is get the Coxswain to forward your request to the Captain through me.'

Loud laughter. 'Some chance!' shouted someone at the back of the room.

'No, fair dinkum. That's what the rules say.'

Untamed was due to leave the Yard and go down the river for her first sea dive next morning.

Looking around the Control Room during her farewell party, it was easy to see that it was the third year of the War. The paintwork was blotchy and thin. The ladder up to the conning-tower hatch was made of iron, not brass, as were most of the fittings. Rust was already showing. A visitor from the Admiralty was in the middle of telling Gus the story of the disappearance of *Vandal*, a sister ship commissioned at Barrow-in-Furness two months previously.

1 The author as a Lieutenant during work-up in *Untiring*, Scotland, 1942. Note acceptable wartime uniform.

2 HMS *Repulse* escorting a troop convoy including the P & O liner *Strathnaver* southwards across the Bay of Biscay, a rare break from Scapa Flow and points north.

3 Loading 3″ ammunition in Holy Loch, 1943.

4 *Untiring*, May, 1944, with Jolly Roger showing thirteen ships sunk.

'It wasn't till next morning they noticed she was gone. A chap from the Flotilla Torpedo Office in the depot ship wanted to have a look at a fitting in her tube space but couldn't find her lying alongside either of the depot ships. So he went down to the Staff office and asked them where she was lying. And that was the first time she had been missed. Apparently she was doing an independent exercise up Inchmarnock Water the day before, due back alongside that night. But she never came back and no one noticed it.'

Next morning *Untiring* was alone alongside with first call on men and materials needed for her completion. The job of teaching the crew something about their boat now began in earnest.

'Now then,' the Chief ERA said in a preliminary lecture to all the junior rates, 'if something goes wrong in a motor car you can stop, get out and call for help; or drive it into the hedge. On this bastard the brakes are not too good. There may only be ten seconds between doing the right thing and going on down. You can't wait for the friendly Automobile Association patrolman to arrive on his bike and sidecar. When we're dived it's the nearest man to the source of an emergency who will be the one most likely to save his shipmates' lives. Sea water coming in through even a small hole under the pressure at periscope depth – around 15lbs/sq inch – will flood a compartment in no time. The pressure increases in direct proportion to the depth, so the further one goes down out of control due to flooding, the quicker the water comes in.'

He took them through each compartment in turn, starting for'ard. Through the next bulkhead were the Petty Officers' and Engine Room Artificers' Messes, and the galley range in the after corner. Each was the same size and layout as the Wardroom; one fore-and-aft bunk against the ship's side and two athwartships settee-bunks either side of a narrow mess table. The backs of the settee-bunks swing up to form another two athwartships bunks. These messes were about seven feet square. Each held five men off watch using the hot bunk system to give everyone a place to sleep.

'They seem to be coming on well,' the Cox'n reported to Number One a week later. 'Mind you, I've got my eye on three or four skates who see this as a quiet number and have no intention of going to sea. They'll draw their lodging allowance until the last day and then slap in with a compassionate request to help out with the birth of their next baby in nine months' time, or something like that. Don't worry, sir, a couple of them will have been disqualified from further service in submarines by the doctor after a close look at their wedding tackle. And don't forget, a warrant to DQs★ is a one-way ticket back to General Service. We'll be all right on the day.'

The Yard now began to make real progress too. The battery tanks, under the crew-space and control room, had been coated with rosbonite, as protection against acid spilt from the cells, and squared by the joiners. From the battery-shed 224 cells, each shoulder-high and eighteen inches square, were lowered down into the boat, packed into position in two battery tanks by long wooden wedges. Once linked up, they were ready for the charging trials using the boat's own engines and generators, all to be carried out under the supervision of the Yard.

Finally our primitive air-warning radar was wired up.

O'Hara snorted. 'Have you seen Charlie Tulk who's in charge of that contraption? Reckon he doesn't know his arse from his elbow. Used to be a dustman. Well, it doesn't matter, the set's useless anyway. Couldn't pick up the Old Head of Kinsale before you hit it. Useless. Except for one thing, Titch. If you get a girl to stand in front of it when it's transmitting she's safe for 24 hours. Better than two condoms on top of each other. The Wrens at the Signal School believe it.'

Titch blushed, wondering how Mick would go about persuading a girl to climb up the periscope standards to get in front of the antenna. She'd show her knickers in the process.

After the battery explosion and go-slow campaign, the Captain sent everyone away on a week's leave partly to prevent the lads from thumping a few dockyard mateys in the Royal George during the dinner hour.

On return from leave, the ship's company found an amazing change. The shattered remains of No. 1 battery had been replaced and most of the structural damage in the living accommodation repaired. The shipyard gangs were obviously working overtime, and the boat was recognizable as a submarine.

'What happened?' I asked Number One.

'Air raid. It works wonders. Been going at it for dear life ever since.'

At nights the painters were giving the boat a few more freshening coats of flat white, usually sprayed on with cheerful disregard for any fitting which should be left unpainted. One painter even covered an area which had a workman's coat hanging on a peg against it, spraying the whole coat white with the rest of the bulkhead. It turned out to be his own.

★ Detention Quarters

Finally came the sure sign that completion was near at hand. The chargehand of joiners was in the office every lunchtime discussing details with Number One.

'An extra bookshelf for the Wardroom? Mahogany's very scarce,' the chargehand said, whilst Number One absent-mindedly topped up his Scotch, '. . . that's enough, sir, thank you. But I've got some put aside for the Captain's cabin in the cruiser; I think we might manage it.'

The engine trials and further charging trials were all completed satisfactorily, and then came the first movement under power down the river for the basin dive in a dock.

Number One caught his trim quickly enough. He turned to the Stoker Petty Officer waiting with his blank new trim-book to record the exact amount in each tank.

'Take all-round readings, Stoker P.O. Then we'll surface and go back to the Yard.'

The dive had washed all the waste and left-over material out of the casing, and also burnished the paintwork so that externally she looked ready for an Admiral's inspection with her brass ensign-staff and tiddley lettering around the conning-tower picking out her name.

Once alongside, an army of charladies swarmed aboard and worked through the night with a few joiners to give the whole boat a showroom' polish. The ensign was broken out and the boat ceased to be J 6444 and became H M Submarine *Untiring*, henceforth referred to as 'she', not 'it'.

The programme allowed two days to embark stores and ammunition. Put like that it sounded easy, but the lads worked till after dark on both days. All the gear which the Stoker Petty Officer had been brooding over for the past three months in the Lay-Apart Store had to be carried down on board and stowed neatly and securely. The locked trucks from the Victualling Yard at Preston were broken open and the mess traps, crockery and galley utensils uncrated and portioned out amongst the messes. Blankets, warm clothing, ropes and wires, binoculars, tins of dehydrated peas and meat, 3-inch shells, clocks, spare gear for all the auxiliary machinery . . . they all had to be checked on board, sorted out and stowed. Looking at the haphazard fashion in which most of the gear had been stowed, the Captain was philosophical but resigned.

'Only one thing will teach them, and that's a gale between here and Holy Loch. If they're kept out of their hammocks during their watches below to secure stores which have broken adrift, they'll soon get the knack of doing it right next time.'

At six o'clock next morning *Untiring* slipped and proceeded down the river for the last time. Gangs of workmen gave a cheer.

On the bridge no one had much to say, chiefly due to the effects of the farewell party the night before. The Captain was screwing up all his concentration on negotiating the twists and turns of the river and missing the tugs which rushed madly backwards and forwards without regard to the Rule of the Road.

Clear of the breakwaters, the Captain ordered 'Patrol Routine' and two watches went below. The generator revolutions went up and she started lifting to a nasty ground swell over the bar. Down in the Control Room several faces were drained of colour.

Fortunately the first leg of the trip was soon over, with *Untiring* secured alongside the submarine training base at Blyth to embark torpedoes for the trip round the coast of Scotland. The sailing orders specified that the boat be 'in all respects ready for war', so a full armament was embarked, with warheads.

'In case of a chance encounter with a U-boat at night or if the *Tirpitz* should break out of Trondheim,' the Captain explained, with fingers crossed.

After the trip round from Blyth to Holy Loch, even the excitement of joining an operational flotilla did little for *Untiring's* morale. Coming so soon after the disappearance of *Vandal* in Kilbrennan Sound, *Untamed's* unexplained loss hit the crew like a shock wave. Even the quiet example of the Captain and the Coxswain's knockabout humour could not bottle it up. The lads were rattled.

'Shit, there must be something wrong with this new group of boats when the first two have bought it without going anywhere near Jerry,' the Outside Wrecker* told the Chief ERA. 'What mods have we that the earlier "U"s did not incorporate?'

'The only one that matters is the tappet hydroplane control gear, but that wouldn't sink a boat. Anyway, just you do your job and we'll be OK.'

'Funny, I heard the skipper saying that he thought that nearly half our wartime losses are accidents that could just as easily happen in peace. You have near misses all the time.'

'Not in a boat where the Outside Staff are on top of their job.'

The crew were not given long enough alongside the depot ship to brood over *Untamed's* loss. After unloading personal kit, we slipped and proceeded up to the Gare Loch for the acceptance dive – the final formality before the submarine was taken over from the builders.

The Captain took the dive very gently, but even so several

---

* The ERA responsible for all moving parts outside the engine room.

members of the ship's company seemed to expect the roof to fall in. Metcalfe, the Outside ERA in charge of the diving panel in the Control Room, was sweating and made his reports unnecessarily loudly. He handled the vent-levers as though he was afraid of snapping them off. She took on a fairly sharp bow-down angle on diving, hovered at 24 feet for a few seconds with all eyes on the bubble, and then straightened out level at periscope depth. Despite all the unspoken forebodings, the boat behaved like a perfect lady. It was too shallow to go below sixty feet, but everything functioned smoothly down to that depth, so the Inspecting Officer pronounced himself satisfied and gave the order to surface. On the way back to the Holy Loch, there was a little ceremony in the wardroom. Vickers' representative produced a certificate for the Captain to sign, officially accepting *Untiring* on behalf of Their Lordships.

'Well, jolly good luck to you, sir.' Mr Brown, the Works Sub-marine Foreman, raised his sherry glass and toasted the ship. It was only the second time he had ever dived in a submarine.

'Will there be a chance of seeing *Untamed* this evening? I'd like to see how she's getting on.'

'No, she's away for the moment,' said the Captain evenly.

Back on board the depot ship the Flotilla Operations Officer outlined the programme ahead.

'Let's see now. Who are you? Oh yes, *Untiring*. Forgive me, but we get so many boats up here I sometimes lose track of them.' Like *Vandal*, the Captain thought grimly. He ran his finger down the chart. 'Yes, working-up patrol in July. You should be ready to sail for the Med end-August after a Norwegian patrol on our nursery slopes. Three months in all, and don't blame us if you don't get much sleep during that time. Four days' leave to each watch either side of your patrol.'

The green scrambler 'phone rang. 'Yes, sir. Liverpool and Glasgow Salvage have been alerted about *Untamed*. They're sending a man up overnight. The Admiralty has ordered that she be raised to find out what went wrong.'

'I hope they do the same for us, only a bit sooner,' the Captain muttered. 'Tell Number One he can pipe normal shore leave, but be ready to slip at 1600 tomorrow with three days' fresh provisions on board. You offload all torpedoes and replace them with four in the racks with blowing-heads. Leave the tubes clear for watershots. The rest of the time's your own.'

Next morning the Coxswain reported to Number One in the wardroom.

'Got one for you this morning, sir. Returned on board drunk, improperly dressed. Committed a nuisance on the quarterdeck and created a disturbance on the mess-deck.'

'Who is it?' Wilson asked wearily.

'Able Seaman O'Hara, sir. Fore-ends' crew. Feeling sorry for himself now. The doctor saw him in the cells this morning and declared him fit for duty. You could have fooled me. He's got a shiner in one eye and his right hand is the size of a grapefruit. Also two loose teeth. And,' he added, 'a hangover, sir. When will you see him? He's our first defaulter since leaving the Yard. So we have got to do him proud.'

'Ask the T.I. to have the fore-ends cleared up by 1130 and I'll see him then. Any witnesses?'

'Yes, sir. The chef says he happened to be passing at the time. Apart from him, there were just the four stokers from *Upstart* whom he took on in the Argyll Bar in Dunoon. She sailed at 0800 this morning for 14 days at Larne. There's a written report from the Regulating Staff in the depot ship. I'll arrange for their Officer of the Watch last night who greeted him to be down here.'

'No report from the Shore Patrol or the Pier Patrol?'

'No, sir. I gather he had no fight left in him by the time some of the lads from spare crew carried him home. And he managed the quarterdeck ladder from the liberty-boat on his own. Wonderful how you go into auto-pilot at a time like that,' the Cox'n concluded, thinking back to having returned on board unchallenged from the Fleet Club in Kowloon after *Clyde* had won the Flotilla Boxing in '38. Next day he couldn't even recall how he got his points decision over that beer-barrel Chief Stoker from *Olympus*, let alone what happened afterwards.

'What's the scale?'

'Well, sir, KRs say he's got to have a day's pay stopped for being drunk. The rest's up to you. We can't charge him with fighting ashore. No reliable witnesses. He didn't hit the Jaunty or the Officer of the Watch. On the books he returned before leave expired, and we can't charge him with having any booze on board, so he's a bit lucky. No previous offences on his Conduct Sheet here. But he's only been on board three weeks.'

'Well, we'll hear what he's got to say. I don't particularly want to pass him on to the Captain so soon in the commission.'

At 1130 the junior ratings were piped away to early dinners in the depot ship and the Coxswain set the scene for the First Lieutenant's Defaulters. O'Hara was smartly dressed in a neatly pressed uniform, his cap squared off over his short back and sides with the gold 'S' of

'H M Submarines' in his cap tally dead centre over a closed purple right eye. 'Cost you a tot for that lot,' said Charlie Tulk as he fitted him out in his own Sunday Divisions kit for the occasion.

I joined the group as the accused's Divisional Officer, and had a brief word with O'Hara, after reading the report from the depot ship Regulating Office.

'You know that the Officer of the Watch has the final say on whether or not a man is drunk or unfit for duty, so there's not much point arguing the toss over that one.'

'Well, sor. I tink there's been an awful misunderstanding. Perhaps the First Lootenant will see it differently. He's a real gentleman.'

No. I clattered down the forehatch as the Cox'n called everyone to attention and reported: 'One defaulter, sir,' and barked, 'Able Seaman O'Hara . . . Off caps! Two paces forward . . . march.'

He rattled through the charges written in his own spidery hand in HMS *Untiring's* Request and Defaulters Book.

'O'Hara, sir. Able Seaman, D/CX0778259. One, did return on board HMS *Forth* at 2340 drunk. Two, was improperly dressed in that he had no cap and no silk or lanyard and his uniform was dishevelled and torn. Three, did commit a nuisance on the quarterdeck of HMS *Forth*. Four, did create a disturbance in the stokers' mess-deck.'

'What do you have to say to that, O'Hara?' Number One asked, beard jutting out, both hands in his reefer pockets, like Beatty on the cigarette cards.

'Well, sor, he,' pointing at the RNVR Sub-Lieutenant Officer of the Watch in the depot-ship the night before, 'says I was drunk, so that's the end of the matter according to King's Regulations. But it's a hard world, sor. You see, I've been taking these pills for my headaches and perhaps three pints of mild did not agree with them. As for the rest, I tripped over a bollard on the pier, hurt myself and my cap got blown away in the blackout. When I got on the quarterdeck they kept me waiting so long out in the cold that I just could not hold it any longer, and you wouldn't have wanted me to wet my trousers, would you now, sor? I don't know where the stokers' messdeck is, so I can't see how I could have created a disturbance there. It's all due to those pills our village doctor gave me to take to sea.'

'Had you been fighting?'

'Who, me, sor? Not exactly fighting. There was this bunch of stokers off *Upstart* who said that *Untiring* was full of brown-hatters – including you, sor, begging your pardon. I could not let that go.'

'Any witnesses ashore, Cox'n? Stoker Bradshaw, what did you see of this whole affair?'

'Well, sir, Mick – sorry, sir, O'Hara – and me were having a quiet game of dominoes together in the Argyll Bar, all peaceful like, when these four stokers from *Upstart* came in. They were looking for trouble. After that it was like O'Hara said. We felt it was best to return on board quietly, not wanting to break our leave on our first run-ashore together. I was with him when he fell over the bollard. It was pitch dark and raining. I'm surprised he was not more seriously injured.'

Number One offered no comment to this bland recital. Instead he turned to the accused. 'You're lucky, O'Hara, you're not charged with any offences ashore. Would you like the charges stood over until *Upstart* gets back?'

'No, sir, they wouldn't tell the truth. And that's the truth, sor.'

'Did you speak to the Surgeon Lieutenant about the pills when he saw you this morning?'

'No, sor. It so happens I took the last one yesterday evening, and I don't remember their name. I was feeling dizzy after having worked so hard getting those eight fish out of the boat.'

The Officer of the Watch gave formal evidence of Able Seaman O'Hara stumbling on to the quarterdeck, blowing a kiss at the Bo'sun's Mate, pulling down his front and urinating against the wardroom door.

'In my opinion he was drunk, sir. I consider he had been fighting, but there is no Patrol or Police report to support such a charge.'

I had already heard on the lower-deck grapevine that O'Hara was well pleased with his night's work, having evaded the police in the back yard of the pub after thumping the animals from *Upstart* to a standstill.

'I let him go below,' went on the Officer of the Watch, 'because I felt sure his mates would turn him in quietly. Then I heard he was on the rampage on the stokers' messdeck looking for *Upstart's* stokers. So I had the Duty Regulating Petty Officer put him in cells for his own safety.'

'Lieutenant Coote, what opinion have you formed of Able Seaman O'Hara?' the First Lieutenant asked.

'Absolutely first-class, sir. Always keen and smart. On top of his job. I find the charges hard to believe of him. The T.I. also thinks most highly of him. I'm sure this is a lapse which he will regret for as long as we serve together.'

The only regret I have, thought O'Hara as he listened in growing amazement to this eulogy, is that I didn't flatten all four of the fuckers.

'Well, O'Hara, I don't believe a word of it. On the very first occasion we grant leave alongside our operational depot ship, you get involved in a drunken brawl, bring the name of *Untiring* into disrepute and end up in cells. I should put you in the Captain's Report for a heavier punishment than I am empowered to inflict. Next time I shall, and you'll likely end up being sent back to General Service. You can thank your Divisional Officer's fine report that you are being let off lightly this time. One more run-ashore like last night and I'll have your guts for garters. Fined one day's pay for being drunk and ten days' No. 11s★.' Pause. 'And fourteen days' stoppage of grog.'

The Coxswain repeated the sentence as though he was addressing a parade. 'On caps, left turn, double away. Report to me in the Chiefs' and PO's mess.'

Somehow everything was ready for sea when the Captain stepped on board five minutes before sailing time and climbed up on to the bridge.

On the way down the Clyde he explained the programme of independent exercises he had in mind. During the next three days every conceivable breakdown and emergency drill was rehearsed and played back at various speeds until it came close to being second nature. Suddenly we were, for better or worse, a team.

'Charlie,' the Coxswain told the radar operator after he had sat beside him on the wheel for a whole watch, 'as a submarine helmsman you'll make a bloody fine Spitfire pilot. Why did you ever leave the Old Kent Road?'

'Buggered if I know, 'Swain. Let's 'ave another butchers at this 'ere magnetic steering what-ave-yer. It's daft to turn the wheel to the left when you want the boat to go the other way. Corse, somethink technical like the Radar set I'm all about; this steerin' job's for common seamen, not highly skilled men. Oh . . . don't 'it me, Coxswain. It's an offence, and I have witnesses.'

Charlie's knowledge of the Radar set consisted of a five days' course in which he had been taught how to switch it on and look for echoes, though he had no idea of classifying one. He could confidently swing off on the aerial training-wheel for dear life and give the impression of having been taught privately by Sir Robert Watson-Watt. A contact report coming out of his little kiosk at the after end of the control room was greeted with gales of laughter.

Another character who soon emerged was Leading Stoker Putnam,

★ Extra work and drill – almost impossible to enforce in a submarine at sea.

one of the few old-time submarine ratings on board. He volunteered as Cook of the Boat in place of Albert, who was unanimously voted out of the galley and put back in the Watch-bill after the trip round. Putnam believed in real submariners' food. Under his régime the meals got bigger and heavier. His Cornish pasties ('Tiddy oggies') looked and tasted like small rugger balls filled with Irish stew. He did most of his Cordon Bleu cooking after he had had his tot and stood stripped to the waist in the galley singing hymns. After a few minutes the songs of praise would give way to a stream of fo'c'sle language as he reached for a pan that was too hot. Then the hymns would go on: 'Jesus loves me, that I know . . . repent and be saved, you bastards . . . come and get it, you sons of Satan!' he shouted for'ard, 'Grub's up.'

During a lull in the galley, I asked him where he had learnt his hymns.

'Seven years a Salvationist, sir, but the Devil tempted me one week when I was collecting the insurance money. The magistrate gave me the option of joining the Navy or going inside,' he explained simply. He was rolling out some pastry which had the consistency and appearance of asbestos.

'That our supper?'

'No, sir, this is for my special clients. One or two of them gannets in the fore-ends will part with sippers of their bubbly at tot-time tomorrow for this little delicacy. It's an apple pie. A slice costs you sippers, a slab gulpers, and the lot for two tots.'

The work-up ran its pre-ordained course with increasingly difficult dummy attacks against screened targets. The crew's confidence only faltered when they were exposed to a live depth-charge dropped 200 yards away. The detonation and whiplash made us wonder what it would be like when a full pattern landed close by.

Sunday evening alongside the depot-ship gave *Untiring* her first chance to mix with all but one of the other eighteen boats there. *Syrtis* was overdue from a patrol off Norway. Three had just returned from long, blank patrols off the North Cape, protecting the flanks of two Murmansk convoys. *Tactician* was painted olive-green all over, ready to sail for Trincomalee and the Far Eastern flotilla next morning. *Ultimatum* had the cobalt-blue livery of a boat earmarked for the Med. Horse's necks or dark-brown whiskies in hand, all the officers settled down to watch a Pinewood epic about one of our submarines breaking into the Baltic through the Skagerrak. John Mills sweated faintly as the bow of his submarine impaled itself into a heavy underwater wire net which abruptly stopped her progress eastwards.

'Group up. Full astern together,' Lieutenant-Commander Mills barked. The submarine shuddered for an age whilst Able Seaman Attenborough stared helplessly at the tachometer building up to full revolutions on both shafts. Suddenly she jerked clear and backed away from the net. A loud cheer went round the wardroom, at which moment the film snapped and spewed itself on to the deck, the lights came on and there was a rush for the bar.

'Won't be a moment, sir,' the operator reported to the Commander, reaching for his splicer and glue. 'This one gets a lot of running. According to the log it's been shown thirty times in the last two weeks down at Rothesay.'

Lights out again, and our hero's boat plunged forward again towards the net. This time she got half-way through before being brought up all standing. Again she wriggled astern and lined up for her third pass at the growing hole in the anti-submarine net. The roar that greeted her break-through into the Baltic had hardly died away when a voice at the back ordered: 'Mark that spot carefully, pilot. We'll need it for coming out next week.'

He had recently returned from the real thing, when two boats from the flotilla attempted to break into the Skagerrak. His own boat touched off a mine at 250 feet but got home – without her bows. Later it was found that the field had only been laid a week earlier. It featured trailing tentacles hanging down to the seabed which triggered off the mine when tripped by an unfriendly intruder.

So to Larne for two weeks, playing the role of a U-boat attacking the graceful *Philante* as Commodore's ship in a 'convoy' protected by a succession of Western Approaches Escort Groups, limbering up between North Atlantic operations. *Tantalus* and *Upstart* patrolled adjacent areas either side of *Untiring* between Islay and Rathlin, whilst the convoy steamed through. By day in shallow, tide-ripped waters the three submarines had it all their own way, once they found themselves in the grain of the convoy.

But night attacks on the surface seldom came off, even taking full advantage of the low silhouettes of the two U-class. By 1943 our escort groups had high-definition centimetric radars which put the attackers firmly on to their plots from the moment each exercise began.

It was no use asking Charlie for any news from *Untiring's* radar. The first the Captain knew of the escorts was a red light shone at him from close range, the signal to dive and be hunted until three underwater signal charges called it off an hour or more later, ordering the boats up on the surface.

At the wash-up (post-exercise conference) in *Philante* the Convoy

School staff evaluated the preceding three days' exercises. When it came to his turn, our Captain, as usual, wasted few words:

'What you're saying is that it's the same here as it is when you join an inbound convoy from Halifax at 40° West. The first you know of a U-boat by day is when his salvo hits. But on the surface at night I give Jerry no chance, having to operate against your radars.'

'Never mind,' the Number One of *Tantalus* consoled me on the train to Belfast for a late evening run to the Officers' Club, 'neither the Germans nor the Japs have radar worth a damn, so we'll find it a piece of cake when we get there. Have a swig,' he offered, holding out a bottle of Remy Martin. The real thing. Pre-war VSOP Cognac must have cost all of ten bob a bottle duty free. 'Got a corkscrew? No? Well, here goes.'

He lowered the heavy mahogany-framed carriage window by letting up on its strap and shaped to break the neck of the bottle across the sill.

'Oh no, it's too good for that. Besides we're coming into a station,' Sandy pointed out as the rattler came to a halt at Glynn. 'Excuse me, Station Master, do you have a corkscrew?'

'Now, it happens I don't, sir. If only you'd asked yesterday.'

'Perhaps you could ring our next stop and alert them?'

'That'll be Belfast Central, sir. But I'll see what I can do.'

A shrill peep, and the Will Hay train lumbered on its way along the western shores of Loch Larne. Ten minutes later it pulled into Ballycarry. There on the platform, resplendent in top hat, frock coat, gold braid and frogging stood the Station Master.

'Which of you gentlemen needed the corkscrew?' he asked, walking along the train, holding a silver salver with four glasses, a deer-horn-handled corkscrew and a small pitcher of water.

Ten minutes and three stiff drinks later, the Station Master whistled the train away, waved his little green flag and lifted his top hat to his new friends in First Class. Such gentlemen!

At the barrier at Belfast a Chief Petty Officer from the Shore Patrol was waiting.

'Are there any officers or ratings here from *Untiring*? Sorry, sir, but you must return at once. Captain's orders.'

On board, the submarine was being readied for sea. The signal read: 'From S 3 to *Untiring*. Proceed forthwith to Campbeltown so as to arrive not later than 0700 tomorrow Sunday. Report to Naval Officer in Charge.'

Early next morning *Untiring* slipped through the gap between Davaar Island and the mainland into the limpid waters of Campbeltown Loch. There was the conning-tower of a submarine showing just clear of the water between two lifting craft with 'Liverpool and Glasgow Salvage Association' painted on their sides.

The paint on the conning-tower was beginning to peel, but not enough to conceal the number 'P58' or her name – *Untamed*.

Alongside one of the salvage vessels was a small landing craft, to which *Untiring* secured. The NOIC Campbeltown was a passed-over submariner called from retirement to the uninspiring chore of running the port as a base for elementary anti-submarine training. He came down to the wardroom accompanied by Arthur Pitt, the Commanding Officer of the submarine *Taku*, then under refit at Troon, after nearly having her bows blown while penetrating the Skagerrak under a deep minefield.

'Morning, Bobby. You know Pitt?' The Commander introduced the officer appointed by the Admiralty to liaise with the salvage company. 'He's in charge. We'll want a working party of two officers and sixteen ratings to clean up down below in *Untamed*.'

'Why us, sir? My ship's company all have friends in her. They're already pretty shattered by having the two sister ships ahead of us off the line lost with all hands in the Clyde areas.'

'We've thought of that. Your lads won't have to do down below until the bodies have been removed. That's being done by a spare crew working party from *Forth*. They're getting an extra tot before they start. All you have to do is have an officer gather in any Confidential Books or classified signal logs which might be lying around. The others are to collect all personal effects and put them on the deck of the landing craft in separate piles, one for each compartment from which they were removed. Get out all consumable stores and tidy up as best you can. Anything else, Pitt?'

'Yes, sir. The reason we called you over here from Larne is that the salvage team and the divers want a live pattern, a precisely similar boat with the same systems and hull fittings as *Untamed*. So, can we have a sight of your docking plan? I should keep your boys down-below until I give you the word to go on board. That should be in a couple of hours.'

'Do we know what happened to her?'

'Not yet. She completed a straightforward three-hour anti-submarine practice run for training classes aboard *Shemara* on a Sunday forenoon. Clockwork mouse stuff on pre-ordered courses, with buffs streamed and showing on the surface. After a break of three-quarters of an hour on the surface, she was ordered down again for another three hours. Soon afterwards *Shemara* detected her speeding up and heard noises which could have been blowing main ballast. But she did not become unduly worried until an hour later when she got no reply from interrogating charges and failed to surface after being ordered to do so by three charges. All machinery noises ceased at 1745, but a large bubble of air came up at 2212, when it was still light. By the time the divers got down to her there was no sign of life and no response to hull-tapping. It took three days to get the lifting craft up from Liverpool – the same ones used on *Thetis*. Then they used the same method to get her here – heavy wires slung round for'ard and aft and secured tight to the lifting craft's bollards at dead low water. As the tide rose she came off the bottom and the whole party was quickly towed towards shallower water, when *Untamed* grounded and we all waited for the next low water.

'With only a little over 12 feet rise and fall it's not surprising the whole operation took over five weeks from where she sank in 164 feet of water.'

'Don't we know anything about the state of the boat down below?' the Captain asked, as two divers joined the discussion in the wardroom, with a set of hull drawings spread out on the table.

'Well, we know the engine-room is flooded, because one of the Navy divers managed to open the engine-room hatch three days after the accident and the body of their Chief ERA floated out. He had the breathing bag of his Davis escape gear shut off, so had no hope anyway. There were other bodies packed so tightly in the hatch-trunking that they could not shift them, so he dropped the hatch shut. The fore-ends are certainly flooded all the way back to the control-room bulkhead, including the accommodation space. Here are the air samples we've taken after drilling through into each compartment.'

These showed traces of chlorine gas, but no more than would be expected with sea-water having got into the battery tank. The killer was the level of carbon dioxide in the engine room, over $4\frac{1}{2}\%$, enough to render everyone comatose, if not unconscious.

'What we're doing now,' said Pitt, 'is to put an air pressure of 9lbs into each compartment. Then the divers will swim around her bottom to identify which, if any, hull-valves have air escaping through them and thus could have been the cause of her flooding. We've already checked the obvious big openings like the bowcaps and the other hatches. They're all shut.'

'Off you go then,' said the Captain. 'Let us know when you want our help. Number One, detail off the working party. Johnnie, you head for their wireless office and pick up their classified logs and cypher books. Have a good look round the wardroom.'

Presently the divers reported back.

'It's the Ottway log. Seems they withdrew it without the sluice-valve being shut. Only three inches across, but that did it, with seawater pressure at 75lbs per square inch at that depth. Anyway we've driven a plug into the hole, and the pressure's now holding. Now we'll open each hatch in turn and pump out the flooded compartments. Should be clear for you in an hour.'

On *Untiring's* bridge the signalman finished taking a signal from the shore station. Then he looked over at *Untamed*. Black oily water was being sucked by portable pumps through big juddering armoured hoses led out of the forehatch, polluting the loch with an ever-widening slick. The swans seemed to know, gliding clear of the glistening, spreading surface sludge. The spare crew working-party were already down inside the engine room, whilst others were spreading out tarpaulins along the deck of the salvage vessel. The tank-landing craft lying alongside had a row of thirty-five empty coffins on deck.

Presently the salvage vessel's derrick was plumbed over the hatch and the purchase-wire lowered down inside. After a few minutes a man shouted up for them to hoist away. A limp sackload was hauled up out of the hatch and deposited on to a tarpaulin. It was a terribly bloated seaman in overalls, wearing a Davis Escape Set. A sailor with his cap flat a'back and a cigarette drooping out of the corner of his mouth sprinkled disinfectant over him, whilst Lieutenant Pitt searched his clothing to find a few sodden letters and other evidence of identification. The tarpaulin was then wrapped around the body and lifted into a coffin. *Untiring's* working-party stood by and watched as, one by one, they recognized the various friends they had made in Newcastle. After thirty-three bodies had been recovered from the engine-room, our sailors went down below to start sorting out the mess.

Down in the engine room it was half-flooded and smelled pungently of diesel fuel. It was from here that the whole ship's company, except two, whose bodies were yet to be recovered, had gathered to make their vain attempt to escape. They had sat in rows along the top of the engines whilst the compartment had been flooded up as part of the drill before opening the hatch through which they had hoped to get out. But everything was stacked against them. The secret of any successful submarine escape has always depended on getting out as quickly as possible before the atmosphere becomes lethal.

In 1939 the Dunbar-Naismith Committee on Submarine Escape pin-pointed the increasing danger of breathing CO_2 under the sort of pressure needed to equalize a flooded compartment, which is directly proportional to the depth. He postulated that the maximum tolerable limit at 165 feet was a little over $1/2\%$, but *Untamed*'s survivors were sitting there in the cold, dark engine-room inhaling a lethal dose seven times above the limit when the decision was made to start flooding and nine times over when the Chief ERA made his bid to lead them out. Ten of them did not have Davis Escape Sets on. They were found in sealed lockers for'ard. All their wristwatches were stopped at 2217, just a few minutes after the last bubble of air was seen from *Shemara*'s bridge.

That was the moment when the drowning Chief ERA momentarily forced the hatch open, only to have it slam back on him, whilst four others fought desperately to follow him out of the escape trunk.

In the control-room everything was uncannily normal. The boat might just as well be lying alongside the depot-ship from all appearances. No water had got into this compartment, as the watertight doors either side were firmly clipped and all the bulkhead shut-off valves correctly shut. Everything was exactly as it had been left. It was rather like the *Marie Celeste*, right down to the remains of lunch laid out on the wardroom table. Even the brasswork was still fairly bright. I picked up the control-room log:

'1358 Flooded for'ard' with a firm line drawn underneath and the pencil left inside the folded book on the seat locker.

It was written neatly and deliberately, just as the previous entry telling of an alteration of course had been. The watch-keeper who was keeping the log completed his last entry before joining the others in the engine-room, no doubt confident of making good his escape. The pin-up girls in the Wireless Office and over the Asdic control position smiled their fantasy messages. One of the telegraphists had been in the middle of writing a letter:

'. . . coming down the line soon on four days' leave. I can't wait to take you in my arms and tell you how I've missed you. Tell Bert and the others at the Crown to stand by with a few big pints for me.'

Binoculars, sextants, watches and other valuable stores were mustered in the wardroom. There the signalman had wasted no time and already had the wine-locker open. The cans of beer were in prime condition. Broadbent, the Chief ERA, appeared and helped himself to a drink.

'I've got just the thing to go with your beer. I've just picked this out of the engine-room bilges. Nothing like a good fresh lobster.'

He held up what looked like a shrivelled colourless human hand with dirty fingernails.

'All right, all right,' the Signalman said, looking closely at it, 'but what about the mayonnaise to go with it?'

There didn't seem to be much point in trying to match it up with one of the bodies already crated up on the landing-craft's deck, so I told the Chief to throw the hand over the side.

'Maybe the swans will enjoy it.'

Meanwhile the fore-hatch was unshipped, by burning off its hinges, and salvage men went down to find the other two bodies there. The first one was hoisted out in a sack and laid out on a tarpaulin. A seaman sprayed disinfectant over him as if he were watering a window-box. He was wearing a sub-lieutenant's reefer, so had to be Peter Acworth, for, apart from that, he was completely unrecognizable, as most of us would be without any hair.

The other body down in the fore-end was the T.I. Both were sitting in the Chiefs' and P.O's mess, apparently without having made any effort to escape. A strong smell of shale oil pervaded the fetid atmosphere. Loaves of green bread and mouldy seawater floated on top of the water. The Torpedo Stowage Compartment was half-flooded, almost up to the level of the hammocks which were slung fore-and-aft. Here were the first signs that something had gone wrong suddenly. All the hammocks looked as though they had been left in a hurry. Blankets were dangling over the edges into the oily water. Any sailor leaving his hammock will stop long enough to lash it up into some sort of a roll, if only to prevent his bedding from being nicked.

Clearly there had been some panic. Even though it happened only ten minutes after diving, I reckon most of the hands off watch had already crashed in their hammocks, with the compartment lighting cut down. Then the water spouted out of the auxiliary machinery compartment (AMC) and they evacuated the fore-ends at the rush. They didn't even shut the tube space bulkhead doors, but they did get the AMC hatch shut and all six clips hammered home.

When the salvage crew finally got the hatch open and had pumped the water out, it was clear to see the cause of the trouble. The log shaft mechanism, instead of being mounted in its guides down through a hole in the ship's bottom, was lying in the bilges some distance away. The hole through which the log normally projected was thus left open to the sea. Only three inches across, but that was enough. The presence for'ard of the two people responsible for the log – Peter, the Navigating Officer, and the T.I. – was evidence enough that they had been investigating some defect in the log when the accident had occurred. It was odd that such a potentially dangerous operation had not been supervised by more experienced men – or even that it should have been done at all whilst dived.

'What I don't see,' Number One remarked, after summing up all the evidence, 'is why the whole for'ard end of the boat should flood up when they had shut off the Auxiliary Machinery Compartment so thoroughly . . . or did they?'

'How about the ventilation to the compartment?' the Chief ERA said.

That was it. Although they had shut the hatch, they had not shut off the two ventilation trunkings either side, thus letting the seawater flood in through the vent louvres like a giant sprinkler system under 75psi pressure. With the best will in the world, they could not have shut them, for their valves were inaccessible behind reload torpedoes, as the Board of Enquiry later admitted. On top of that, one of them was labelled 'shut' when it was wide open – further evidence of lack of skilled supervision at the yard.

'Poor bastards,' the Chief said, 'they were on a hiding to nothing. That AMS compartment was only tested to 10 pounds per square inch, so the hatch would have burst open even if the vent trunkings had been shut off. As it was, all three compartments flooded through the ventilation. And even if they had shut off the tube space, it looks as if they were unable to get the bulkhead door to the accommodation compartment shut. Here's the four-part tackle they used trying to pull the door shut. There must have been something wrong with the door itself.' It was one of many deficiencies glossed over in the subsequent official report.

'So what?' Number One said. 'The cubic capacity of those three compartments was well over the amount they could blow or pump out of all the ballast tanks, even if they had all systems opened up. No chance, unless they'd hit the main ballast blows as soon as the panic began. But they were probably worried about breaking surface in front of *Shemara*.'

'Beats me why they haven't designed an interlock to prevent the log being withdrawn with the sluice valve open,' the Chief said. 'As it is, it's crazy. The indicator moves down as the log comes up.'

'Don't worry, they will now,' Number One said. And they did.

Before leaving Campbeltown, this macabre interlude over, the Captain cleared lower deck:

'Now I know what you're all thinking; that there's a bogey about these "U" Class boats. You've seen two boats go in the Clyde recently, and you're beginning to think there's something wrong with them. Well, we don't know about *Vandal* because they haven't found her. But we do know how *Untamed* was lost, and it was nothing to do with the basic construction of the boat. It was due to faulty handling of the log by two members of the ship's company . . . and that could happen to us. Faulty drill will sink any

34

submarine. As for the class suffering from some design weakness or being built sub-standard, remember that the Tenth Flotilla, which consists almost exclusively of "U" Class, has already sunk nearly a million tons of Axis shipping in the Med. And we'll add to that tally.'

But not every member of the ship's company saw it that way.

'T'isn't natural,' the T.I. muttered in his strong Geordie accent. 'Men were never intended to go about under water, so this is the price they pay for trying to.'

All the way back to the Holy Loch, Metcalfe sat in the control-room near the foot of the conning-tower ladder. He was chain-smoking and talking nervously, always on the subject of disaster. When the Captain pressed the klaxon unexpectedly, the Petty Officer of the Watch quickly opened all the main vents and everyone carried out the correct diving drill. But Metcalfe jumped across the control-room and started shutting them. However, his mate, a Leading Stoker, pushed him out of the way and yanked them open again. Everything went smoothly after that and the Captain soon ordered her to surface. But it was clear that the visit to Campbeltown had left its mark. Next morning the Coxswain reported to Number One. 'Metcalfe's missing. He sold his camera and a leather jacket last night and was seen going ashore with a suitcase. Best place for him. I've reported him to the Flotilla Regulating Office. Whatever happens we don't want him back here.

'And, if you'll forgive the description, there's a helluva stink going on about *Untamed*'s bodies. In that hot weather they decomposed so quickly that they were all buried last night in a communal grave in Campbeltown. Now some of the next-of-kin have turned up demanding to see them.'

A week later there was a confidential signal from Fort Block-house:

'Metcalfe J. R. D/MX 702881 ERA
borne on the books of *Forth* for *Untiring* surrendered himself to civil police in Warminster six days absent without leave. Medical and psychiatric reports recommend immediate reversion to General Service ashore. Propose no disciplinary action but that he be placed under report.'

'Christ, the old man's soft in the head,' Bunts said, showing the Coxswain the reply drafted in the Captain's own hand.

'From *Untiring* to S5 repeated FOS and S3. Your 131223Z concur.'

'Let's all catch the next liberty boat and bugger off on leave.'

But the last word on the loss of *Untamed* was not said for a long time. While *Untiring* was back at Larne finishing off her time with the Convoy Battle School, a Board of Enquiry was convened in HMS *Wolfe*. Its report did not emphasize the extent to which the crew's inexperience and the various deficiencies built in by the Yard had contributed to the disaster. The most lethal of these was that the main valve used to flood up the engine-room at maximum rate for an escape had its flap valve indicating it to be open when it was shut. Both the Yard Manager and the DSEA Coxswain from the depot ship whose job it was to check its function swore on oath that they had verified it. The Board blandly accepted the explanation that one of *Untamed*'s crew must have unshipped the valve lever to clean it and replaced it the wrong way round, which ignored the fact that it could just as easily be polished – if it ever was in wartime – in place. The Board's Report was finally forwarded to the Admiralty with Flag Officer Submarines' own comments, ending with:

'In all the circumstances Their Lordships need not feel unduly concerned over what occurred on this occasion.'

But that unconcern – possibly excusable in the context of sustaining morale throughout the Fleet – was not shared by those of us who suspected that *Untamed* had sailed from the Tyne as a submarine disaster waiting to happen. We were no better prepared, but survived long enough to expose and put right our potentially lethal mechanical deficiencies and to learn enough as a team to shade the odds in our favour when called upon to face any emergency short of a direct hit by the enemy.

Would we have made a better shot at getting out of a sunken submarine? We did not know the whole answer until after the War, when the Ruck-Keene Committee on Submarine Escape released the chilling pronouncement that breathing pure oxygen under high pressures carried a rapidly increasing risk of fatality below 100 feet. Our Davis Escape sets were charged with pure oxygen. Our training tank at Fort Blockhouse was only 25 feet deep.

As it happens, none of this mattered much because submarine captains had to weigh up other risks. There had been reports of escape hatches lifting under heavy depth-charging, so we preferred to have them bolted shut from outside the hull before going on patrol.

During my time in *H.43* I happened on the best use for Davis escape gear. We were entertaining some RAF pilots from Valley during a weekend visit to Holyhead. They prescribed pure oxygen as the best cure for a hangover, so we broke out four sets and sat around the wardroom table being slowly revived. This became a matter of routine for the rest of the war. Some officers needing to sustain the pace of being on leave in London resorted to benzedrine. But I had no trouble spotting a charioteer at the Bag-of-Nails in the small hours: one of a two-man crew who rode human torpedoes. He pulled a familiar black metal flask out of his jacket and bit its copper stem off as though about to light a cheap cigar. The oxlet giving its life-saving oxygen was identical to those fitted in our Davis Escape sets.

The same Flag Officer Submarines who had expressed himself satisfied with the state of operational readiness of our boats had assured Their Lordships that there was no call for high-definition surface-search centimetric radar to be fitted.

A year later *Untamed* was recommissioned as HMS *Vitality* but never went on a war patrol. Our work-up was intended to stretch the boat and her crew during the next few weeks, and did so. But *Untamed* was soon forgotten, as confidence grew, whilst the evenings drew out and the mist got warmer.

After finishing our time at Larne, we returned to the Clyde, when Commander (S) of the Flotilla came to sea with us for our Final Sea Inspection. Ben Bryant was already a national hero through his exploits in *Sealion* off Norway and *Safari* in the Mediterranean, for which he should have got a Victoria Cross. We expected Ben to crack the whip and expose our unreadiness by probing questions. But the conversation was mostly about brothels all over the world and the day passed agreeably. Evidently he was satisfied after we had gone through our paces, for his report concluded with the words: 'I consider *Untiring* is in all respects ready for operational patrols and should do very well.'

★ 3 ★

CHEFOO TO THE KOLA INLET

Our working-up patrol off Norway did not yield the chance encounter with a U-boat we hoped for, but going back up the Clyde exactly three weeks later seemed like coming home after a foreign commission. All the things we missed most at sea were waiting for us: mail, clean laundry, hot baths and good, well-cooked meals. We were to sail for the Mediterranean in a week, but half-way through our preparations for sailing Italy surrendered. Next day the Captain had a letter informing him that *Untiring* was to be relegated to a training flotilla and that he was being sent out as a Spare C.O. to Malta. Then a signal arrived confirming that we were still intended for the 10th Flotilla at Malta and would sail as originally arranged.

Before doing so, some new faces reported on board. Ordinary Seaman Winchester admitted to having been an actor before he got his call-up papers, so was looked at askance from the start and didn't last long. But the new chef was another matter; a real qualified cook straight from being the pastry chef at the Norfolk Hotel in Bournemouth. Leading Cook Hazzard quickly became the most popular man on board, because he told the depot-ship victualling staff to stuff their mildewed wrapped loaves and baked hot fresh bread every other day on patrol. He served up our basic rations disguised as gourmet dishes and never missed producing a birthday cake – for a consideration at tot-time.

From the day he joined he slept on the deck in the galley, with his neat auburn beard outside a blanket. In the early hours of one morning in harbour I was frying up a batch of eggs and bacon for a wardroom card school when I missed the frying pan with a cracked-open egg, which plopped on to his beard. He never moved, but reported sick to the Coxswain next morning: 'Something's wrong. I spewed my ring up during my sleep.'

If decorations had depended on the vote of the crew, he would have got his DSM before the Coxswain.

With each news bulletin giving further rumours of Allied landings up the coast of Italy, it certainly looked as though there would be very little enemy coastline left to operate against. Like wartime holiday travellers with guilty consciences, we wondered if our journey was really necessary.

Nevertheless, we painted the submarine dark blue all over and then sailed at six o'clock in the morning, mostly with such prodigious fat heads from our last night ashore in the U.K. that we didn't care much whether we were bound for Malta or Mandalay. Off Ailsa Craig we met two submarines homeward bound from the Med., both due to receive, as we knew, a highly organized reception from the Flotilla, the Press and the newsreel cameramen we had seen hanging about the depot-ship.

'Anything left for us?' the signalman flashed to them.

'Not a thing. Good hunting.'

We felt very small indeed as they passed close enough for us to see the innumerable white bars on their 'Jolly Rogers', one for each ship sunk by torpedo. The leading one, a 'U' class like ourselves, had two Italian cruisers to her credit.

The boat rolled her way down the Irish Sea keeping close station on the escort, when we could see it through the rain squalls. It was a depressing start to our foreign commission.

Clear of the Scillies the escort signalled farewell and abruptly turned back northwards. We dived almost immediately.

As the Bishop Rock lighthouse dipped astern it seemed like a good moment to take stock. It might just be the last time I saw England.

If anyone had said four years earlier that I'd soon be a regular Lieutenant in an operational submarine in the Royal Navy, rather than entering chambers as a graduate pupil to a barrister, I would have dismissed it as fantasy.

I was born in Adelaide within sight of the Test cricket ground, hemmed in by the steeples of Anglican churches, and thereafter lumbered with an Australian passport, with all its concomitant delays at Heathrow; I still have to argue my case for entering Britain. alongside the latest plane-load from Pakistan. I lost my British citizenship sometime in the 'sixties, following the passage of one of the British Nationality Acts. The first I knew of it was when I renewed my passport in 1972.

I have an open and shut case to enjoy the protection and European Community immigration privileges of an Irish passport but never made the move.

My grandfather suffered from various pulmonary weaknesses, so emigrated to New Zealand around 1890 from the family home at Ballyfin in the heart of Ireland, half-way to Limerick on the road from Dublin. There his father presided over the dwindling family fortunes, living in grandeur in a Georgian mansion with Palladian facades on an estate of 50,000 acres, many of whose tenants could not pay the rent.

He doubled as an ordained minister in the established Church amongst a largely Catholic community. If I didn't know that already, I found out one night in the wartime blackout in Belfast. Taking a leak against the base of a statue of a severe-looking gentleman wearing a spade beard and carrying an open book, probably not *Raceform*, I chanced to read the inscription by the light of a passing car: it was dedicated to the leader of one of Ireland's many lost causes, the Temperance movement. His name was Sir Algernon Coote, Bart. My grandmother told me how he often had ornate Connemara marble drinking fountains installed in the surrounding villages. The drill at his home town of Mountrath in what was then Queen's County was typical of many. A line of open horse-drawn carriages clattered to a halt in the main street lined with pubs, all shut with their curtains drawn out of respect to the occasion. According to the *Leinster Express* a thousand attended the ceremony at which Father Brennan thanked the Rev. Baronet for his generous gift for the good of the people amongst whom he lived. This was not a meeting at which political matters should be referred to, he declared, but if they had more men of the stamp of Sir Algernon Coote, men who lived in their midst, who derived their income from them but spent it freely (cheers) . . . resident gentry who took an interest in the people's welfare, how much better it would be for the country (loud cheers).

The conscientious local newspaper reporter then noted the intervention of A Voice: 'A long life to him' (cheers).

Winding up his Vote of Thanks, Father Brennan observed that, given the fountain's unfailing supply of pure water, the people would have no need to resort to the public house to quench their thirst (laughter and applause).

The ageing Baronet got back into his carriage and all the men doffed their caps and the women curtsied as the procession drove off to the sound of pub doors being opened. No doubt Father Brennan was first through the nearest one. Peter Sellers might have re-enacted it beautifully.

Unhappily, few of the family remained as Irish residents long after The Troubles. By the time the 13th Baronet died in 1940, he had blown much of the family money in the cause of Christian Scientists in Southern California, and his home had become a Catholic nunnery. Ironically my grandmother also fell prey to religious extremists, as I saw for myself when I was fifteen. She had dipped heavily into capital to make the long journey from New Zealand to Oxford for a meeting conducted by Frank Buchman, the founder of Moral Re-Armament (the Oxford Group). She took me with her. The proceedings were orchestrated to relieve the consciences of its mesmerised congregation through public repentance of sins which did not sound to me would merit more than a tut-tut in a confessional box. The MRA fund-raisers clearly expected to relieve them of large donations as the price of this spiritual balm.

My mother's side also sprang from Ireland. In 1858, at the age of three, her father had sailed to Australia aboard the clipper *Lady Augusta* commanded by her grandfather Captain James Henry Crowe of Cork. They left behind a dubious enterprise in the shape of the local bankers, Crowe, Littleton and Giles, from which the last-named partner had absconded to the USA with most of the bank's realizable assets. Its creditors were paid in full, making considerable inroads on the Crowe estates. My mother's father settled in Elliston near Adelaide where she was the youngest of five daughters, all of them delivered by aborigines. In the early years of this century, they lived in the style which recent Australian movies have portrayed in a home not dissimilar to Scarlett O'Hara's. There were plenty of servants, everyone dressed for formal dinner by candle-light six nights a week and, after the men emerged from punishing the port decanter, sat around for whatever musical talent could be deployed in the drawing-room. One was a handsome young baritone, a junior member of the cable company, whose repertoire peaked on 'The Dashing Sergeant-Major' with heavy declamatory gestures. He swept up the youngest daughter and became my father.

I knew little of my family background until much later, otherwise I might have headed for a career at sea earlier. Besides Captain Crowe and his family sailing across the Southern Ocean in *Lady Augusta*, there had always been Cootes in the Navy List since the days of Nelson. Three of them became Admirals. One of them wrecked his flagship when he was C-in-C on the South Atlantic station. Another became Governor of New York and is buried near the Battery. He brought the notorious Captain Kidd to the gallows (probably didn't get his cut). In my time the 14th Baronet became a Rear Admiral in the British Pacific Fleet.

It was not till after the War that I learned of another reason why I should have embraced the sea – I had been born with a caul over my head, so would never drown at sea. 'Now you tell us,' the crew of the yacht *Toscana* told me after the 1979 Fastnet Race in which fifteen participants lost their lives. If only my mother had followed the practice of Cape Horners and handed me the caul to be made up as a tobacco pouch, I might have felt a lot easier about some of the events described in these memoirs.

By my fourth birthday I was embarked on a nomadic life all over the Far East and Australasia, wherever my father's job with Cable and Wireless took him.

Kindergarten in Singapore was followed by a local school in Batavia, capital of the Dutch East Indies, where not a word of English was spoken. Within a few weeks I had fluent Dutch, but it was all beaten out of me at the junior house of King's School in Auckland, where I boarded whilst my father was doing a tour on Cocos Island.

Three memories survive: seeing the great Maori full-back George Nepia kick the winning goal against the touring English XV at Eden Park; being pitched into the boxing ring horribly mismatched against a heavier boy who beat me into whimpering submission; finally making the acquaintance of the first man whom I shall push in front of a tube train at the earliest opportunity – a precocious bully called Thorburn who was in my dormitory and got his kicks at the expense of my misery. The least of the indignities he inflicted on me was to lower his pyjama pants in front of my face whenever the mood or his diet took him.

Still not ten years old, I then made the long sea voyage to rejoin my parents in Shanghai. I became a boarder again, this time at the China Inland Mission School at Chefoo in Shantung in North China, an austere establishment founded in the 19th century for the children of those spreading the Word in Szechuan and points west. Chefoo was then the summer base for the US East Asiatic Fleet, with dozens of old four-stackers anchored in the bay just 40 miles west of the British naval base at Wei-Hai-Wei. Their crews amused themselves with 'Russian bares', as we called the pathetic white prostitutes who were hostesses in all the clip-joints along the waterfront. Over the back wall was a peasant farmer living in terminal poverty in a makeshift tent next to a tall circular tower with an external staircase up to its gallery 30 feet up. Baby girls were dropped into it at birth.

In the winter it was so cold that the school quadrangle was flooded and became an ice-rink for four months. We queued up each morning to take a double tot of cod liver oil with only an inch cube of bread with salt on it to kill the taste.

The staff were all English missionaries, somewhere in the bigoted fringe of fundamentalist Baptists; but they were well qualified and excellent teachers. The Headmaster's name was Bruce; he was reputed to have played cricket for Gloucestershire. He certainly had the wrists of a county batsman when laying on the cane for offences such as sniggering during bible classes. Before I left I knew that my name would survive there on the varnished board recording those who had gained Distinctions in the Oxford Junior School Certificate. Not too far above mine was Henry R. Luce's name in gold leaf.

Sundays were strictly observed. In between morning and evening services there were bible classes. Only books approved for reading on the Sabbath were permitted, mostly biographies of early missionaries or Christian Saints. No organized games were allowed, although approved walks in groups of three or more were. There wasn't a wide choice of preachers to deliver the sermons, so the one about there being graves of all sizes in the cemetery came round a bit often, especially if there was a diphtheria epidemic about. Evensong was the only time we clapped eyes on the 150 girls from their school up the hill. One of them later married Ben Bryant, the great wartime submarine captain.

At first my holidays were spent in Tientsin, looked after at night by a gentle old lady who was named Serica after the crack tea clipper in which she had been born whilst her father was its master. Later we moved to Hong Kong, where my father was a leading yachtsman and set me firmly on a lifelong obsession. I knew every ship that sailed the China Seas, from the beautiful white Canadian Pacific Empress liners, which were reputed to steam through fleets of fishing junks without pausing, to the small tramp steamers on the coastal trade, either with the black funnel of Butterfield and Swire or the red one of Jardine Mathieson. Mostly I sailed in them to and from Chefoo, locked behind bars on the centre island of the superstructure with armed guards in place to deter hijackers. The term after I left, the schoolchildren returning from Hong Kong and Shanghai were in a ship which was taken over and held by pirates for three days.

At 13 it was time to head for home and further education. Chefoo was overrun first by local warlords, then the Japanese and later the Communists. The school was evacuated to Malaysia before the war and may well be there still. The old buildings are now government administrative offices.

One trip home began with a visit to Japan with my mother from which I retain two abiding memories: there was a slot-machine area on the rooftop of our hotel in Kyoto. Amongst its attractions was a coin-operated dummy machine-gun which one fired using a cartwheel foresight to aim off against film of combat aircraft in flight. The trigger stopped the film and black dots showed where one's shots would have gone. The targets were all the very latest RAF and US fighters, then barely in front-line service. Assessments of 'kill' or 'damaged' flashed on the screen in two languages.

Later we were directed to the best sukiyakis in town, eaten on a dreamy verandah beside a limpid pool illuminated by soft-coloured lanterns. I think I spotted before my mother did that the obsequious geishas in hissing attendance had more to offer than raw eggs, fish and paper-and-scissors games. Although I was only 4'11" at the time, I imagine the girls took me for fully grown.

I arrived in London at the end of November, 1934, on the day of the Duke of Kent's wedding to his beautiful Greek Princess. Marina blue was the chic colour and Woolworths sold Marina berets at half a crown (12½p) each. At Victoria Station the pea-soup fog was new to me, but we made contact with an uncle by marriage who took us down to his home in Shirley Park where he was a G.P. Every Sunday he played golf with one of his patients, John Gordon, the editor of the *Sunday Express*. He showed me round one Saturday evening and sternly warned against ever being involved in newspapers. 'It'll kill you, laddie.' He was still there when I became General Manager of the *Sunday Express* thirty years later.

Throughout the late 'thirties we were brought up on stories of the endless summer of 1914, a prelude to all that mud and blood in the trenches where the Flower of England was butchered. But the strawberries in that hot summer of 1939 were every bit as plentiful and juicy as they had been a generation before. The roses had never been so spectacular, nor the lawns greener.

Mr Duff Cooper appeared for Speech Day at Felsted with his elegant wife in a chauffeur-driven Rolls. Recently having been First Lord of the Admiralty, after being Secretary of State for War, he must have known a thing or two when he assured us all that we would soon be in the trenches ourselves. Julian Bickersteth, the Headmaster, positively beamed and repeated the message in his sermon to school-leavers during Evensong the following Sunday. He wore his military chaplain's stole and Great War medals for the occasion. Later he followed his father as Archdeacon of Canterbury, but not before one enterprising member of Stock's House had locked the door to his celibate bedroom from the outside and cycled to Chelmsford in the middle of the night to mail the key to the only pretty Housemaster's wife. Unfortunately the culprit was fool enough to own up when mass reprisals were threatened on his House. He was mercilessly flogged, which stood him in good stead

44

when he was tortured by the Gestapo as a guest-artist in the French Resistance.

Duff handed me three prizes, which lie unopened on my bookshelf to this day. They were law text-books to take up to Jesus College with me in September. The History Prize was for a bit of investigative journalism on the origin of the Bayeux Tapestry, which I was not to set eyes upon for nearly 40 years. One of the others was for an essay discussing the proposition that sculpture is frozen music. I fancy the third was for fiction.

Our knowledge of post-Versailles Germany was sketchy. On the whole we didn't rate the Germans too highly. Not long before, we'd been shown the Lilienthal film of the 1936 Berlin Olympics. The commentary was given in perfect English by a sallow cultural attaché from von Ribbentrop's embassy. In between shots of blond Aryan athletes, the camera cut to the tunnel leading into the stadium. A knobbly-kneed emaciated figure emerged at the end of the 50km walk with that ridiculous heel-and-toe action of the long-distance walker. The audience erupted in laughter. The commentator held up his hand. 'Don't laugh. That was the only gold medal Britain won in athletics.'

We had one German in my house, a harmless pasty-faced refugee called Rudenberg who wore steel-rimmed spectacles and worked mostly on his own, because his maths were so far ahead of our sixth formers. Once a fortnight he received a heavy flat parcel with a Hamburg postmark which we backed away from as though it was a letter bomb. It was a supply of dried bananas which made him noisily flatulent. He went to the States at the outbreak of war and became a distinguished professor, one of the team working on the H-bomb.

The Auto-Unions and Mercedes lapped our ERAs with ease, but an Englishman won Wimbledon, beating the blond German Baron Von Cram in the final.

I ran a half-mile in 2.01 on grass to win the Home Counties' Schools' 2 × 880 relay. Walking through the main gates on our return from the meeting, word had reached the Cricket XI who were fielding against the MCC and well on their way to victory. They turned and clapped, which made me feel foolish, as I was carrying a bouquet of sweet peas, pressed on me by our overjoyed athletics master. This was held to be proof that I was his partner in unspeakable acts, not excluding sodomy.

I had supper with T.S. Eliot and four other members of a pretentious literary society, affecting to have unscrambled the message of *The Waste Land*. It was not until years later that I learnt what hang-ups lay behind his brooding introspection.

The last OTC Field Day was more than usually bewildering. I simply never got the big picture of what we were supposed to be doing lying in the stinging nettles, except waiting for an officer to arrive on horseback and announce we were all dead, releasing us to slope off to the finish line. Our issue of blank cartridges was spent on firing pencils through the tops of our caps. I had just been demoted to private for showing up at the General's inspection wearing slippers instead of boots. All I remember of the OTC camp at Tidworth was that we beat Sedbergh in the final of the rugger competition.

A spluttering RAF Hawker Hart circled round low over the school and landed safely on our playing fields. 'Just as well it's the summer term,' the pilot remarked nonchalantly as he climbed out, 'no rugger posts.' The aircraft had to be dismantled before it could be taken away.

In a staged criminal trial held in front of the whole school I was defence counsel and won an unexpected acquittal for the accused by introducing a bogus witness with a trumped-up alibi, against the odds – and the script. A rosy future at the Bar awaited me.

The Tory candidate was swept into power in a mock by-election, but one of my eccentric friends standing in the interests of the Communist Party saved his deposit and finished ahead of the Labour candidate. I handled his publicity, which consisted mainly of lurid pudenda ripped out of *Men Only* or *Health and Efficiency* with the simple message: 'Vote Communist and get your share'. Filling out a form during a Ministry of Defence Positive Vetting procedure later, I mentioned this episode, but my security clearance was unimpaired. I would not have been so lucky in the States.

The last night of term was enlivened by someone touching off the fire alarm and getting us all out on to the cricket pitch at three in the morning. So we caught the single-track London North–Eastern Railway rattler from Dunmow for the last time, past the halt at Easton in the middle of a field. The guard remembered a one-coach train stopping there at dusk to offload the familiar bearded figure of Edward VII smoking a cigar, who stomped off towards the gates of the Countess of Warwick's country home.

My last two years at school were happy ones, partly because I enjoyed some of the privileges of seniority, but mainly because Alastair Andrew, my enlightened dilettante sixth-form master, introduced teaching by tutorials, a form of self-discipline I was not due to enjoy until I got to Cambridge. Fortnightly essays were researched in the school library, quite unsupervised. Looking for something new to write about – say, the Hundred Years' War – I occasionally turned up books which had evidently got past the arbiters of taste who approved each new addition to the shelves. *Untrodden Paths of Anthropology* became a cult, mainly for its specific description of how ageing Annamese got their kicks by an anal violin whose single string could produce delicious vibrations in the vicinity of their prostate.

War came to me on the golf course at Cranleigh School during a break from playing in the local tennis tournament on the village green. There could be no possibility of swotting up Roman Law or Early Jurisprudence whilst all my friends stepped forward to answer Duff Cooper's call to arms. For me, it had to be the Navy. So I hastened to a recruiting office near Trafalgar Square, wanting to join the RNVR as an officer candidate. It seemed they were not taking anyone but Officers' Stewards on long engagements. I did not share the Chief Petty Officer's confidence that I would soon be picked out of the wardroom pantry to become a Watchkeeper in a destroyer. (In 1945 I was able to get our Steward in the submarine *Trespasser* released from the remaining two years of his service on the grounds that he had been conned into being a Steward in the Fleet Air Arm as a short cut to a flying commission.) His record showed that, every time he had put in a request to enjoy the opportunity promised in September, 1939, he was promptly drafted to another Fleet Air Arm wardroom. No one believed his story until I met him.

To go back to the outbreak of War, I then found I was within a few weeks of the age limit to sit the Special Entry exam in December for a permanent commission in the Royal Navy.

My tutor at Jesus College wished me well. One look at the syllabus pointed me in the direction of a crammer at Haywards Heath. I had just ten weeks to make up for not having done any maths or science subjects since School Certificate in 1937.

Autumn at Haywards Heath dragged on. There was little to do but work. The fighting war receded to the point where I reported to Harrow School to sit the written examinations in the Old Schoolroom with my enthusiasm on the wane. After the examinations, including the oral at Burlington House, I was looking forward to going back to Cambridge. Before taking the exam one had to list one's choices of branch of the service in case of passing in among the also-rans. Without giving the matter too much thought, I put the Royal Indian Navy and the Paymaster branch as my second and third choices, which intrigued the interviewing board. I left the room certain that I was heading for Bombay – or, better still, Cambridge.

Two weeks before going up for the Lent Term in pursuit of my immediate aim of getting Blues for cross-country running and squash, the results were published. My name came first in the list of cadets accepted for the seaman branch; then it dawned on me they were not in alphabetical order.

At Gieves I met young Rodney Gieve who assured me that red tabs on a uniform were for a Surgeon-Midshipman (actually a Midshipman in the Royal Naval Volunteer Reserve). There was a huge man being measured up for a uniform, fully 6'5", and hefty with it. I was liberal with the 'sirs' in our casual conversation, sure that he was a Lieutenant.

The next time I saw him was on Platform 1 at Paddington Station on 17 January, 1940, as one of the Special Entry Cadets heading for initial training at Dartmouth in the West Country, then in the grip of a Siberian winter. None of the five others who had joined my house at Felsted in January, 1935, survived the war.

It was August when most my Term of newly-promoted Midshipmen made the 24-hour train journey from King's Cross to Thurso in the far north of Scotland, on our way to join the Home Fleet in its anchorage at Scapa Flow.

The old fishing-boat skipper from Buckle driving the battle cruiser *Repulse*'s tender slowed to a stop short of her port quarterdeck ladder, pulled down his wheelhouse window and gave the dozen of us new midshipmen his parting advice: 'Noo remember, sirs, ya dinna swear and ya dinna drink.' Soon we were doing plenty of both, especially once we got to sea in the Iceland-Faeroes gap. The quarterdeck was awash – so was our gunroom flat underneath it. Going on watch in the main armament spotting-top was a teeth-gritting challenge to my poor head for heights. Having to climb the last fifty feet from the bridge up iron rings outside the mast, high above the funnels with a following wind, meant climbing through the smoke from her forty-two boilers.

Our part in chasing the *Bismarck* ended by having to anchor in Conception Bay, Newfoundland, to await a tanker for fuel replenishment. Then we had a week of pure peacetime in Halifax before giving surface cover to a major convoy to the Clyde. On return, it was time for half of us to do time in destroyers. Cards were cut to decide which group in the gunroom should go right away. I got the one-eyed Jack and soon found myself in HMS *Eclipse* of the Third Flotilla on the very first Russian convoy. *Repulse*, with her gallant Captain Bill Tennant but without air cover, was no match for the swarms of Jap torpedo-bombers three days after Pearl Harbor. She took down with her five of the gunroom including my closest friend. Kit Bros Captain of rugger at Rugby and fullback for Scottish schoolboys, who got a posthumous mention in despatches in place of the Victoria Cross he was recommended for after calming

5 *Untiring* entering harbour in La Maddalena, after a blank patrol, 1943.

6 Loading torpedoes at La Maddalena, 1944. J.O.C. holding steadying line.

7 German escorts firing every weapon at *Untiring*'s periscope after the latter had sunk an ammunition convoy off the Italian Riviera.

8 German minelayer (ex-F/S *Heureux*) after being sunk in Monaco, 14 December, 1943.

down a panic in the 15- inch TS (control centre) below the armoured deck and the waterline. He had taken over my Action Station there when I left. His crew got out just as the armoured hatch slammed down on him.

The destroyer *Eclipse* had been commissioned three years before the War and still had many of her original crew; the remainder were reservists who still wore their peacetime uniforms as postmen. Her Captain was a brilliant shiphandler, but unlucky in the opportunities that came his way against the enemy. During one confused action in fog off North Cape, she suddenly found a damaged German destroyer dead in the water. A classic torpedo attack was carried out, but when the firing levers were pulled on the bridge nothing happened. The Gunner (T) had fired them all in local control during an earlier skirmish without the bridge – or the enemy – being aware. By November, 1941, I had finished my destroyer time and was sent to the cruiser flagship HMS *Edinburgh* to get sharpened up for the first of the examinations for Lieutenant.

We were on Murmansk convoys almost without a break, mostly in weather I never want to sail through again. Christmas and New Year were spent at anchor in the Kola Inlet waiting to take a convoy home. The ship was in a low state of training and discipline. One forenoon I was playing bridge in the gunroom, since no formal instruction was offered, when the air attack alarm rattlers sounded for a lone German bomber flying overhead, probably on reconnaissance. Our first salvo demolished a farm building ashore, because the guns had not been lined up with the director before they were fired. During one convoy I caught a bridge look-out in a wing shelter reading a magazine, so I had him relieved and led before the Officer of the Watch as a defaulter. The sailor was cautioned to keep a better look-out in future, whilst I got a rocket for not supervising the look-outs efficiently.

I was not in the least bit surprised when she was sunk on the very next trip after my group left to go south for Sub-Lieutenants' courses. We nearly sailed with her, but waved our appointments at the Commander who had us put ashore as she weighed anchor.

Proficiency in Gunnery, Torpedoes, Anti-Submarine Warfare, Signals and Navigation had to be certified in each of the famous Naval Schools. At the RN Gunnery School at Whale Island in Portsmouth we were fallen in on the parade ground when the Course Officer announced that our entire group was due for conscription to the Fleet Air Arm as pilots or observers, with the exception of those who had already been accepted for submarines. I had vivid memories of being on the screen of the carrier force in the White

Sea which launched three Squadrons of lumbering Albacores and Swordfish biplanes in a daylight attack against an alerted enemy at Petsamo and Kirkenes, from which fewer than half returned. I led the rush to the phone box at the far corner of the parade ground as soon as we were fallen out.

The Drafting Officer at HMS *Dolphin* denied having received my letter volunteering for submarines, which was not surprising as it was yet to be written. A dozen of us escaped the Fleet Air Arm by similar ruses and were sent railway warrants with orders to join HMS *Elfin*.

Many are disconcerted by the Royal Navy's practice of giving ships' names to shore establishments. Perhaps that's why they have been known as stone frigates for centuries. But to me there is something incongruous about calling a headquarters building near Moor Park golf-course in the outer suburbs of North London HMS *Warrior*, when the genuine article is secured alongside in Portsmouth Harbour, having been lovingly restored to exactly how she was in 1860. So it was with HMS *Elfin*. When I joined submarines in 1942, Flag Officer Submarines found it necessary to conscript a growing number of officers and ratings to replace heavy losses in the Norwegian and Mediterranean campaigns.

My Officers' Training Class assembled at the hutted camp on the outskirts of Blyth in Northumberland, formerly a boys' remedial school. Among our numbers were half-a-dozen Reserve Sub-Lieutenants arbitrarily plucked out of the Belfast Lough Anti-Submarine Trawler Force. Most of them headed for the little harbour looking for an A/S trawler, for no one had bothered to explain to them that they were about to become submarine officers after a course at HMS *Elfin*. Two left the next day, followed by another later.

They missed a lot of fun. Not only did the base enjoy Duty Free privileges, but it was staffed by gently complaisant Wrens and friendly young instructors who had survived to pass on the lessons of our losses in those early campaigns, fought either in unsuitable boats or before it was generally recognized that pre-war training had its priorities all wrong. As the war dragged on, officers and senior ratings were often given a few months on the training staff at Blyth to recharge their batteries before their next operational appointment.

On leaving as qualified submariners, most of us headed north for Rothesay on the island of Bute in the Clyde approaches to join HMS *Cyclops*, the depot-ship for a flotilla of First World War vintage 'H' and 'L' Class boats which acted as clockwork mice for the Anti-Submarine school at Campbeltown. My appointment was to *H 43* which had been first commissioned in 1916. She was not allowed to dive below 100 feet and, like many a damp old house, had flickering electrics and inadequate plumbing. When the attack team closed up, I parked myself on the heads pan and pulled the upper panel of the door on to my lap. There I constructed the plot to solve the enemy's course and speed. When I forgot to take dividers and parallel rulers in with me, I had to make do with a toothbrush and spread fingers. Her Captain was Robert Boyd.

After a couple of months he was appointed to stand by a new submarine then building at Vickers' Walker Yard on Tyneside. He agreed to take me with him. I wouldn't put it stronger than that.

★ 4 ★

FRUSTRATION OFF TOULON

My story moves on to *Untiring* outward bound as an operational boat destined for the famous Tenth Flotilla in Malta. The trip to Gibraltar from Bishop Rock is about a thousand miles. A photo-reconnaissance Mosquito could do it in three and a quarter hours. It took us eighteen days, including a ten-day anti-U-boat patrol off St Nazaire.

Those ten days were similar in all respects to the patrol off Norway, with monotonously bad weather thrown in. The usual nightly cyphers told of so many U-boats moving through our area that, when plotted on our chart, we were, it seemed, permanently surrounded by whole packs of them. Then one night I sighted one. No doubt about it this time. The Captain was equally convinced and shaped up for a deliberate attack on it. Just as he was about to fire a full salvo at point-blank range, the target leisurely hoisted his mainsail. It was a tunny-fisher out from the Gironde.

Eventually orders came from Gibraltar to proceed on our journey and we made off southwards, diving by day and pressing on by night on the surface.

The nights got warmer and calmer as the days got shorter and stuffier. When I came up on to the bridge for my watch one day, it was to find we were already threading our way through the lines of trawlers, corvettes and Harbour Defence patrol craft which sought to bar the Med to intruding U-boats. Down below our crew were climbing into their best uniforms. The Coxswain alerted Captain's requestmen to be ready on arrival. One was Charlie, coming up for rating as Able Seaman at last, after having been held back as an Ordinary Seaman. The order was given to switch off and secure radar. Next came a bellow down the voice-pipe, too late to save the antenna from being mangled on the jumping wires as

Charlie lowered it without first lining it up fore-and-aft. The door of his shack opened: 'All right, 'Swain. Forget about my request, I wouldn't want to waste the skipper's time.'

That left only one item of formal business – to draft Ordinary Seaman Soames Winchester quietly out of the submarine on suspicion of being a queer.

'Well, he has to be with a name like that,' the Coxswain explained. 'Some of the lads are afraid he'll touch them up.'

The Rock of Gibraltar looked more like an Insurance Company's advertisement than ever, throwing its shadow across a harbour filled with a huge fleet of carriers, battleships and cruisers, most of them licking their wounds after Salerno.

The officers moved into a flat for visiting submariners up Scud Hill. The time there was divided between sleeping, drinking sherry and visiting bars in the Main Street in company with the Officers of *Upstart*, which had arrived from UK the day before we did.

We soon looked forward to sailing from Gibraltar, which was beginning to pall, for all its glorious weather, shops stocked with smuggled Swiss watches, its duty-free exports from UK, its fish dinners washed down with white wine as cheap as draught beer, its parties at the Rock and in the flat at Scud Hill.

After six days, the ship's company had finished cleaning out the boat and re-stowing it for our next patrol. They had also gone through all their money in typical Jolly Jack fashion preferring good old English wallop at 3/6d a pint to local wine a quarter the price. The sailor's attitude to life has altered little since Nelson's days. They live like lords for five nights and then want to get away out to sea again. Their morale and offensive spirit had increased from the moment we left the Clyde. At home they were always brooding on some domestic trouble, wondering when they were next getting any leave or thinking up some scheme to dodge going abroad. By the time we reached Gibraltar most of them conceded that they enjoyed serving in the boat, which in their eyes was the finest submarine that ever sailed the seas. A good deal of furniture in the Capitol Bar was smashed driving home that point to *Upstart*'s libertymen.

Our orders from Algiers came at last. From Captain (Submarines) 8th Flotilla to Senior Officer (Submarines) Gibraltar:

'Sail *Untiring* to patrol in area SU, thence as ordered by me.'

'Area SU is this one,' – Gus unrolled his chart of the south coast of France – 'from Marseilles along the coast eastwards as far as the Hyères Roads.'

The Captain looked quickly along the coastline. 'That means, in effect, Toulon Bay. Well, you can tell the T.I. that I'll need his torpedoes this time.'

Toulon had become the prime target for the Eighth Flotilla ever since the Salerno landings, because it was the principal naval port left to the Germans in the Mediterranean. Almost all their U-boats were based on Toulon, as was most of their A/S fleet.

Intelligence reports showed a ring of heavy coastal defence batteries stretching right around the bay from Cap Sicié to the Porquerolles. Radar stations, infra-red sniffers and searchlights completed the defence of the harbour against intruders on the surface, whilst shore Asdic installations, hydrophone buoys, nets and minefields guarded the harbour approaches against submarines.

We sailed at teatime on Sunday afternoon. *Upstart*'s four officers were the only people to see us off. They appeared in fancy dress and played us out with a doleful rendering of 'Nearer my God to Thee' on an accordion, to the astonishment of the officers on the flagship's quarterdeck who had long since decided that all submariners were certifiable.

My first watch that trip was unforgettable. It was a pitch-black moonless night. We were proceeding on the surface just east of Gibraltar wondering if the R.A.F., who had asked us to do an exercise with some of their maritime aircraft, would show up. I was on the bridge waiting to take over the watch from Number One when it happened. A blinding white light rushed at us out of the darkness, followed by the roar of four Liberator engines passing twenty feet overhead. The light went off as the sound of the aircraft died away into the night.

'At least it would be quick and merciful,' Number One remarked.

The aircraft had tracked in to us by radar, switching on its Legh light – the size of a destroyer's 36-inch searchlight – just as it came over us, in time for the bombardier to release his pattern. She also set us up as a target for the U-boat which had been reported patrolling the area for the past week.

Two days later and the Balearic Islands were left behind on our starboard quarter. The weather was all that we expected of the Mediterranean in late summer: flat, calm, cloudless days and cool hazy nights. Without air-conditioning, the atmosphere when dived was hot and humid. Whilst we were eating supper on the surface during the night when we expected to make our landfall off Toulon, a cypher arrived from Captain (S) 8.

'U-boat expected to arrive Toulon dawn 15th.' That was next morning. It was based on an enemy report from *Unseen* after a

U-boat had passed outside torpedo range. It was filed in the Log on top of the dozens of U-boat reports we had received on our two previous patrols.

On the bridge, during the two-hour watch from midnight, I could plainly make out a line of hills across the northern sky, with one particularly distinctive headland right ahead. The Captain was on the bridge.

'That's Cap Sicié, on our radar at nine miles. Keep on steering 030°, speed half-ahead together group down, zigging thirty either side every four minutes.'

I thought we must have been a large echo on the enemy's shore radar sets. The look-outs evidently thought so too, for their eyes never left their glasses the whole watch. Being right on the enemy's doorstep for the first time was like walking into a cave full of reptiles. Somewhere ahead were German anti-submarine vessels sweeping round the bay. High on the blacked-out cliffs were guns' crews and coastguards peering out to seaward. It did not occur to me that they were bored, cold and disinterested, or that the officers in the corvettes sweeping the bay were most probably looking at their watches and thinking it was about time they started back towards the harbour entrance. They would have had intelligence from their agents at Algeciras, who had seen us sail eastwards from Gibraltar four days ago, but hadn't taken it any more seriously than we did the report of the U-boat due to arrive at dawn. That U-boat might, I suppose, also be sighting Cap Sicié about now.

We edged in towards the land on our motors with everything on the alert. In the tube space the T.I. sat up all night beside his firing panel, with the bow-caps open and everything in readiness for a snap shot at a passing shape. The Asdic (sonar) listener swept round for the tell-tale beat of an enemy's propellers. Charlie's radar was only being used intermittently. At that time most submariners were over-impressed by the Germans' ability to detect and fix foreign radar transmissions.

By five o'clock on 15 October the eastern sky began to pale and it was time to dive to seventy feet to await sufficient daylight to see through the periscope. The Captain ordered the boat down to 200 feet, looking for any thermal layers beneath which we would be able to hide if we were hunted during the course of the day. Hot surface water in the Mediterranean produce layers which Asdic beams bounce off. We found pronounced layers at 35 feet and 120 feet. Winter gales disperse the layers and leave good A/S conditions.

'That'll do,' the Captain said after twenty minutes. 'Bring her up to periscope depth.'

The boat came slowly back towards the surface. In the wardroom, Gus and I were having our breakfast, discussing the quiz column in *Good Morning*, the daily parish magazine produced by the *Daily Mirror* during the last years of the war.

'Korinthos is a brand of toothpaste, a Turkish coin, a port in Greece, or a perennial flower . . .'

'Faint HE [hydrophone effect] bearing Red 130, Sir.' It was the HSD* on watch.

'Hullo, the reception committee are out early,' Gus murmured.

'Sounds like fast diesel, Sir,' the HSD went on. That decided the Captain.

'Half-ahead together, periscope depth.'

As we came up through the fifty feet mark, he already had the periscope up ready to see what was there as soon as it broke surface.

'Thirty feet, Sir. . . . Twenty-eight . . . twenty-seven . . .'. Number One reported the depths as he steadied the boat.

The Captain swept round with the periscope. 'Bring her up further . . . twenty-four feet.'

'Bearing now Red 110.'

'Diving Stations! Port twenty. Bring all tubes to the ready.' The Captain was ranging through the periscope.

'Range is seven minutes on twenty feet. I'm seventy on the starboard bow of a 700-ton U-boat. Down periscope.'

As I juggled with the wheels on the fruit-machine (torpedo control calculator), over the headphones I could hear the T.I. raging at the fore-endmen to get the bowcaps open and the firing reservoirs charged. One by one the 'ready' lights came on.

The H.S.D. continued to report the bearing of the H.E. 'Red five-oh. About 360 revolutions.'

'Use that,' the Captain snapped. A quick look at the German U-boat revolutions-for-speed table – 360 revs was 13 knots. 'Up periscope. What should I be on the bow from the Asdic bearings?'

'Eight-five, Sir, on a 130 track.'

'Right, that'll do. Midships. Steady. What's my D.A.?'

'Red one six.'

'Set me on.'

A rating swung the periscope round till the bearing pointer showed that the Captain was looking along a line sixteen degrees to port of right ahead – the amount of aim-off required to hit.

* HSD: Higher Submarine Detector, the most senior sonar operator in the boat.

'Stand by . . . fire one!'

I flicked the tube order-instrument to 'Fire'. There was a shudder through the boat and the T.I's voice came over the 'phones: 'One fired, Sir.'

'Fire two!'

Another shudder. The HSD could hear them.

'Two torpedoes running right ahead, Sir.'

The firing interval was prolonged by the ship's head swinging a degree and a half to starboard during the salvo, as the control room log showed. That was one lesson learnt the hard way.

'Fire three . . . fire four!'

The Captain had a quick look round the horizon. 'There are two corvettes or destroyers over against the land about four miles away bearing *that* . . . green four-oh . . . and there's an Arado seaplane circling ahead of the U-boat. Shut off for depth-charging.'

It had all taken two and a quarter minutes from the time of the first look through the periscope till the torpedoes were fired. Half the ship's company were only told then for the first time what the target was. Meanwhile, Gus had plotted the actual distance the torpedoes had to run to hit. It was nearly four miles. Running time for a hit was seven minutes. The Signalman was counting out the minutes whilst the Captain told us more:

'Only really saw the conning-tower on the first look. It was a Jerry all right. Two banks of anti-aircraft guns on a bandstand abaft the bridge, no gun on the for'd casing. There seemed to be an awful crowd of chaps on the bridge. Gus, giving our fish an extreme running range of 12,000 yards, in what depth of water will they end their run? Will they hit the beach?'

'They'll stop just over the hundred-fathom line, a mile off Cepet.'

'Good! Then we won't hear them go up on the putty. Can you still hear them running, HSD?'

'Yes, Sir. Still running straight.'

'Seven minutes, Sir.'

Another look through the periscope. The U-boat was still steaming on towards the land.

No one spoke for a few seconds.

'Blast and damn! We've missed. Take her down, Number One, sixty feet.'

He stood back as the periscope was lowered. We had just got to forty feet when there was a sharp explosion, followed by a rumbling sound like a building collapsing.

'Periscope depth. Quick as you can. Up periscope!'

The Captain was trembling with excitement. All the control-room personnel were smiling incredulously. Over the 'phones the T.I. was shouting, 'We've hit! Tell the Captain. We've hit her!'

It seemed an age before the periscope broke surface and the Captain searched towards the U-boat.

'She's not there. . . . The two corvettes are . . . and there's the Arado. One hundred and fifty feet. Silent routine.'

'H E of the target has ceased, Sir,' the HSD reported.

All the noisier auxiliary machinery was stopped and the crew squatted on the deck at their Diving Stations. Course was ordered to take us clear out to seaward. It was then just six o'clock. We had been dived for one hour on our first day's diving on the billet for our first Mediterranean patrol. It was unbelievable luck, if we had hit. But if that explosion hadn't been our torpedo, what was it? The chart showed that the torpedoes finished their run in six hundred feet of water, so it could hardly be them hitting the shore.

Five minutes later there were two distant muffled bangs. Then silence.

'Probably the Arado dropping its charges along the tracks of our fish,' the Captain said. 'But they're a long way off.'

There were still two destroyers, or corvettes. The aircraft could direct them along the wakes of our torpedoes, which must have shown up on that glassy sea like vapour trails in the sky. But they never came. Possibly they were picking up survivors. After an hour the boat came back to periscope depth. The Captain could see nothing. There was a heat haze in towards Toulon which cut down visibility, but the destroyers were not in sight. It was safe to carry on reloading torpedoes, but not at periscope depth. In that crystal-clear water an aircraft passing directly overhead would see us as if we were on the surface. So he took a fix, which put us three miles to the southward of Porquerolles Island, and ordered sixty feet and a course towards Cap Camarat to the east.

In the fore-ends the crew were jubilant. They were manhandling all the hammocks, sacks of spuds, clothes and lockers out of the compartment to make room for reloading. It was difficult to impress on them that silence was essential, that German A/S vessels were undoubtedly listening for us. The job of handling torpedoes is much more tricky whilst dived, as one can never rely on the boat remaining on an even keel. A torpedo halfway loaded might run out again if a bow-up angle developed. A ton and a half of high explosive taking charge in that confined space did not bear thinking about. Preventer tackles have to be rigged and manned, all of which prolongs the job. Luckily, the air was still fresh, so the physical effort of hauling on the loading tackles was no greater than doing it in harbour. In the middle of loading in the third torpedo, a whispered order came for'ard from the control room.

'From the Captain! There's something overhead. Stop loading. Keep silence.'

Everyone sat on the deck and waited. There was a pitter-patter of a ship's propellers passing over the top of us. It was obviously something small, probably an E-boat or chasseur. The seamen loaded in the last torpedo as if it was Venetian glass.

During my afternoon watch I got my first look at the French coast in daylight. We were moving slowly along about a mile and a half to the southward of the Hyères Islands, a chain of small islands stretching from Toulon to Cap Camarat and the entrance of the Gulf of Fréjus. There were a few white houses with red-tiled roofs standing out clearly in the brilliant sunshine. Outlined against the skyline were big mattress-like radar aerials and several large gun emplacements. Through the high-power periscope it was possible to see men standing by the guns and people in the grounds of their houses. It was all very peaceful and reminiscent of a seaside holiday on a fine August day. Arado and Heinkel seaplanes were buzzing about over the area looking for us, but only came near enough to force us deep twice. A line of R-boats passed eastbound behind the islands. Surprisingly, there were yachts' white sails moving lazily across the Roads.

A long post-mortem on our attack was taking place in the wardroom. Gus and Number One were convinced that we had hit her, but the evidence, overwhelming as it was on paper, would not persuade the Captain to claim it as more than a possible.

'But I didn't see the thing blow up. He might have dived just as the torpedo exploded prematurely somewhere in his wake.'

We later came to know this self-deprecating side of him well; his claimed tonnage of ships we sank always erred on the low side.

At night we surfaced off Cap Camarat and went out ten miles to charge our batteries in peace. The early part of the night, when both generators were going flat out to recharge the batteries, was always the most dangerous. The enemy were known to have a nasty habit of sending R-boats out to lie stopped all night in areas where our submarines were suspected. The throbbing of our generators carried across the night like the noise of machine guns in a crypt, or so it seemed as I strained my eyes in the blackness for an R-boat's white bow wave, almost certain to be the first indication of their presence.

We dived at first light in towards Cap Camarat. From there we worked along the coast into the Gulf of Fréjus, up as far as St Tropez.

Our track took us serenely through areas Gus had shaded in pencil on the chart with a marginal note, 'Believed mined'.

We looked in at the Golfe de St Tropez, but there was nothing there except small fishing boats and yachts. St Raphael harbour was empty, but there was a seaplane hangar with a slipway which was noted as a possible target for our gun later on. For two days of flat calm weather and extreme visibility we patrolled backwards and forwards along a line across the gulf. We might as well have been off Torquay, which indeed the coast resembled. There was nothing moving on the water, but we watched the steady stream of trains hauling munitions towards Italy. The only consolation was that we were confident that nothing had slipped through our area.

On the fourth day the mast of a small vessel was sighted coming from the direction of Cap Camarat. The Captain began to carry out a dummy attack on it, just to keep his eye in. It was soon apparent that it was one of the F-lighters we had read about at Gibraltar. A long, low vessel, heavily armed, probably carrying several hundred tons of supplies. It was not doing more than eight knots and took nearly twenty minutes to reach us. By then the periscope estimations had given such a good plot that the Captain decided to give it a couple of torpedoes. Two were fired at a range of eight hundred yards, set to run at four feet. The Captain kept the periscope up to watch the torpedoes running, waiting for the bang due 30 seconds after firing.

'Both tracks have passed under our target,' he said quietly. 'Anyone want to have a look?'

The squat counter of the F-lighter looked very close in high-power. Three sailors were sunning themselves beside a wicked-looking 88mm. The Nazi ensign streamed out from its masthead as it steamed slowly on its way. They had not seen either our periscope or the broad aerated tracks of the torpedoes.

'Now we know; they are shallow-draught vessels all right.'

Probably one of the fish had passed just ahead and the other had dipped a few inches under its set depth of four feet.

During the night the Captain decided to try his luck in the Toulon area again. So we zig-zagged gently eastwards past the Hyères Islands and dived for a patrol off the steep bluffs of Cap Sicié.

Once again the visibility was extreme and all the houses on shore stood out plainly. Two R-boats came past inshore of us, towing something behind them, probably minesweeping.

We were well inside the hundred-fathom line and slap in the middle of another shaded area on the chart. 'I wonder if they're doing a clearance sweep for a ship to pass through here later on?'

No one thought much more about it. We had done nearly a week on patrol by this time and were despairing of ever seeing anything reasonably large as a target. Over lunch we were all saying as much when the telegraphist of the watch brought a pink signal into the wardroom.

'Enemy report from the R.A.F., Sir.'

'One merchant vessel, two A/S trawlers in position 42° 40′N 5° 15′E, course 120°, speed 7 knots. Time of origin 1132,' the Captain read. 'That sounds more like it. Plot that on the chart, Gus, and let me know how far away it is.'

He went into the control room to have one of his periodical looks-round, whilst Gus fixed the enemy's position.

'Giving him 7 knots he should be about 20 miles away bearing 300°, Sir. Coming from Marseilles, maybe.'

'Yes, that's about it . . . and there's his smoke, if I'm not mistaken. Diving Stations.'

Amplifying information was slow coming from the periscope.

'Smoke bearing red six-oh . . . and a mast. Start the plot.'

Slowly the target identified itself as, first, its funnel and upper-works, and then its hull appeared over the horizon. We lay in wait just over a mile off the land, where it was almost certain to pass to get into Toulon.

'There are two escorts, one on either bow. Target appears to be in ballast. Set both torpedoes to six feet.'

This attack was quite unlike the one against the U-boat. It took nearly two hours for the seven-knot merchantman to reach us. By then the plot had its course and speed worked out with very little margin of error, which was just as well, since we only had two torpedoes remaining. More details from the periscope:

'Three-island, medium-sized merchantman. About five thousand tons. Nazi ensign.'

From the way the Captain kept the periscope away from the target we knew he was passing inside the escorts. It was a point-blank attack with the range on firing under 400 yards.

Two shudders from for'ard and the torpedoes were running. Everybody tensed themselves for a big explosion, but none came. The Captain ordered rapid changes in course, depth and speed to evade the counter-attack from the A/S trawlers, who must see our torpedoes explode on the beach. Two minutes later there were two faint plops, no louder than a couple of electric light bulbs bursting.

'That'll wake up the escorts,' the Stoker P.O. muttered as he shut off a sea-connection for depth charging. 'I don't mind getting a plastering after we get our hits, but this is a bit one-sided.'

For half an hour we crept silently to seaward at two hundred feet. The H.S.D. reported the H.E. of the target and its escorts fading on a steady bearing. It slowly dawned on us that no one had noticed our torpedoes, not even those manning the semaphore station on Cap Sicié, directly above the explosions at the foot of the cliffs.

Back at periscope depth, one by one, we all had a look at the fat prize that had slipped through our fingers. It would go into Toulon, load up with ammunition, guns, stores and tanks to prop up the Naples front, where the issue was still in doubt.

There was only one possible explanation – we had fired from too close. When a torpedo leaves the tube it is set to plunge deep before recovering, in a series of porpoising movements, to its pre-set depth, normally about 300 yards from its point of discharge, but sometimes further. Doctrine lays down 500 yards as the minimum practicable firing range for submarines for that reason.

'So you see,' the Captain summed up, 'I made a balls of both those attacks, so what right have I to claim the hit on the U-boat?'

His depression was shared by most of the young crew who expected every salvo to strike. No. 1 was consoling: 'Don't forget Wanks missed with his first twenty-two torpedoes fired in anger . . . but he didn't do so badly afterwards.' The ace 10th Flotilla marksman had gone on to sink two U-boats, two destroyers and over 120,000 tons of merchant shipping after those early blank patrols which almost led to his being relieved from command of Upholder. Nevertheless, we persuaded the Captain to claim the U-boat in the signal which was then sent to S.8 at Algiers, reporting all torpedoes expended. Later that night we got a reply:

'To Untiring from S.8. Well done. Return to Algiers by direct route, arriving first light 21st.'

The signalman was already busy stitching a skull and crossbones out of wardroom table napkins on to a black flag. Then he added in the top left-hand corner of the flag a red 'U' with a broken bar through it. But the Captain could not be persuaded to fly it. 'Wait until we have more to show for our efforts.'

Off Algiers we surfaced and rendezvoused with a trawler who escorted us towards the harbour entrance.

'Wish we could find something like this off Toulon,' the Captain said wistfully, looking at the fleet of merchant ships lying calmly at anchor in the open sea, protected only by a few patrolling corvettes and MLs.

Down below, the ship's company was washing and shaving, mostly for the first time since leaving Gibraltar. Clean white tropical uniforms came out to replace unspeakably filthy overalls. Up on the bridge sallow faces blinked at the harsh sunlight. The depot ship was lying at the detached mole opposite the long waterfront of tall modern buildings. From the sea the appearance of the town is deceptive, a lovely symmetrical façade of white buildings masking one of the most squalid and vicious ghettos in the world. The inner harbour was crammed full of shipping unloading weapons for the drive from Tunisia to Italy. The trot of submarines alongside included two who had got in ahead of us that morning and were flying their Jolly Rogers, one with eleven and the other with nine bars. We had not earned our place. This was the depot-ship from which Commander Linton had won his Victoria Cross in *Turbulent*, whilst *Splendid*, *Sahib*, *Saracen*, and the other 'S' boats had made their devastating contribution before being sunk themselves.

Over the wardroom mantelpiece there hung a smiling portrait of the Supreme Allied Commander, Mediterranean, signed: 'To the Eighth Submarine Flotilla, whose gallant efforts did so much to hasten victory in North Africa – Dwight D. Eisenhower.'

★ 5 ★

THE CASBAH TO THE GUT

The depot ship at Algiers, HMS *Maidstone*, under Captain Barney Fawkes, turned out to be the happiest one we ever lay alongside.

Every department was run towards one over-riding goal: to bring submarines just returned from sea back to the first state of readiness in the shortest possible time. Their repair staffs pitched into our defect list as if their lives depended on it. The humblest members of her company – the Writers in the offices, the Stewards, the Cooks, the Ordinary Seamen – all looked upon the submarines as being part of their team. They shared the good moments – when a submarine entered harbour with more bars on its Jolly Roger – and the bad ones when boats were overdue, and personal effects had to be mustered and packed away before being auctioned off for prices inflated by emotion. Our matelots spent four days unshackled by discipline or routine at a large seaside villa and came back with lurid stories, none better than Dickie Bird getting plastered at the local bistro and turning in with the old Arab caretaker's sister. Nothing unusual in that, until the lady mentioned that she had a son who fought in the First World War.

Ashore we made useful contacts in two American Army Officers who ran a transportation pool in a back-street garage. They apparently had cornered a stock of jeeps, staff Chevvies, cigarettes, blondes and quiet bathing beaches along the coast. We supplied the whisky, which they drank like draught beer. One day I mentioned that I could use a reliable motor-cycle. Next afternoon Sergeant Ricky called me up to come and see him. There he produced a freshly painted 250cc motor-cycle.

'All yours, and here's a U.S. Army gas permit that'll get her topped up anywhere on this goddamn continent. Yes, sir.'

It was a beautiful machine, obviously not American, probably German or Italian loot, I thought. A closer look at the engine

9 J.O.C.'s wedding to Sylvia Syson, 18 September, 1944.

10 Robert Boyd outside Buckingham Palace after receiving the DSO and Bar in command of *Untiring*.

11 Signalman Bert Allen amidst the rubble of the Submarine Base, Malta.

12 HMS *Otway*, built in 1925 for the Royal Australian Navy, was J.O.C.'s first appointment as Executive Officer.

13 First Command, HMS *Truncheon*, on a visit to St Peter Port, Guernsey, 1948.

14 "Uncle" Rouse with lucky Robert Borwick in *Golden Dragon*, 1949.

15 On promotion to Commander, 1952.

16 Wardroom guest night, R.N.C. Dartmouth, 1950. J.O.C. to the left of Commander Vere White-Boycott.

17 Torpedo tube doors, HMS *Amphion*, 1950.

18 *Totem* showing totem pole with J.O.C. and John Fieldhouse, then First Lieutenant.

19 The Bishop of Fulham blessing *Totem* on commissioning at Chatham Dockyard.

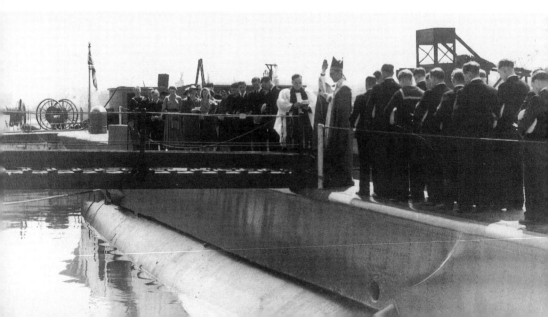

revealed the logo of Britain's most popular make engraved on the crank-case casting – 'B.S.A.' Ricky didn't bat an eyelid.

'I guess I've got the fastest spray-painter in town. My top-sergeant found this one parked outside the Aletti only two hours back.'

As I rode it back to the jetty opposite the detached mole, I kept one eye open for a dismounted Army despatch rider. The motor-cycle became communal property for the Third Hands of all the submarines there and remained in the *Maidstone* long after we left, along with two jeeps which the Americans gave to the flotilla.

We also shared with the Yanks difficulty in establishing rapport with the French. An uneasy mix of Gaullist and ex-Vichy forces in the town led to continual fights and shootings among themselves. To us it seemed that the whole French Army had been re-equipped by the Allies on a lavish scale, only to sit about in Algeria waiting for their leaders to settle their political differences. It particularly annoyed Ricky and Butch to see Moroccan troops dressed in G.I. combat uniforms. They were always stopping their cars to give lifts to what they took to be stranded Yanks, only to get a *'Pardon, m'sieu?'* in answer to their 'Where you come from, bud?' Our sailors reduced these differences to simpler terms. One night there was a bloody pitched battle on the Quai Transatlantique between them and the matelots of the battleship *Richelieu*, no doubt harbouring bitter memories of our shelling their fleet at Oran. Next morning *Maidstone* had to send a doctor and two officers over to recover several battered British seamen.

Soon after we reached Algiers, the Captain took Number One and me to one side and told us that we were not being credited with the U-boat at present.

'Black market information [i.e. Ultra] is that a wireless message transmitted on German U-boat frequency was picked up just after the time of our firing, reporting having been missed by torpedoes.'

That led to an official verdict against our claim.

However, postwar analysis was conclusive, and I have a tie to prove it, depicting the emblem painted on *U.616*'s conning tower – a red devil wearing seaboots firing two six-shooters from the hips. Her Captain, Oberleutnant Koitschka, spotted our torpedo tracks and evaded them without difficulty. One went up in his wake, but the others were spread well apart, no doubt due to our ship's head swinging slowly with the target as the salvo was fired. In the heat of the moment the last order had been 'Amidships,' without a steadying course specified. In May the next year he was trapped by six USN destroyers backed up by three RAF Wellingtons and was hunted to exhaustion. Forced to the surface, where she was scuttled, the crew abandoned ship and were put in the bag. Although I was unable to attend their reunion in Hamburg forty years later, they sent me the tie.

Two weeks after our long-range hosepipe shot, *Ultimatum* was luckier. Patrolling at first light in the same area, she scored a hit at 7,000 yards on *U.431* returning from her sixteenth war patrol. There were no survivors.

Another U-class which was due back from a patrol off Bastia just before we arrived was still overdue. It was officially posted as lost, and there was the usual depressing sight of a steward in the wardroom removing the officers' names from the letter rack.

We sailed during the first week in November under orders to join the 10th Flotilla at Malta on conclusion. None of us were altogether sorry to leave. Life ashore was ruinously expensive. A stroll along the Rue Michelet in search of presents to send home showed handbags for thirty pounds, evening shoes for forty, more than a month's salary for a Lieutenant drawing submarine pay. For the equivalent cost of an evening out in wartime London one could have a few glasses of wine at the Aletti and then watch a middle-aged floor show at the 'Bosphor', where the only drink was 'champagne' – aerated white wine at 250 francs a small bottle. At 4,000 francs a (short) time, the tarts of the town were expensive luxuries even for the Americans, although one of them left me with my happiest memory of Algiers. Sergeant Ricky was leaning up against the front door of his garage when a classic peroxide blonde street-walker swept past, with wiggling hips and miniature poodle. She propositioned him and mentioned a price. Ricky shifted his cigar to the other side of his mouth: 'Who pays? You or me?'

The officers' brothel was 'The Sphinx', an imposing four-storeyed building with tiny rooms reeking of potassium permanganate leading off the internal verandahs around its covered courtyard. It was a boisterous, sordid production line. 'You pay your money and they thread you on,' was an Aussie's description. One night some of the Junior officers from the 8th Flotilla set fire to the place, having smuggled in a basket of limes concealing half-a-dozen underwater recognition flares which no ordinary fire extinguisher could douse. Everyone made good their escape in the ensuing riot among the sirens and whistles of U.S. Shore Patrols, except for a few Americans. They got the blame and had the place put off-limits to them for their pains. Next day one of our boats sailed with a wrinkled dildo strapped limply to its for'ard periscope.

The ratings found their runs ashore dangerous as well as expensive. Apart from the occasional café brawls with French matelots, they were liable to be castrated, should they press their advances on a veiled Arab woman. In spite of warnings and out-of-bounds regulations, they frequently woke up next morning in some dingy hovel deep inside the Casbah area, broke and beaten-up.

However, once at sea, they appeared to look back on Algiers as Hollywood later made it out to be – an exciting melting-pot of Eastern and Western civilizations where exotic adventures lay just around the corner.

The look-outs on the bridge enlarged on their squalid evenings in the native quarter till they sounded like an unexpurgated version of the *Arabian Nights*. A half-anticipated complication arose on the second day out. The coxswain came into the wardroom and told the Captain that the H.S.D. had reported sick.

'What's wrong with him?'

'Well, sir, you'd hardly guess after the way that Romeo's been carrying on ashore, but he's got a tear – a dose.'

'Gus, get out the Submarine Temporary Memoranda. There's something in there which will help.'

'Here it says we are to give him forty M&B693 subphanilanide tablets spread over three days, lots of water to drink, no sugar, no starch.'

'And no tot,' the Coxswain added, practical as usual. 'Right, that course of treatment will shake him. Just you leave him to Doctor Willoughby, Sir.'

For the next three days a pale, dejected Dickie Bird crept around the boat looking as though he would welcome The Reaper. The treatment was as efficient as it was drastic, and he was duly cured. Knowing there was no substitute for him as an Asdic listener, he never missed a watch.

Our patrol area this trip roughly extended from Cannes to Monte Carlo. We made our landfall at night by the distinctive Mont Agel above Monaco. For the first few days we patrolled in the bay between Nice and Antibes, looking for coastwise traffic cutting across from Cap Ferrat to clear Antibes. Sure enough, on the third day we sighted smoke and two masts clear of Cap d'Antibes. We waited confidently for it to alter course towards Nice, but unexpectedly it held on out to sea outside the range of protective shore batteries. We went deep and closed at full speed – eight knots with our screws audible all over the Western Med. At the next look it turned out to be a French destroyer of the *Terrible* class at long range, going hell for leather eastwards. Two looks through the periscope had not generated a satisfactory plot, so the Captain let it go, hoping she was on her way to pick up a westbound ship from Genoa.

But it was not to be. By day we strained our eyes through the periscope towards the Italian border, where a ship could be lost against the dark background of the hills. We plotted various conspicuous buildings on the coast on the chart to help our pilotage. The huge white Musée Océanographique on the headland at Monaco, the domed roof of the Casino, the hotel on Cap Ferrat, the promenade at Nice, crowded with Wehrmacht officers on leave, and the cliff railway at Menton were all inspected at close quarters. I often thought of old men huddled in front of fireplaces in London clubs daydreaming about their pre-war winters on the Riviera.

At nights it was unexpectedly cold. I wore two sweaters under a heavy kapok-padded suit, with fur-lined sea-boots, balaclava and two pairs of gloves. We used to surface three miles off the coast and head out to seaward for the charge. The day's accumulated garbage was not ditched until we were as far offshore as we would go. No. 1 had snap inspections of each bucket waiting to be swung up through the conning tower hatch for disposal, looking for anything which might leave a trace on the surface. I thought he went a bit far when he threatened the stokers' mess with disciplinary action for putting in a broken 78 rpm record without first steaming off the HMV label.

Once the battery was full we would creep back in to the coast and lie stopped in waiting for a convoy coast-crawling by night.

Time was marked only by diving in the mornings and surfacing at dusk. Large meals, regular sleep, books to read and desperate crib or uckers matches in the dogwatches followed each other in inexorable sequence.

When our recall came it seemed almost a pity to upset the peaceful routine. We set off to the south not having sighted or heard a thing that floated during the whole patrol, except for that one destroyer. The Captain was, as always, full of self-recrimination.

'Nice start to our time in the Tenth Flotilla. They will already have had our last patrol report with S/M8's covering letter telling them how we squirted off eight kippers for no hits. Now I'll have to break it to them that we let a destroyer go by.'

We touched in at Bizerta for the night, but that collection of bombed mud-huts was not enough to lure anyone ashore. From there we sailed in a Malta convoy to comply with the R.A.F.'s policy of assuming all submarines in the Mediterranean to be hostile. It was a lazy two days' surface trip devoted to sunbathing. Slowly our yellow complexions darkened. Passing through the boom into Sliema Creek was like coming home for the Captain. He had been serving in submarines based there on and off since Christmas, 1940.

As we passed in through the narrow entrance twenty-three days out from Algiers, the signalman produced our Jolly Roger and asked the Captain's permission to fly it.

'Whatever for, signalman? We don't fly it for a blank patrol.'

'But it wasn't blank, sir. Look.'

He unfurled the flag and showed us a little white circle which he had stitched in the bottom right hand corner. On it was printed 'M&B693'.

Home for the Tenth Flotilla was a damp stone building on Manoel Island, which juts out into the middle of the harbour. It used to be Lazaretto Quarantine hospital. We secured alongside what was now little better than a heap of rubble. The harbour was deep enough to allow submarines to lie right up against the building. There were two other 'U's secured to pontoons just off the shore.

Even though it was many months since the last bomb had fallen on Malta, little had changed since the dark days of the siege. The wardroom might have been a medieval stone barn, in dark damp contrast to the glaring sunlight outside. The local insipid beer or gin, when there was any, were drunk out of sawn-off bottles. Crockery, cutlery and furniture were all improvised or scrounged. The combination of a hard-headed Maltese messman, a lack of fresh food and an Admiralty victualling allowance intended for other days ensured that the food was bad and insufficient. We, who were just out from the relative plenty of England, had no right to complain. We could only marvel at those who had kept going out on patrol from here throughout the dark days.

At the time few realized the crucial part then played by submarines of the Tenth Flotilla. The Governor at the time failed to acknowledge their existence in his autobiography. From the end of 1940, when the first two 'U' class arrived out from England to start Lazaretto as an advanced base for the First Flotilla at Alexandria, a handful of submarines under the inspired leadership of Commander 'Shrimp' Simpson strangled the Axis supply-lines to North Africa. For some time they were the only Naval forces left on the island, and for even longer they were the only offensive threat to the enemy at sea in the central Mediterranean. They returned from patrol with the prospect of having to turn around and go out for more under constant enemy bombardment. The base staff was short-handed and lacked spares and equipment. Stocks of modern torpedoes were soon used up, and boats went out with obsolete practice fish. Soon the Italian Regia Aeronautica was backed up by Kesselring's Stukas. Then the Flotilla went through its most critical days. Two boats were sunk alongside their harbour berths by bombing, so it was decided that the remainder should spend the hours of daylight on the bottom of the harbour, surfacing to work all night at getting ready for sea once more. Dog-tired officers and men who had to spend their spells in harbour working round the clock in this fashion often turned their eyes to the two unfinished tunnels cut into the cliffs of Valletta opposite Lazaretto. They were planned in peacetime as submarine shelters, but abandoned due to their cost, said to be one million pounds – the price of waging the war for just under one hour.

In spite of all, they continued to come back from sea with their Jolly Rogers flying, a sight to thrill everyone, especially the bewildered Maltese looking out from their cave shelters. The only restaurant left open in Valletta offered a champagne supper to the officers of every submarine that came back after sinking something – until the bubbly ran out.

In the wardroom – and now in the Submarine Museum at Gosport – there was a framed score-board, giving a diagrammatic tally of each submarine's successes. *Upholder, Utmost, Urge, Unruffled, Unrivalled* were names with a string of little outline sketches of sinking cruisers, U-boats and merchant ships after them. The total damage to the Axis in merchant shipping alone amounted to just under one million tons. The cost to the Flotilla had been high – only two of its first fifteen submarines, lived to complete a tour. But, in the words of the Admiralty communiqué which announced the loss of *Upholder*, '. . . the ship and her company are gone, but the example and inspiration remain'. The inspiration was right there on that scoreboard. The bottom line had a new name on it, *Untiring*, followed by a blank space.

The changed situation in the Western Med after the landings on Sicily soon made it possible for submarines operating along the Riviera to be based nearer their patrol areas. So, no sooner had we arrived in Malta than there was talk of moving to La Maddalena. None of us had even heard of it. The chart showed it to be in the Bonifacio Strait between Corsica and Sardinia.

'Looks like a Wop version of Scapa Flow,' someone said, with uncanny prescience. A member of the advance party which had gone up there to spy out the land brought back a depressing tale.

'There's nothing. Just a rocky island with a church, a wine shop and a brothel. In peacetime it's where Italian naval officers were sent if they made off with their Commanding Officers' wives.'

★ 6 ★

JACKPOT AT MONTE CARLO

For our fifth patrol we were sent back to the area off Nice again.

A signal from S.10 warned us of a ship due to pass through our area at night, but, even though we lay stopped on the surface within a mile of Cap Ferrat for much of the night, we never saw it, even with a bright moon to seaward of us, which made us vulnerable to anyone looking out from ashore. At 0100 it was flat calm and the Captain decided our target was behind schedule. Fifteen minutes later we were in the grip of our first mistral, a vicious wind we endured four days a week throughout the winter. The same gales dissipated the thermal layers which protected us against Asdic pings in summer.

Next day keeping periscope depth was awkward, with vision frequently obscured by steep waves. The Captain took the boat close in to Monte Carlo for the day to get under the lee of the land.

During the afternoon Gus sighted a mast coming from the direction of Nice. The Captain looked at it for a long time.

'Looks as though it might be a medium-sized coaster – tall single funnel and two masts. Start the plot.'

For the next hour and a half we waited for the enemy to reach us. The plot gave the unlikely target speed of 2 knots. She was steering an erratic course, possibly due to the bad weather. Abreast of the headland of Monaco she turned sharply to port and scuttled into Monte Carlo harbour. The Captain followed the enemy towards the harbour entrance where she was seen to berth alongside the northern jetty.

'That'll be the *Quai de Plaisance*,' Gus said, looking up from the chart. 'It used to be the straight coming out of the tunnel during the Monaco Grand Prix.' I leaned over his shoulder and saw that the harbour was in the form of a square, entered through the breakwater forming its eastern side. It was plain that only a vessel berthed against the western wall would present a clear target from the harbour mouth. The Captain had other ideas.

'How much water is there two cables outside the breakwater?'

'Fifteen fathoms, sir.'

'Can do. Now, what's the least depth of water between the target and the harbour entrance?'

'Twenty-one feet.'

'Well, Coote, so long as the fish is fired far enough outside the breakwater to allow it to find its true running depth, there should be no question of it exploding on the bottom.'

After another long look at the target the Captain then headed out to seaward.

He has decided it's an impossible shot, I thought, along with everyone else in the Control Room. Then the Captain came over to the chart-table and placed the parallel rulers through the harbour entrance to a point half-way along the *Quai de Plaisance*.

'Now let's see. There are probably nets across the harbour mouth. So we'll have to fire one to blow them open and then another to go through and hit the target. We'll let him have it nearer dusk at 1700, so that we'll be able to get away on the surface. By the way, where's *Jane's Fighting Ships?*'

The Captain opened it up at the French section and started working through.

'It's flying a Nazi ensign, but the funnel cowling looks French to me. Besides, the Germans can't send ships this size by rail, and I'm damn sure this one didn't slip through the Straits.'

He paused at one picture. 'Quite like that, only more old-fashioned, and it's got a whale-back ramp over its counter as if it were a . . . that's it! A mine-layer!'

'Of course,' Gus said, 'that is why it was steering that crazy course at such a slow speed along from Cap Ferrat. It was on a lay.'

'At least we know not to go back along that way tomorrow. This picture is the one, I think, "One thousand tons, length 275 feet, draught 12 feet – carries at least one hundred mines. Also employed on net-laying duties".'

A pencilled track of a torpedo through the entrance of the break-water on an oblique shot showed that we needed half a degree accuracy from the torpedo's gyroscope.

'The nearer we fire from, the wider the margin of permissible torpedo error – but if we get too close the kipper will hit the bottom in shallow water before it has recovered its depth. Besides, we've got to allow room for ourselves to turn away after firing. We'll squirt off the first one here,' – he marked a point five hundred yards outside

72

the harbour – 'and the second one, if necessary, here. That's three hundred yards off. If one of those two runs off its course and hits the breakwater it will sound mighty loud in here. Number One, go to Watch Diving now and go to Diving Station at quarter to five.' He turned to me, 'You're Officer of the Watch now, aren't you? Keep on out on 140° till quarter to four, then turn back on to 320° and call me. Don't use too much periscope and don't spend your time goofing at the pretty girls on the promenade.'

It was odd looking through the periscope at the peaceful Sunday afternoon scene which we were to interrupt so rudely at five o'clock. The long grey ship was lying alongside with some washing billowing from a jackstay on her fo'c'sle. Seen against the background of plane trees along the quayside and white buildings rising up the steep hill behind, she looked more like a pleasure steamer than a warship. The only other boats in the harbour were yachts laid up for the duration.

At teatime we started back towards the harbour again, our course once again being plotted through an area marked as 'Mined' on the chart. One worry was whether the Germans had laid a controlled minefield off the harbour, linked to hydrophones or Asdics ashore which could trigger off the whole minefield on hearing a submarine's screws.

By the time the ship's company went to Diving Stations the boat was approaching its firing position.

'Yes, everything seems much the same as before. Set the torpedoes to six feet. Take down this fix.'

He swung the periscope round, taking bearings of the breakwater light, the Musée Océanographique and cathedral spire.

'Three hundred yards to go for the first one, sir.'

I quickly thought of all the things which could go wrong with the torpedo. The balance chamber might be flooded, in which case it would plunge straight to the bottom. Or the relay valve of the gyroscope might be seized up, causing the torpedo to swerve off course and blow up on the breakwater. Worse still, the propeller clamps might still be on, or the air vessel stop-valves shut, but I was confident we had followed the correct drill before the rear doors were shut after loading.

'Now, gunlayer, this is up to you,' the Captain said to the helmsman. 'If you go so much as a quarter of a degree off your course I'll break your neck. Steady as you go on 321 degrees. Remember you're the chap who decides which way the kipper will run.'

Len, the gunlayer, scratched his beard and grabbed the wheel tighter. All eyes were on the compass repeater tape in front of him. 321½ . . . it jerked back to port, 321 . . . 321½ . . . Len gave the wheel half a turn . . . 321 . . . the tape was steady.

'Fire one!'

Again that shudder as the torpedo was blown out through the tube.

'There's one to knock down the door,' the Captain said, still looking through the periscope. 'I do wish all those people sunning themselves on the quay would get away from that minelayer. If they only knew. There's a woman with a pram just near the bows . . . Jesus!'

A violent thunderclap explosion rocked the boat as though we'd been straddled by a pattern of depth charges. 'Controlled mine-field' flashed through my mind, but no water was coming in.

'Quick, Number One, your camera.'

The Captain stood aside from the periscope as Number One held up his camera to the eyepiece and snapped the mushroom of smoke that was rising out of the water where the minelayer had been.

'I think we can save the other torpedo,' the Captain remarked. 'It looked as though that chap still had most of his eggs on board. One torpedo would never make a bang like that. Any damage, Number One?'

'No, sir, just a few lights.'

'I expect most of the blast was contained inside the harbour. That *Quai de Plaisance* doesn't look too pleasant now. Half the trees are down and there are bits of wreckage all over the place. Hullo, I see the buildings round about have lost most of their windows, too. Hope we didn't upset the wheel in the Casino.'

He let us each have a quick look through the periscope as we hurried away from the harbour. Through the narrow gap in the breakwater, I could just see a tangled heap of metal sticking up above the water. The line of trees along the quay was interrupted by gaps where the force of the mines counter-exploding had uprooted them. The branches of those still standing were covered in clothing and debris. People were running down the hillside to the harbour.

When I first re-visited the Côte d'Azur in the early 'fifties the little man running the newspaper kiosk at the end of the quayside remembered it well. He had nipped off to a Bar Tabac for a pastis and returned to find his stall had been wiped out. Bowing to commercial and political pressures, the Monegasques have renamed the beautiful quayside avenue in turn after the Liberation, John F. Kennedy, Charles de Gaulle and now des Etats Unis. On Grand Prix day you pay £1000 for a place on one of the motor yachts berthed stern to the wall where we blew up the minelayer, then the *Quai de Plaisance*. Before being commandeered by the Nazis and renamed *UJ2213* she had been FS *Heureux*. The archives in Monaco insist she was a minesweeper, which would not account for the force of the explosion.

The news would have been flashed along the lines to Nice. All available destroyers and E-boats would soon be raising steam for full speed to come after us. The Captain thought so too, for he took the boat deep and increased speed. During the hour that was left till it would be dark enough to surface he presided over our usual post-mortem in the wardroom.

'There's just a chance they didn't see the track of the fish, in which case the whole thing might be put down to sabotage or an accident. Just the same, we mustn't take any chances. We'll get out of this area tonight and go round towards Genoa. How about your photograph, Number One?'

'Should be a good one. The light wasn't too bad.' It turned out to be a clear snap of some officers standing on the balcony of the mess at Lazaretto with a vague blur of smoke and houses superimposed. Evidently he had forgotten to wind on the film.

In the Torpedo Stowage Compartment the lads had cleared away everything in readiness for reloading. The Signalman was busy cutting a piece off the tail of a red shirt belonging to the gunlayer. It was to make the red bar on our Jolly Roger, to indicate a warship sunk. The gunlayer took full credit for having pointed the submarine accurately at the target and was reminding the tubes' crews that it took a gunnery rating to aim their torpedoes for them.

'Mind you all bring your tots round when we're back in 'arbour to show your appreciation.'

The new torpedo was loaded in with a very rude message to A. Hitler chalked on it.

We surfaced five miles off Menton, expecting to spend an uncomfortable night dodging angry E-boats and being put down by hunting aircraft. But the weather took a hand. Within an hour it was blowing a gale once more, with driving sleet reducing visibility to a few cables. Unpleasant it may have been for those on the bridge, but there was a comfortable feeling that no hunting craft could find us in that weather. All night we steered what we hoped was a course parallel to the coast. By dead reckoning we should be to the north-east of Cape Noli at dawn – just short of the large minefield protecting Genoa itself.

The weather moderated slightly during my watch, and when I came down at 0430 it was choppy with occasional rain squalls. I

75

could make out the snow-covered peaks of the Alpes-Maritimes, without being able to identify any one single point. Just after I turned in, the night alarm sounded.

An attack quickly developed. From the information passed down it sounded like a fast-moving ship coast-crawling north-eastwards. In a break in the visibility the Captain recognized it as a destroyer moving at over 20 knots. It was too far away to attack, and soon crossed our bows and disappeared. As we would be diving soon, Gus and I sat down to a cup of cocoa and a game of crib in the wardroom instead of turning in for the short remaining period of darkness. The charge had been broken and the boat was proceeding dead slow in towards the beach on its motors. Suddenly there was a shout from the Control Room:

'For Christ's sake, torpedoes approaching!'

Gus and I shot over to the Asdic where a shaken operator was holding out his earphones at arm's length.

'Torpedoes! Green 110, sir!' He pointed wildly out across the Control Room, as if he expected something to come bursting in through the boat's hull at any second. No mistaking the torpedoes. The noise coming from those earphones sounded like a tube train approaching a station.

'Hard a-port. Tell the bridge torpedoes approaching on the starboard beam.'

The operator put his earphones on again and picked up the noise of the torpedoes.

'Very loud; bearing Green 85, sir,' he stammered and took off the earphones again. The bearing was growing for'ard, so they were going to miss ahead if they ran straight.

There was a series of clatters and bumps as the look-outs came tumbling off the bridge, followed by Number One.

'There's a bloody great destroyer lying stopped beam on to us with her tubes trained outboard. Range about fifteen hundred yards. We've seen the tracks of his fish. They've missed ahead,' he told us breathlessly.

The Asdic operator soon confirmed that, but they still sounded right on top of us. For a moment I wondered if they might be the new acoustic torpedoes, which would home in on the noise of our propellers. I was badly rattled.

'Why the hell doesn't he dive?' I asked.

The answer came down the voicepipe. The Captain sounded as calm as though he was still in Inchmarnock Water.

'Bring all tubes to the ready.'

I wondered if the Captain had taken leave of his senses. He had sent the look-outs and the Officer of the Watch down below, and now he was staying on the surface to argue the point with a destroyer, which had a surfaced submarine in its sights, having just fired three kippers at us. Now it would turn in and ram us.

'Set all tubes to eight feet,' he ordered calmly.

The H.S.D. had taken over the Asdics now and could hear the torpedoes still running faintly in the distance. He swept round on the bearing where even Charlie on the radar set had an echo the size of a house at 500 yards.

'Turbine H.E. increasing,' he reported.

That would be the destroyer speeding up as it came in towards us. The faint patch of light under the conning-tower hatch was blotted out as the Captain stepped down off the bridge. Urr . . . urr. The klaxon sounded like an air-raid siren. No one needed any urging to get the boat under. By the time the Captain had got down below we were already passing twenty feet.

'Ninety feet, shut off for depth-charging. Silent routine . . . And hold on to something,' he added quietly.

'Transmissions on Green 30, sir. In contact,' the H.S.D. reported. 'H.E. increasing.'

We were at seventy feet when the destroyer passed straight over the top of us, the thrash of her propellers plainly audible throughout the submarine. You could see it written on everyone's face: this is it, here it comes. A straddle first time. Ten feet a second to sink. That's ten seconds for a pattern set to a hundred feet. Seven . . . eight . . . nine . . . ten . . . counting too fast . . . probably only five seconds so far . . . seven . . . eight . . . nine . . . ten.

'Vessel lost contact, sir. He's sweeping on Red 120. Transmission interval 2500 yards.'

What had happened? There was no ear-splitting crash . . . nothing. The Signalman rose to the occasion.

'Maybe those depth charges were made at the Skoda works and filled with sand.'

'Or M. and V.' the Gunlayer put in.

We squatted on the deck, waiting for the destroyer to pick us up again. The Captain was wearing a head-set plugged into our Asdic and could hear the enemy's transmissions as he swept round to pick us up again. It wasn't long coming.

'In contact, sir,' the H.S.D. said casually. 'Red 90.'

We listened while he reported that the destroyer was coming in again, speeding up and cutting down its transmission intervals as it closed on us unerringly. Perhaps that first run had only been a sighter. This time we were for it. Once again the thrash of propellers overhead. The noise died away and the counting started again. But nothing broke the suspense.

For an hour the destroyer hung about, making fewer and less accurate runs over us as time went on. Then the H.E. faded altogether. We waited another half an hour and then came cautiously up to periscope depth. Just because the noise of his screws had faded, it did not necessarily mean that the enemy had departed. He might easily be sitting somewhere near, waiting for us to make the next move. The Captain searched swiftly round with the after periscope.

'Not a sausage. Well I wonder what all that was about. Now we've got to find out where we are.'

He identified a cliff against the barren line of hills as Cape Noli and gave Gus a fix which put us four miles off the beach. When we had fallen out from Diving Stations and were seated round the wardroom table having our breakfast, the Captain produced his theory.

'I didn't like to say this in front of the troops, but I think they may have been using depth-charges with contact pistols. Not the usual ones set to go off hydrostatically, but maybe a large pattern of small charges with graze fuses like our hedgehogs. It wouldn't take more than one direct hit by a very small charge to blow a hole in our pressure-hull. Nice chaps. Now, what's Jane up to today?' He picked up the *Good Morning* newspaper and settled back to enjoy the strip cartoons with his coffee.

The thought of those small contact bombs sinking all round us without exploding like any decent depth-charge was creepy.

'Give me an honest-to-God pattern of 450-pounders any day,' Number One said. 'At least you know after the explosion where you stand, or if you do.'

If we thought we were to be left on our own for a quiet day patrolling at Watch Diving we were mistaken. The lights in the wardroom had only been out a few minutes and we had barely settled in our bunks when Gus, who was on the watch, came in and shook the Captain.

'There are some masts and some smoke coming down from the north, sir.'

'Oh dear. I suppose that destroyer has rustled up a few of his chums to continue the good work.'

He went to the periscope and tried to make out what went with the masts. But it was still blowing hard, with spray continually clouding over the upper window. It was some time before the Captain could see.

'Just as I thought. Three of the bastards, sweeping in line abreast. Heard anything, Asdics?'

'Yes, sir,' the operator replied, 'I can just hear transmissions sweeping.'

Wearily the ship's company went to Diving Stations as we went deep and waited. At least this time the enemy could only hunt for us in a general area. He hadn't seen us dive, as he had earlier in the morning and been able to go straight for the patch of bubbles where our main ballast tanks had vented themselves. They might miss us altogether.

'In contact, sir.'

They had us again. It was a repeat of the earlier performance, with three sources of H.E. and pinging, making their attacks in turn, though not with the deadly accuracy of our old friend. In all they kept us deep for a further two hours. Everyone's nerves were a little on edge. The Coxswain, squatting in front of his after-hydroplane handwheel, could stand it no longer.

'If those Wops want an A/S exercise, why don't they use their own bleedin' submarines? We didn't come all the way out from U.K. to be a clockwork mouse for training their Asdic ratings,' he muttered to the Second Coxswain.

When we came up again, the Captain was able to identify one of the three hunting craft as it went away to the south.

'They look like those sketches we have of UJ-boats: converted coasters, with a big gun for'ard, a tall single funnel and a pronounced sheer.'

'UJ' stood for Unterseebotjaeger. We had recently been warned they were nasty customers. They were more efficient as anti-submarine vessels than destroyers and carried large quantities of depth-charges. The patrol report of the first British submarine to encounter one told how it surfaced to gun down what was taken to be an unescorted coasting-vessel; she was quickly put down again by heavy and accurate gunfire. 'They carry at least 84 depth-charges,' the report ended laconically. We were glad to see the last of them.

At last it really did seem as though they had given up. We had lunch in peace and I took over the afternoon watch. Quickly the lights went out for'ard as all hands turned in to catch up with their sleep. The Captain decided it was not worthwhile trying to get away from the area, even if it was compromised. Better to lie in towards the land till dark, and then shift patrol elsewhere on the surface. There was not very much chance of the Germans sending any shipping past Cape Noli for a while, when they knew there was an enemy submarine off there.

I looked across the troughs of the waves at little villages each with their prominent church towers spaced at intervals along the coast. I was wondering vaguely how Napoleon ever coaxed his armies across those peaks when I saw what at first I took to be a stick on the water. There was another mast near it. The boat pumped up to 24 feet with the swell and I saw that there were two squat vessels plunging in our direction, not very far away. With difficulty I awoke the Captain who took over the periscope, threatening a horrible end to the next Wop who disturbed his afternoon's sleep.

'More UJ-boats, I suppose.'

He stared at them for a while and went on: 'These look like a couple of dressed-up canal barges. Might be UJ-boats though. Wait a minute. What have we here? A couple of R-boats or chasseurs on either bow. Good enough – Diving Stations.'

When the order was given to get all tubes ready, the crew knew we were no longer on the defensive and were going to hit back for having been kept on the hop all day.

The targets were two cargo vessels, with their engines and super-structure aft, very like the little Dutch coasters in the English Channel. These two were on their way towards the war front, so they were for it, and their escort of chasseurs were not going to stop us, especially after the way we had eluded the much more formidable UJ-boats. The Captain fired a full salvo from eight hundred yards. He was still looking through the periscope when the bang came. It was followed by a succession of small explosions like a string of Chinese crackers going off.

'No doubt about what those two were carrying. There are shells still bursting all round the spot where that chap blew up. Looks as if we've missed the other one.'

He was not in the slightest perturbed by the presence of the two chasseurs. Instead of going deep he stayed up to watch the fun.

'They're not much more than motor boats, and they're making heavy weather of this sea. Get one tube reloaded as quickly as possible, I'm going to trail this other fellow – I think we can keep up with him.'

The plot showed the target to be making good not more than seven knots against the head sea, so we would be able to keep pace submerged whilst our batteries lasted.

In under a quarter of an hour I was able to report to the Captain that we had one torpedo ready. We had managed to overhaul the target, so were able to turn and fire at our leisure. The Captain watched the torpedo's track cut across the waves to its mark.

'Damn! Missed ahead,' he said savagely.

20 HMS *Totem* coming alongside at Oban for the Coronation celebrations, 1953.

21 *Totem* fore-ends, home for 20 sailors, 8 torpedoes and most of the stores.

22 After a brief encounter in the fog. Medway River, 1952.

23 HMS *Totem* alongside HMS *Forth*, submarine depot ship at Malta, September, 1953.

24 C.-in-C. Mediterranean (Admiral Mountbatten) being saluted on board *Totem*, Navarin Bay, October, 1953.

'A series of small explosions all round, sir,' came from the H.S.D.

'Lord, yes, someone's firing at our periscope. Is there an aircraft about?' Another look round at the periscope. 'Well I'm buggered. It's the chasseurs. Both of them are firing every gun they've got at our periscope. There's a chap manning an Oerlikon on the bows of that one who is getting very wet indeed. They've got the wind-up properly. The target's turned away and is heading in towards the beach.'

He watched as the ammunition ship bolted like a scared rabbit for the shore. The two chasseurs must have fired every round of Oerlikon they carried before they too went in after their charge. The Captain was now determined to dispose of the remainder of the ammunition convoy. We loaded in our last three torpedoes and then nosed in to the shallow water. The ship had beached itself stern on to us, so it would only be possible to get in an oblique shot set to run on the surface from further up the coast. The first torpedo blew up on the bottom just under the stern of the target.

'That's shaken them. They're all jumping over the side and wading up the beach.'

The second torpedo hit it fair and square. There was another sharp explosion, and once again bursting shells and rockets put up a Guy Fawkes show. This was too much for the chasseurs. With one accord they both turned and ran. Judging from the direction they headed, it seemed as if they were making for the little village marked on the chart, appropriately enough, as 'Finali'.

Disposing of those two ships had cost us six torpedoes, but as they were carrying well over a thousand tons of ammunition between them, it had been taxpayers' money well spent.

We made best speed to get away from the area. It did not take much imagination to foresee what the local German naval commander's orders for that night would be. All shore leave for destroyers and UJ-boats based in Genoa would be cancelled. I wished them a pleasant night flogging backwards and forwards off Cape Noli in a gale. By then we should be well on our way back to Maddalena. A signal was sent telling Captain (S) that we only had one torpedo remaining and were accordingly leaving patrol. It was then just under twenty-four hours since we had fired through the breakwater into Monaco harbour.

★ 7 ★

CHRISTMAS AT LA MADDALENA

The average submariner's attitude towards the fighting qualities of the Italian Navy was much the same as that of the rest of the Mediterranean Fleet, which had spent three years trailing its coat outside bases in which numerically superior fleets lay at anchor. But in one aspect of naval warfare they were acknowledged to be masters – Italian minelaying was gruesomely efficient. Even deep water, outside the hundred-fathom line, was often found to be mined. Consequently we approached our landfall for the trip through the Bonifacio Strait to Maddalena very gingerly.

Several of our submarines were thought to have met their end there. Although we had been told before sailing from Malta that a minesweeping flotilla was starting to clear a channel through the Straits, it would take months before the job could be done thoroughly.

In addition, making a landfall on the south-west coast of Corsica, with its succession of similar peaks and capes, was speculative. Ironically we were compelled to remain dived by day for fear of U-boats from Toulon which were thought to patrol off the Ajaccio area. At length, the morning mists cleared away and we could pick out the Monachi Rock Lighthouse in the Straits. We surfaced and verified our position by a fix, which put us comfortably in the mined area.

With all spare hands on the upper deck wearing life-belts and with watertight doors shut and clipped throughout below, we set course for a line of dan-buoys marking the narrow channel already cleared by our sweepers. Soon a light flashed from the eastwards. It was a motor gun-boat which Captain (S) had sent out to escort us in.

'Congratulations on your success. Follow me in.'

We duly took station astern of M.G.B. 660 and made our way

along the twenty-mile channel to Maddalena, which now appeared as a row of rocky islands on the horizon.

The closer we got to the island the less inviting it looked. The barren shore of boulders and scrub was horribly familiar – it was indeed the Mediterranean's Scapa Flow. There was nothing to show that any living thing moved on the island except that a few dozen barrage balloons glistened overhead.

The channel twisted its way past a series of small islets and brought into view a line of sparse whitewashed buildings along the waterfront. One or two small ships at anchor in the harbour gave us a desultory cheer when they saw our Jolly Roger flying from the after periscope. The only sign of it having been an important Italian Naval base was the topmast of an 8-inch cruiser sticking out of the water where it had been straddled by B.17s.

In a small corner of the harbour bordered by the heap of rubble that had once been the Royal Dockyard were the submarine berths. There the advance party of depot-ship's staff from Malta were waiting to greet us. Groups of Italian sailors and Carabinieri pointed excitedly at our Jolly Roger and white ensign. It was the closest any of them had ever got to an British warship during the war.

Captain (S) already knew from Intelligence all about our having disposed of the ammunition ships. In fact, he told us quite a lot about the attack which we didn't know ourselves, including the contents of their cargoes and their intended destination. Our lads were the centre of admiring circles of spare crew ratings who lapped up their highly-coloured accounts of our patrol waiting for the invitation to 'come down below and have one out of the bottle'. Sacks spilled out the Christmas mail from home – enough to go round for everyone, for we had had none since Algiers. One of the fore-endmen held up an airgraph with the news of the birth of a daughter over a month ago. Most tots having been bottled throughout the patrol, there was no lack of Nelson's blood with which to celebrate. By noon silence settled throughout the boat as they slept it off.

As we went through the dockyard to our quarters, scruffy Italian sailors in clogs jumped out of the way, saluting ostentatiously. '*Viva Inglese*'. I couldn't see Jack doing that to a German naval officer in Pompey dockyard, if the war had gone the other way. The White Ensign flew outside a stone compound marked 'Caserna Favelli'. It was the old Italian Naval detention barracks, but it would have to do for us, as every other building in the dockyard area had been flattened in the town's only air-raid – ten minutes during which the U.S.A.A.F. carried out a devastating saturation attack.

The 'Caserna Favelli' had been designed to make life uncomfortable for serious offenders, so the accommodation was, even by Italian standards, sketchy. Our seamen had to sling their hammocks in damp stone stables with only lockers for furniture. Plumbing and sanitary arrangements were open plan, hole-in-the-ground type, involving a weekly visit from an unhappy Italian with empty tubs on a bullock-cart. The lot of the officers had been softened by the Royal Marine Engineers who had knocked up a wooden hut in the central courtyard as our wardroom. We slept four or five to a small tiled room.

Our first meal brought us face to face with another reality of life in Maddalena: there was no fresh food on the island. The familiar 'M and V' ration had followed us ashore. There was fresh meat and vegetables in Sardinia, but AMGOT★ regulations forbad its export, even though only half a mile of water divided us from a land of plenty.

The town itself was typical of so many in the Western Mediterranean. It had no apparent reason for existence except as a garrison for the thousands of Italian troops stationed there – now officially designated as collaborators. These dejected flotsam of the Desert campaign stood about in their soiled green uniforms pathetically asking for tobacco. They squatted down in bored sullen groups. They were all waiting . . . waiting for the day when they could all stop being gladiators and go back to their vineyards or their fishing. An atmosphere of total inertia hung over the town. None of the inhabitants seemed to register any emotion one way or the other on seeing their enemies walking unarmed through their streets. The Germans had been in the island for two years. They had gone. Now it only remained to be seen if the British administration would mean more food, or less. That was all. One could see in the faces of the children that it had better not be less. The only houses of any size were the former officers' quarters. The local Admiral's residence was second only in size and grandeur to the officers' brothel. The Germans had requisitioned all the more comfortable homes and two of these had been shrewdly taken over by our own Coastal Forces, who reached the island a week before the 10th Flotilla's advance party.

All Allied forces including the Submarine Flotilla were under the Naval Officer in Charge, Captain George Phillips. Early in January he was relieved by the elegant but aloof P.Q. Roberts. In a previous appointment in the Operations Division of the Admiralty, he had used his initials to designate the convoys to Murmansk. Besides

★ Allied Military Government of Occupied Territory

our submarines he had under him flotillas of British, American and Canadian Coastal Forces, an R.A.F. barrage balloon unit, the R.M. Engineers, the minesweepers and American A.A. gunners, whose performance to date was most reassuring – in one raid by the Luftwaffe the week before their Bofors shot down seven out of twenty-five aircraft and winged several more. Thereafter the Luftwaffe only visited us singly and at a respectful height.

If the 20,000 demoralized soldiers lolling about the streets were pathetic by day, at night their spirits perked up a little. They roamed the streets with guitars singing 'Lilli Marlene' and once even plucked up the courage to fire a tommy-gun through the window of an empty ground-floor cabin in our quarters. Reprisals in the form of a curfew and a rocket delivered by the Captain to the local General put a stop to that sort of bravado for a while. For good measure P.Q. commandeered the Italian General's immaculately groomed and caparisoned white charger and used it to move around the town. It was a shrewd psychological and symbolic move, making it clear to all who was now in charge.

Next day *Upstart* came in from sea, flying its Jolly Roger to mark a hit on a large merchant ship off Cannes. It was followed by another on Christmas Eve with a tanker sunk off Leghorn to its credit. It all added fuel to our Christmas morning cocktail party in the wooden hut. American officers from the P.T. squadron were greatly impressed. They had not been in the Med long and could hardly believe such targets still existed. They looked at the flotilla scoreboard with its little tonnage thermometer nudging the million mark.

'Is this what's been sunk by the whole British Navy in the Med?'

'No, just the 10th Flotilla,' said someone with studied casualness.

The Americans were to be our nearest neighbours on the Island. Strictly non-controversial remarks were exchanged over cocktails, until one American led with his chin:

'Pity the Yank subs didn't operate in the Med. Those boys would have shown you the way, like they are doing out in the Pacific.'

'Not with you in one of them,' his chum quickly cut in.

Our Paymaster was telling another group of Americans that their concern with our troubles in India would be better directed at their own black problems. The Pay was a bank teller in peacetime. Reading the *Morning Post* for ten years on his commuter train had set his political views in concrete. As the gins passed round he ploughed through his repertoire: the race problem, intimidation in American labour unions, the acquisition of British assets in the States under duress and the behaviour of American servicemen on leave in London.

'D'you ever hear the story,' he asked, 'that's going round the town? They all say that there are only three things wrong with the Yanks . . . they're over-paid, over-sexed and over here – Ha! Ha! Jolly good, eh? Over here.'

I warmed to a Lieutenant (j.g.) who choked back a natural impulse to knock him down on the spot. A loud-mouthed American and an insensitive stupid Englishman very nearly put an end to our entente then and there. Fortunately being washed up on the same desert island gave us a common interest in being good neighbours, so we clinked our glasses to a happy sojourn at Maddalena together.

Christmas festivities went on all day. After lunch in one of the motor gunboats where their ever-resourceful cook produced a turkey, probably nicked from the U.S. Navy Admiral's pantry, it was time for a return visit to the American mess. Their regime is as dry as Scotland then was on a Sunday, so we expected Coca-Cola and ice cream during a quiet evening round the radiogram and ping-pong table. Yet the singing and shouting suggested some stimulant other than the Christmas spirit had taken over. Two black waiters brought round a fruit cup. I hesitated . . .

'G'wan, Sir, take one – it's grapefruit juice . . . laced with a little something.'

We all drank their health, expecting anything from methylated spirits to high octane fuel, but it was pure grapefruit juice. Why, I wondered, do we need so much alcohol to liven up our parties when these chaps can work up the atmosphere of the Mardi Gras on grapefruit juice? There were roast peanuts, sweetcorn, honey-baked ham and pumpkin pie to liven up reminiscences of visits to each other's countries. Crap dice were spat on and rolled for untidy piles of dollar bills. Glenn Miller and Benny Goodman's music barely held their own against the rising background level.

It first struck me that there was something wrong when I saw Georgie Hunt doing his sword dance. He was the C.O. of *Ultor*, normally shy and retiring, not one to take the lead in noisy festivities. I sniffed my grapefruit juice again. It was odourless, so I asked the American doc standing beside me if it really was innocuous. He turned a glazed eye on me.

'Innocuous? It'll inoculate you! It'll make you high as a church steeple. It has me already.'

'What's in it?'

'It's the best goddam ninety proof pure torpedo alcohol Uncle Sam ever made. They put it in our tin fish as fuel but sometimes we bleed a little off to spike our grape-fruit juice on special occasions.'

Geordie went through the steps of his dance flawlessly. Soon he had the Americans doing an eightsome reel as a break from some athletic jitterbugging.

The day faded to a blurred dissolve. The next thing I knew was a rasping across my face. Like some nightmare sequence in a horror movie I looked upwards, transfixed by a long wooden pole which seemed to have grown out of my head. At the other end of the broom-handle was a grinning black messboy sweeping out the debris of the party. There seemed to be others in Royal Navy uniforms stretched out like bodies recovered from the rubble of a bomb-site.

The story was painfully pieced together. Those who had fallen where we drank our last tumbler of torpedo alcohol were relatively lucky. Some sixth sense propelled Gus back towards the submarine pens in the mistaken belief that he was Duty Officer. He was helped on board and tucked up in his bunk after the Duty Petty Officer had forged his signature in the Night Rounds Book.

Meanwhile the First Lieutenant, Digger, remembered that he was Duty Officer and set off towards the boat, collapsing in a heap on the road outside. Sailors returning from the brothel picked him up and manhandled him towards his room in the barracks. Unfortunately he was spotted by the one man he needed to avoid. Commander(S) was never one to make any allowance for human frailty or bother to look for evidence beyond his eyes, so he placed Digger under arrest and set in train the proceedings for a court-martial.

Before the ceremony was held and the necessary sword found to be placed on the President's table, our Captain sought an audience with P.Q. So when Digger was called into the room a few days later and found the sword pointing at him, no one was unduly worried. The sentence of a Severe Reprimand meant nothing to a sheep farmer from the outback of New South Wales. Nor did being dismissed his ship, as he had been temporarily drafted from *Untiring* to the Spare Crew, so his dismissal was technically from HMS *Talbot*, the name now borne by the former Italian detention quarters. He was instantly reappointed to HMS *Untiring* and was back on board the next day, throwing his weight around with the finesse of a stevedore as though nothing had happened.

Gus was commended for his initiative in stepping into the breach as Duty Officer. I was privately cautioned by the Captain that I should not always count on such outrageous luck.

Our friendship with the men of the P.T. Squadron never looked back. They had steaks, ice-cream and movies in their mess; we had Scotch, gin and beer in our boats. I fell into a running bridge school. The stakes at a dollar a hundred were far beyond our usual two pence a point, but concentrated our attention marvellously, cutting out those speculative slam bids second time round and other private variations on Culbertson. Bills were settled weekly, showing quite small cumulative swings, but it made a prudent player out of me – for the time being.

Life ashore was so dull and uncomfortable that the ship's company couldn't wait to go back on patrol, just to get away from the unvarying menus, the sickly vino in the taverna, the lack of mail from home, the ration of one bottle of beer a week in the canteen. They had only returned from patrol four days before they all cried out to be sent off to sea again. There was no patrol leave, for the simple reason that there was nowhere to go.

Our stand-off was cut short, so we gladly sailed for patrol on New Year's Eve, knowing that we would miss nothing in the way of a celebration. Even our two Scots on board were resigned to it. Going down the Bonifacio Strait we ran into a full westerly gale. A tank landing-ship struggled past us on its way out through the west channel. Later we heard it had blown up on a mine and gone down like a stone an hour after it passed us. Four minesweepers had been lost in as many weeks and several gun-boats and landing craft had touched off mines.

Our patrol area this time was between Genoa and Leghorn. We reached the billet without incident and spent a week without seeing anything more than a stream of trains running along the coastal railway.

A few F-lighters came through our area, all of them northbound and empty. The Captain did not rate them worth a torpedo, but, after ten days on the billet, he changed his mind.

'We'll sink the next one that comes our way.'

It happened that one fully-laden and southbound appeared next day. It was a murderous point-blank range attack from 700 yards. The explosion of our torpedo hitting blew lamps out of their sockets in the tube space. Not a trace of the F-lighter remained at the next look.

There remained a few hours of daylight, so we made off from the scene of attack, in order to surface clear of any hunting craft that might be whistled up from Leghorn. Their masts duly appeared at teatime, followed shortly by the sound of Asdics sweeping. The Captain watched them till he could make out four in line abreast. In due course the H.S.D. reported one of them to be in contact with us, so we went deep. At least two of them passed over the top pinging all over us without registering any active disapproval.

Although we were slowly working our way out into the deep field of the Gulf of Genoa, the UJ-boats would not be shaken off. There was always at least one of them apparently in contact. The time for surfacing came and went, with the hunting craft still hanging on to our tail. The air in the submarine became increasingly foul, with everyone breathing laboriously and finding any physical exertion a conscious challenge.

Then, just before midnight, the sound of Asdic transmissions died away altogether. We waited another half-hour, but still there was no sign of the enemy,

'Thank God, that's over,' the Captain said. 'Now let's surface.'

I followed him up the conning-tower as the first draught of sickly sweet fresh air came down into the boat. My head was barely out of the upper hatch when the Captain's seaboots crashed down on my shoulders.

'Get down! Press the tit!'

I hit the klaxon and fell down into the Control Room, with the Captain close behind me.

'Ninety feet. Shut off for depth-charging. There are four UJ-boats away to starboard in the moonlight. Hear anything, H.S.D?'

'No, sir.'

We sat and waited to find out if they had sighted us on the surface. But it was half an hour before their transmissions were audible. Then they were groping uncertainly in our direction; it was unlikely they had spotted us during our brief moment on the surface, even though we had been right in the path of the moon. There was no question of being able to run off track from the advancing sweep of UJ-boats, so we settled down dead slow, heading straight towards them, reducing our width as an Asdic target to sixteen feet.

Two of them passed either side of us without giving a sign of having detected anything unusual. They carried right on sweeping round: click – peep . . . click – peep . . . click – peep . . . click – peep. The sound of their screws disappeared to the southward. Less than an hour later we surfaced and crammed on the charge. We also had to get a bit further from the area of A/S saturation, so altered course to close the coast off Cape Noli, the scene of our affair with the two ammunition coasters.

It was our last day on patrol, and all on board hoped for something to fire our remaining salvo at. The Captain passed the time trying

89

to read the mind of the German naval officer ashore in charge of convoys and escorts. He drew lines routing imaginary ships on a chart of the Gulf of Genoa.

Accordingly, that night we charged in the middle of the Gulf astride the direct route across from Leghorn to the Riviera. It seemed an anticlimax patrolling in the deep field even though most of the Captain's hunches had come up pretty well so far. I had the middle watch on the bridge, fighting off the false sense of security of being homeward-bound with thoughts turning to what film would be on at the base cinema when we got back and who else would be sharing our stand-off period. Jan Pengelly, the starboard look-out, was declaiming to his opposite number the relative advantages of rough cider over beer.

There was a full moon to the south throwing out a broad floodlit path, but the rest of the horizon was impenetrably black. I readily imagined how we would stand out to a destroyer away to the north of us. So I had another search round that sector.

'Cut out the talk, you two.'

Silence for a few seconds, then:

'Ship there, zur, and he's a big 'un. Red one – two – five.'

It must have suddenly come out on to the edge of the bright moon path, for it was clearly visible to the naked eye. A square dark shape with a smudge of smoke.

'Sound the alarm! Captain on the bridge! Starboard thirty.'

The generators coughed to a standstill as the ship's head started swinging round to put us end-on to the target. The Captain's head appeared through the hatch.

'Looks like a single merchantman, sir. Can't see any escorts.'

'Let me know when the tubes are ready.' The Captain leaned down to the voice-pipe. 'Set target course 280 – speed nine knots. Depth, twelve feet. Can the Asdics hear anything?'

Back up the voice-pipe came the answer:

'One source of pinging bearing 095°, sir. That's all.'

We both peered through our glasses again, trying to make out the escort. Although the merchant ship was now quite plain, less than three miles away, it was not possible to make out the source of the pinging. Perhaps it was still in the darkness on the far side of the moon's path. The Captain was thinking out loud while he went on searching.

'If there's a destroyer on either bow of the target, we should be seeing the nearer one. Then we wouldn't be able to fire from his port bow without being silhouetted in the moon for the other. On the other hand we've hardly time to work our way over to the other side without getting tangled up with the escort. Only one thing for it. Get down, look-outs.'

They shot down the hatch, a clatter of binoculars against the ladder.

'All tubes ready, depth set, sir.'

Still there was only the one ship in sight.

'Reciprocating H.E., 120 revs, bearing 087°, sir,' from the voice pipe.

'Two sources of pinging . . . 032° and 091°. Fast turbine H.E. on 91°.'

'Two destroyers, eh? Well, I can't see them. Let's get under. Don't press the klaxon.'

I dropped into the conning-tower, shouting down below to Number One to take her down. The Captain shut the lid and came into the Control Room.

'Set a range of three thousand five hundred on the fruit machine. Keep the reciprocating H.E. up to date. Starboard thirty, steady me on a 110° track for the original estimated course . . . Hullo, what's the matter Number One?'

He was looking at depth gauges which showed us to be below our ordered depth and still going down.

'Little bit heavy, sir, nothing much.'

He flicked his pump order instruments over and speeded up. The Captain waited for the periscope to break surface to get another look at the target. From Asdic reports it would seem the escorting destroyers were disposed on either bow of the merchantman, so we should have been able to see at least one of them before diving. The reciprocating H.E. (the merchant ship) was drawing slowly ahead, as was one source of destroyer turbine. But the other destroyer's bearings were drawing aft, so we had passed ahead of her and were going to get into a close-range firing position between the target and its port bow escort which should have passed close astern, leaving us clear for an undetected attack.

This picture was clear within two minutes of diving, while Number One was still wrestling with the trim, complicated by not being allowed to speed up to gain maximum hydroplane effect, for fear of the boat running blind too close to the target. However, he had got the boat under control and had begun to bring her up to periscope depth when the H.S.D. reported that the bearings of the nearest destroyer's turbine had steadied and was very loud.

'Transmitting on 15 k/cs, interval 2500 yards – not in contact, sir.'

The Captain had a look at the Asdic gyro bearing repeater. 'The brute must have zigged towards.'

With a destroyer so close on a collision course it was time to retreat to a safe depth and let her pass over the top. At 45 feet, leaving about fifteen feet of water between our bridge and the German's propellers, she rumbled slap over the top with her Asdics still sweeping round unsuspectingly. One of her screws had a singing beat, indicating a chip out of one of the blades.

As soon as she was over, we came up to periscope depth. By then we were down-moon from the target and the Captain could see nothing of the target, although he could make out the stern of the destroyer going away only two cables distance and still blanketing our Asdic from hearing anything.

Night vision through a periscope is limited due to the amount of light lost down its 35-foot barrel between the top window and the eye-lens. On a clear moonlight night one can make out the horizon and possibly the shape of a ship in the moon, but the Captain could not even make out whether he was above the water or under it.

'All sources of H.E. fading, sir.'

'Right. Stand by to surface. I want a Radar plot. We'll trail them and give them kippers for breakfast.'

It meant surfacing in the shimmering path of a moon, giving the enemy every chance of seeing us silhouetted. There was also the possibility of a 'weaver' covering the stern of the convoy.

All this was clear in my mind as I climbed up the ladder behind the Captain. We could make out nothing in the inky darkness away to the north-west, but presently Radar picked them at a range of three miles. The generators were started and the chase began. It seemed that we had not been detected on surfacing, as there was no gunfire, star shell or searchlights to greet us.

But the Radar range slowly increased.

'Ring down "Full Ahead",' the Captain ordered. 'Full buoyancy. Tell the motor room this is an emergency.'

That was all the switchboard operators had been waiting for. Their field regulators were wound down to fine limits, and the armature ammeter pointers went past the red lines – indicating 490, 500, 510, 515 revolutions.

'Thirteen knots. Wonder what he's chasing, Nobby?'

'Or runnin' away from,' the more practical Nobby replied. He worked his motor up to 518 revolutions.

Up on the bridge we still could not see a thing.

'Control Room, Radar range, please.'

'Seven thousand eight hundred, sir. Range opening.'

It was obvious we were never going to catch them so we broke off and headed for home. Once again, the Captain seemed to think it had been all his fault. Over our cocoa in the blacked-out wardroom we ran over the unfortunate combination of circumstances he had been up against: the extremes of visibility caused by the moon; that destroyer zigging straight for us at the last moment; and the target making good 14 knots – most unusual for small merchant vessels. But it was no use, and we returned to Maddalena with the Captain convinced that the ship got away due to his error of judgement.

★ 8 ★

OUR NEW ALLIES

On entering harbour we were signalled to go alongside *Paccinotti*, the Italian passenger ship which had served as a depot-ship for their submarines operating before the capitulation. She lay alongside a wrecked jetty, surrounded by workshops which had been flattened during the Fortress raid. Italian sailors crowded her guardrails, nudging each other and pointing at our black Jolly Roger. Her Captain, reputedly peacetime Master of the transatlantic liner *Rex* and a hot Fascist, looked contemptuously down at us from his quarters under the bridge.

'What'd you get?' the Staff officer called out.

'One F-lighter.' The Captain made a gesture with forefinger and thumb, as a fisherman might in describing a minnow. 'Should have thrown it back.'

'Betty Grable's on at the flicks.'

'Good show.'

The smell as we went through *Paccinotti*'s mess-decks to reach her quarterdeck might have been an abattoir, a hospital theatre during a gangrene operation, a sugar-beet factory or an unventilated public lavatory. Her dimly lit gangways 'tween-decks reeked of garlic and unwashed bodies, with an overlay of cheap tobacco.

Out on the quarterdeck, we exhaled and took in long draughts of fresh air. We were piped and saluted by a slovenly-looking piccolo player as we gratefully ran down the ladder to the jetty.

I found myself talking to one of the two spare Commanding Officers who had just come out from England. He was already looking for one of the regular C.O.s to go sick.

'Bobby Boyd's quite fit, I suppose?'

'Never been better.'

'Oh, well, I may be coming out with you on your next patrol to have a look at the areas. My name's Charles – Barry Charles.'

He put me in the picture about what was going on in the war in our theatre.

'The Monte Cassino set-back doesn't look too healthy. We're losing a lot of troops there. So the local Wops are perking up a bit. They sense that the Germans are rallying. Better watch yourself ashore after dark. Been a few beatings-up in the town too. We had a box of sixty revolvers pinched during unloading our gear from Malta. There's a supply of liquor just in from Naples (one bottle per man per month), the promise of a beer ration (one bottle a week) and a new supply of English magazines in the mess.'

There was still no fresh food and tinned rations were beginning to undermine the troops' health and morale. Small scratches or cuts from the football field obstinately refused to heal. In most instances they were accompanied by sinister swellings. The submarine crews, who were already suffering from oxygen deficiency during long days spent dived, were less resistant to infection. Every lunchtime a regular queue of sailors fell in with their meals to complain to the Officer of the Day – who was eating the same food himself, decked out in pastry or mashed potato by a Maltese messman.

At last the Paymaster was authorized to go on a foraging tour of Sardinia. He set off with a lorry, a pile of AMGOT lira, an Italian dictionary and the cheers of the whole flotilla. The sailors confidently told each other of the chickens that grew the size of turkeys on the mainland, of the lemons, the grapes and the sweet potatoes. But next day the lorry returned empty.

'Their prices were too high,' the Paymaster explained, having been guided by the officially authorized victualling allowances. Later a more enterprising Supply Officer in Malta thought nothing of sending us to sea with dozens of eggs purchased on the Black Market, each costing the equivalent of half a day's victualling allowance.

Jack will put up with unimaginable personal discomfort without a murmur, so long as his portion at dinner is large, palatable, hot and on the dot of noon. He does not look for variety. Just a regular roast, with potatoes and cabbage, followed by tinned fruit or a 'duff' – the latter must be heavy and preferably 'figgy'. Then give him unlimited quantities of strong sweet tea and he will endure anything.

In the base at Maddalena all departments were understaffed and had to work overtime, to keep abreast of maintenance and repair requirements. Many found that hard work passed the time and kept alive hope of better times. The small armament staff who lived in remote quarters in the middle of the harbour was at half-strength and had only the tools and test equipment that they could carry with them from Malta. Yet somehow they always came up on time with a full re-load outfit of torpedoes for the boats back from the sea. They had no crane to load them on board, so they commissioned an abandoned Italian steam hoist. An old West Country stoker who had served with steam up the Yangtze stepped in and took immense pride in his rattling machinery.

The engineers had no workshops, so they took over those in the Italian depot-ship *Paccinotti*. Without a word of English being spoken, they soon had the Italian artificers working on the hundred and one defects brought up by the submarines. Their pay was mostly in bars of soap, which bracketed equal with cigarette tobacco as the most valuable commodity on the island.

To those of us in the submarines who were impatient to get to sea again after a week in harbour, it was a constant source of wonderment how the base staff kept going as they did. But they were always there, smiling, to meet us on our return, ready to do whatever they could to put the boat back into operational readiness. No one volunteered to change places with a member of the base staff, no matter how much of a pasting they might have got on their last trip. It was easy to keep our crew intact throughout our time at Maddalena. No one went sick the day before patrol, or requested a draft to spare crew on compassionate grounds or to do a course for professional advancement.

We renewed our contacts with M.G.B.660 and the Coastal Forces boys. They had been having a lean season in their area around Elba with nothing but a few heavily escorted F-lighters to attack. They were also finding that their boats were not fast enough in bad weather to get away from destroyers. But this had not damped their spirits. They had tapped a source of Corsican wine and were dispensing it by the carboy at noisy parties held in their minute wardrooms. Inevitably the Canadians started their crap games; high stakes were the order of the day, but money had lost its value where there was nothing to buy. I was washing in one boat's Captain's cabin when I opened his desk to look for soap. It was piled high with bundles of 100-franc notes.

'Oh, those? I bought them from Corsican refugees. They're all Banque de France notes which the Corsicans are unloading as fast as they can go, because they're sure AMGOT is not going to honour any metropolitan French currency. Most of them are phonies rolled off by the Germans in thousands.'

'What do you pay for them?'

'Three pounds for a thousand.' The official rate was two hundred to the pound. 'And the Paymaster gives me full value.'

'Doesn't the pusser smell a rat having all you boys handing in so much cash?'

'No, he can't. As far as he's concerned, we just won it in crap games with the Yanks. I haven't drawn my pay since October.'

The most resourceful man I met was a cook in an American P.T. boat. At Capri one day he saved and dried all the coffee-grounds from the crew's meals. He then made them up in little packets and took them ashore, where they were quickly exchanged for hand-carved wooden Capri souvenirs. Cigarette boxes, toast-racks, coat-hangers, candlesticks, ink-stands all came his way, each with 'Capri' engraved on it somewhere. When they went down to Bizerta for new engines, it was child's play to dispose of them amongst the P.T. base personnel at the rate of one carton of Camels (200 cigarettes) per article. Base personnel there were provided with more gift cigarettes from the States than they could ever smoke and they were never likely to go to Capri themselves. The next step was easy. Up in Bastia the standard price for a carton of 200 cigarettes was ten Banque de France 100-franc notes. These were quickly turned into good American dollars and the cook cleared rather over $300 for a heap of dried coffee grounds.

At street corners one was pestered for 'tabac' in exchange for Lüger pistols, watches, eggs, chickens, German Officers' caps or Fascist emblems. Storing up for our next patrol, we laid in enough eggs for a fortnight at the cost of two packets of Players from each of the four of us.

Just before we sailed, a Free French boat came in. She was *Curie*, a Vickers-built 'U'-class, manned by the crew of an old French submarine which had escaped from St Nazaire in '40. She had had a long-range shot at a tanker off Toulon and missed. When their officers came into the base the Navigator was missing.

'He's under close arrest in his cabin,' Jean-Pierre told me. He pointed at his Captain, a black-eyed hunchback who had reputedly once returned to France by parachute. 'It's that man. He's going – how do you say? – off his rocket. All François did was to ask him if we couldn't go a little closer to the coast. But it's all right. There's a new Captain arriving from Algiers tonight – one of the lot who escaped from Toulon in 1942. I'm afraid the boys will not like it. In fact they say they will refuse to go on patrol with a Vichy man.'

'Is that him now?' I indicated a tall French Lieutenant who had just come in to the mess. There was something missing about his uniform: he did not wear the Cross of Lorraine over his right breast.

'Yes, that's him. Excuse me, please.' Jean-Pierre hurried off to introduce himself.

It was an odd set-up – either might have shot the other as a traitor if the war had gone a different course; the one had crossed the Channel in a rowing boat in 1940, the other was barely a year out of Toulon. They openly expressed their fear of being sent to Algiers because the French naval authorities there were hostile to Gaullists. Algiers kept on asking for *Curie* to be sent to join their flotilla, but her officers were ready with new excuses to remain with our 10th Flotilla: compatibility of spare parts was always a safe one.

'I'd be sent straight to a shore job in the Cameroons,' François once said, expressing a fear common to all of them that the Vichy French Navy under Admiral Darlan would victimize them for leaving France in 1940. 'No, I am going to see this war through with your people.'

Curie put aside their distrust of the new C.O. and thereafter did her full share with some success. Although built at Barrow-in-Furness as an exact sister-ship to our own U-class, there was an important concession made in order that the French crew should feel at home in her. They always got their daily ration of a litre of wine. There was no stowage problem: they simply filled the two 120-gallon distilled water tanks with whatever red plonk was available.

In the process we were reassured that the pure distilled water we carried for topping-up the 224 cells of our main batteries was not as essential as we had been led to believe. The routine for topping-up always used to be preceded by the Petty Officer in charge producing a sample of the water he was about to add to the electrolyte, along with a chemical test kit and a manual with elaborate instructions and tables. Silver nitrate was one of the drops added to convince the First Lieutenant that it was safe to go ahead without fear of contaminating our prime energy source.

By the middle of the war we all filled our distilled water tanks straight from the same shore supply we relied on for drinking and cooking, without any discernible harm to the main batteries.

★ 9 ★

COUNTER-ATTACK

Next patrol we were booked for the St Tropez area, where we had missed those two F-lighters on our first Med patrol. It seemed about time someone in the flotilla got a really good strike. The post-Christmas patrols had not produced anything more than a few brace of small coasters. Barry Charles was with us as a passenger to have a look at the coast. He was an agreeable shipmate.

The coast around St Raphael looked much the same. The same red and green roofs, evergreen vegetation and backdrop of blue mountains mantled with snow at their summits. We cruised in close enough to see German troops promenading with French girls, but all their war supplies were moving in those never-ending trains. There were, apparently, unprotected flimsy-looking viaducts which could easily have been cut from the air, but, although we frequently heard over the B.B.C. that the Riviera railway was attacked by our bombers, we never noticed an interruption to the stream of eastbound rail traffic in a year off that coast.

After a couple of days of fruitless search between the entrance to the Hyères Roads and Cannes, S (10) signalled us freedom of action eastwards as far as the Italian border. We shifted that night and fetched up off the small harbour of Oneglia. Closing it involved working through a suspected minefield, but the spine-shivering sound of a mine-wire scraping along our side never came, and soon the masts and funnel of a medium-sized merchant vessel were in sight. It was right up against the shore and it was hard to see what it would be doing there. Within a mile of the beach the Captain could see a black hole large enough to drive a submarine into on the water-line. He looked through the back Intelligence files.

'Here it is "April, 1943, attacked by R.A.F. Beaufighters – beached itself; June, 1943, attacked by Dutch submarine *Dolfijn* – two hits; October, '43, British submarine fired two more torpedoes at this abandoned ship"; the official comment ended, "This ship may now be said to be no longer of value to the enemy".'

From a thousand yards further to seaward that ship looked to all the world like a sitting target in undamaged condition. Having missed joining the club of those who wasted torpedoes on a wreck, we turned towards the harbour itself.

'There is a ship in there. Looks like a small tanker, under a thousand tons; its funnel had a cover over it. She may be laid up.'

'Yes, but I don't think it's a tanker – it's probably a coaster or even a UJ-boat. I put its tonnage at 800, no more. Now, let's have a look-see at the chart. Maybe we can let him have one of our Mark VIII two-star cards.'

The Control Room crew all grinned. This was the sort of submarine action everyone dreams about. A nice deliberate, cold-blooded demolition with no unpleasantness to follow. But, try as he did, the Captain could not wriggle those parallel rulers on the chart to give us a clean shot through the harbour mouth.

'We might come back and gun him at the end of our patrol, if we have no better luck. But we won't do much more than blister the paintwork or its superstructure with our bow and arrow.'

Our thoughts were turned from those disappointments by a cypher signal which came in during the dogwatches. Prefixed 'Immediate', it was in a cypher which only the Captain held the key to unbutton. He furtively produced the plain language message. Gus and I were playing our everlasting game of crib when the Captain took the chart off the table. Gus recognized it.

'It's the Toulon chart, chum. I don't want to start any buzzes, but my guess is we'll be steering west tonight to cut off a U-boat before breakfast.'

'Maybe they've got the word that the aircraft-carrier is going to move.'

'You're both wrong.' The Captain had overheard us. 'There's a convoy coming through from Genoa. I think we'll crack it off Cap Camarat, because I don't see how we can make Toulon by daylight.'

As soon as it was dark we surfaced and belted our way along the coast to get off Cap Camarat as soon as possible, working out as we went what time we could expect to pick up the enemy at various speeds of advance. About two hours before daylight was the most likely time. Our best chance of making a successful interception was to lie right in under the cliffs and fire to seaward. Otherwise the enemy might slip along close to the beach with their screw noises blanketed by the continual rumble of waves breaking against the shore. It was a moonless night, so we would have to rely on Asdics picking them up.

At one in the morning we were off the Cape, working our way slowly inshore at low buoyancy on the last reduction of the charge. Two o'clock found us stopped, half a mile off the beach. I had the watch on the bridge. The Captain was there, also trying to penetrate the blackness all round. To make the darkness worse, there was a ground fog settling on the water. 'I remember the instructor on my command course telling me that to lie stopped on the surface was bad submarine practice. He said a lot of people used to do it off Norway in the early days of the war but none of them were left to tell us how they got sunk. Hullo, what's that?'

A light had come on inshore. It persisted for a few seconds, long enough to get a quick bearing.

'Three two seven, sir.'

'That'll be Cap Camarat light. Good. That's significant. No master on earth would try to make that entrance to the Hyères Roads on a night like this without a light ashore. I'll bet a pound to a pinch of shit that light coming on means they're not far off now. Tell the H.S.D. to double up listening watch.'

The chart gave us the light's characteristics as four double flashes every fifteen seconds, but this one was not behaving as advertised. Its beam came down on us intermittently, swung round till it apparently hovered over in our direction and then swung on round.

'It may be imagination, but does it seem to you as if that light was dipping and elevating every time its beam is pointing towards us?'

Yes, sir, it does. Like an Aldis lamp.'

'God, that's it. There it is. He's flickered letter "A" that time.'

Darkness again. Then the beam of light on the cliff swinging slowly round till it paused momentarily over us and flickered up . . . down . . . up . . . down and on round till it faded.

'Bridge! Fast light diesel bearing red three oh,' came urgently from the voicepipe.

A quick look. A white bow-wave filled the binoculars.

'Look-outs below! Dive, dive, dive,' the Captain snapped out. 'Hard a'starboard.'

We crammed ourselves into the conning-tower as the boat angled down.

'Shut off, Number One. Silent routine. Steady on 160.'

A metallic explosion shuddered the boat, quickly followed by another. Bits of a broken lamp hit me on the cheek. Damage Control reports came into the Control Room from for'ard and aft.

'After ends, motor room and engine room correct.'

'You can pass through the boat that was an E-boat. So that was probably his full outfit of depth charges.'

People who had been off watch when we dived were still rubbing their eyes wondering what had happened. 'What's up, sir?' the gunlayer whispered to me. 'That convoy turned up? Cor, I thought we was going to sink something, not get pushed under.'

'Keep silence. One twenty feet. There may be more of those about,' the Captain said.

The H.S.D. had picked up the E-boats screws again. It slowed down and stopped out to seaward. We continued slowly along, waiting for the next move. It soon came.

'Diesel H.E. increasing. Bearing 152 degrees.'

It rattled overhead like a rat scurrying across a corrugated roof. No bang. The Captain had probably been right in surmising those two depth charges to be the E-boat's full load. Once more it slowed down. Evidently it had us in acoustic contact and meant to hold on. Certainly there was no question of hanging around off Cap Camarat. The alarm was up and all hopes of nipping off the oncoming convoy had gone. Barry and the Captain were discussing the situation over the chart.

'They must have had us on shore radar. The light we saw was beaming that E-boat on to us.'

'What now?'

'I'll have to keep on out to sea. Our only hope of getting in an attack on the convoy, if it exists, will be if it decided to go outside the islands. But that little bastard up top will keep pretty good track of us. So things don't look too rosy.'

The troops evidently thought so too.

The Asdic operator continued to report the sound of its screws somewhere between us and the Cape. It made no further attempt to run over the top, but its armament of two torpedoes and assorted artillery was enough to keep us under. This continued for two hours, though there were heartening signs that the enemy was no longer in certain contact. For spells of quarter of an hour nothing could be heard of it at all; then the H.S.D. would pick it up again for a while, just bumbling along the shore.

At 0530 we fell out from Diving Stations and sat down to breakfast. We had moved about six miles away from Cap Camarat and had kissed goodbye to the attack on the convoy. The Captain was unusually despondent; we all tactfully buried our faces deep in *Good Morning* and said nothing. Number One was on watch. He must have imagined he was whispering to the planesman, but in the dead silence in the wardroom we could hear every word of it.

'Just bad luck, that's all. Might have happened to anyone.'

'Don't suppose there is any convoy.'

'Sir, will you send for the H.S.D.?' It was one of the junior Asdic ratings on the listening watch. 'I think I can hear faint Asdic transmissions bearing 030.'

That was enough. Breakfast was pushed aside in the rush for the Control Room. The Captain had already reached the listening position and had tapped in a spare headset for himself.

'Go to Diving Stations and bring her up to twenty-six feet. Alter course to port to 030 degrees.'

'This will be the posse called out by that bleeding E-boat,' Gus whispered in my ear, always the little optimist.

The Captain waited for the top of the periscope to break surface, drooping round the handles like a tired prize-fighter and gazing at the shallow gauge needle as it laboriously climbed down to the thirty foot mark. At no other time did he display his imperturbability better than on occasions like this, when there was an undue delay in getting up to periscope depth. Most Captains made it clear that they didn't like being left just dipped at the vulnerable depth where one is liable to be rammed blind. Other boats described horrible scenes in their Control Rooms, of C.O.s. kicking their First Lieutenants, screaming and shouting to get the boat up. But our man just drooped over the periscope handles and said nothing. Meanwhile the H.S.D. had taken over listening and confirmed enemy Asdic transmissions a long way off, which could mean anything up to ten miles.

'Twenty-nine feet, sir,' Number One reported as soon as the needle was past thirty, 'twenty-eight and a half, twenty-eight . . .'

The Captain was already sweeping quickly round. Evidently satisfied that our shadower of the middle watch was not in close proximity, he concentrated on the bearing given by the H.S.D. There was breathless silence in the darkened Control Room waiting for the verdict.

'Nothing. Not a sausage. Just miles and miles of fuck-all. Sure you can still hear it, Bird?'

The H.S.D. rotated his bearing pointer slowly backwards and forwards.

'Yes, sir. Transmissions bearing 028 degrees. No H.E. Bearing moving left.'

'Well the vis. is not so hot. They may be there,' the Captain said to Barry, who was standing beside him. 'You have a look.'

'It's not properly light yet. I don't like that haze over a glassy calm sea.'

The Captain took the periscope again. Suddenly he stopped on a bearing fine on the starboard bow, hastily rubbed the eye-lenses clear with periscope paper, re-focused and looked again.

'Down periscope. Sixty feet. Full ahead together group up. Steady as you go. Let me know when I've done five minutes at full speed.' The boat took a bow-down angle, the main motor tachometers momentarily fluttered back to zero as the grouper switch went up, then came back together to 300 revolutions – nine knots flat out, making a shuddering propeller beat which we imagined would be heard in Algiers. The Captain turned to Gus:

'Give the enemy a course to clear Cape Camarat by one mile, speed 12 knots. Put him half way between Cap Dramont and Camarat now – give me a course to close.'

'Can you see the convoy?' Barry asked.

'No, but I did see a couple of balloons sticking over the horizon, and I think we'll go and have a look at them, just in case there are fat merchant ships dangling on the end of their wires.'

So we rattled along at nine knots, heading back in towards the direction in which we had last heard our E-boat half an hour earlier. If he was still there, or anywhere within five miles of us, he would certainly hear us coming. But this thought did not seem to bother the Captain nor the troops, who were all smiles and whispers. After five minutes, during which the boat had closed over half a mile, we came up for another look. This involved going dead slow to cut down our periscope feather which might be spotted by an aircraft several miles away. This next look was more instructive.

'Start the attack. There's a forest of masts bearing *that* – Green 26. Take that as the centre bearing. Two ships with conspicuous funnels are on that bearing, each flying a balloon.' He fumbled with the range-finder. 'Can't get a range. I'm probably only seeing their mirage now. They are at least sixteen thousand yards away.' He had another look round for the E-boat. 'Sixty feet. Full ahead grouper up. Let me know after ten minutes. You can bring the tubes to the ready, set depth twelve feet.'

Once again the boat put her head down and ran in. The Captain was drawing a little diagram on the chart of the possible disposition of the convoy. There were the two ships with balloons in line abreast with a screen of some sorts – just masts so far – in arrowhead formation ahead.

'It's the party from Genoa all right. Bit late though.'

During the remainder of the ten minutes at high speed all sorts of problems were gone into. The Captain had to decide at which point it would be pointless trying to press on any closer, seeing that a torpedo would close the target five times as quickly as we

104

could. Against this was the fact that the greater range multiplied torpedo inaccuracies and increased the chances of their four broad aerated tracks being spotted in time for the convoy to take avoiding action. Another consideration was that targets would be making a navigational alteration of course on rounding the Cape; should this occur just after firing the torpedoes on their long run, it would throw all our fruit-machine calculations out. At the next look the log showed we had closed nearly three miles since the beginning of the run in. The Captain steadied for a bearing and range.

'Leading ship of convoy bearing . . . range in high power, *that* . . .' I fed the figures into the fruit machine.

'Range ten thousand five hundred. True bearing 019 degrees.'

'Put me thirty on their port bow.'

He folded up the periscope handles as it slid silently down into the well. Once again he ordered the boat deep for a further burst of four minutes at top speed. Over the chart table he quietly put us in the picture: the screen consisted of three destroyers, large ones, maybe *Terrible*-class Frenchmen; one merchantman was a big chap of seven or eight thousand tons, the other medium-sized around the four thousand mark.

'As they are now, I might get a shot at them overlapping to make a continuous target. Got any speed from those last ranges and bearings?'

Gus spanned a pair of dividers against his speed scale on the side of the plot.

'Ten knots, sir.'

'Give her that. Is all set for'ard?'

'Yes, sir. All tubes ready, depth set 12 feet.'

'Predict a running range of seven thousand yards.'

This latter information was to allow for a gradual falling-off in average running speed of the torpedo at longer ranges.

Provided the destroyers did not hear us on this last spurt of speed, we would certainly get off a long-range 'hose-pipe' salvo at what sounded like a handsome target. The periscope went up for the final look. New ranges, bearings and angles-on-the-bow came in.

'Everything much the same as before,' the Captain said to himself. 'Stand-by . . . fire one!' The boat kicked back as the first fish went away. 'Fire two!'; again the quiver of recoil. Deliberately the Captain aimed each torpedo until the whole salvo was on its way. 'Foremast of the second ship . . . quarter of a length astern. Christ! That one made a helluva discharge bubble. There they go, leaving wakes like battleships behind them. Down periscope, starboard thirty.'

Another burst of high speed to run off track and dodge the

Germans coming out along our torpedo tracks dropping patterns all the way. The torpedoes would take just over five minutes to reach their mark, so with luck we could count on that much time to get away from the telltale bubbles which marked our firing point. At five minutes we slowed down to a silent speed, shut off for depth charging and listened. Dicky Bird on the Asdics was reporting our torpedoes all running straight.

'Five minutes, thirty seconds, sir,' from the telegraphist holding the plot stopwatch. No one moved. I glimpsed the coxswain, holding his jackknife open on his lap and fingering the little row of five notches which he had already cut.

At nearly four miles it was a surprisingly loud bang.

'One torpedo exploding,' the H.S.D. reported quite unnecessarily. The troops went mad. On my phones I could hear someone in the tube space saying, 'That's one of the bastards.'

'Quiet! Silence everybody,' the Captain ordered.

There was another thud and several voices unisoned 'two hits' . . . a pause, and yet another explosion. Three out of four. The Coxswain hacked three fresh notches into the wooden flare-rack. No one cared what happened after that. Grinning faces all round the Control Room defied the Germans to harm us; the Captain had hit both those ships, and, who knows, maybe one of the destroyers as well.

'One torpedo just gone up on the beach, sir,' the H.S.D. reported the dull, almost inaudible plop of a torpedo exploding in shallow water. 'Turbine H.E. increasing 150 revolutions.'

'Well we've made it easy for them,' the Captain commented. 'They can't very well miss those tracks on a day like this. Pass through the boat to hold on to something. We're in for a bit of a bollocking.'

The first destroyers dropped a pattern of seven . . . seven thunderclaps in an intermittent ripple with the concussion hitting flat against the boat's side as if a giant was lambasting us with a spade.

'Up to half a mile away,' the Captain said reassuringly.

The next pattern was louder and obviously closer, but the effect on the boat was not noticeably different. The deck under my feet jumped momentarily, but everything was under control and functioning smoothly. The noise and the unexpectedness with which each pattern went off were infinitely the worst part of the treatment.

The third lot were closer still, but it was only the noise which alarmed us. It reminded me of walking through Hyde Park during a lull in a night raid in '40, when a battery of heavy A.A. went off right in front of me, twenty yards away.

The troops seemed to be taking this, their first major counter-attack, calmly. They sat around on the Control Room deck; the Chief ERA and the P.O. Telegraphist were playing noughts and crosses on the Radar Office door; the Signalman kept his tally of the number of charges dropped; Gus doodled on the plot, while I listened over the phones for any report of trouble in the tube space, the most vulnerable compartment in the submarine. The Captain sat alongside the H.S.D. listening to the destroyers groping round for a contact. Bird's Asdic office was bedecked with pin-ups of all ages, colour and sizes, from his landlady at Tyneside to his Arab 'queen' in Algiers.

'One, *there*, stopped, transmitting with a three thousand yard interval . . . another bearing green 110, moving right, transmitting.' The Captain nodded. All seemed well; he was snaking us out of trouble at two-and-a-half knots, with a gentle zig-zag.

'That one is speeding up for an attack. Two hundred revolutions, bearing moving rapidly right across our stern.'

That was a good sign. They were probably attacking the disturbed patch of water where the Captain had put on a spurt to get off track. The bang of the next pattern was perceptibly quieter than the first three, the moment when everyone abruptly realises that mortal danger is receding, the matelots stick out their chests and tell each other it was nothing to the depth-charging they got in such-a-such a boat off Norway in 1940. Up till that moment each pattern had been nearer than the last, and there was a niggling thought that they might get lucky and straddle with the next. But slowly the conviction grew that he was simply plastering the area at random around an increasingly unreliable datum.

Three more patterns were dropped when the Captain ordered a few more revolutions. Presently their screws could be heard getting fainter. A few minutes later the Captain was at the periscope for his first look and with it a momentary anxiety that our Asdics might have been deceived by one of the hunting craft lying stopped, not transmitting but just listening. He swung round with the small attack periscope. Evidently all was clear, for he lowered it and walked for'ard for a good look through the high-power stick.

'Two destroyers going into Hyères Roads. There's the smoke of the convoy behind the first island. I can only see one balloon.'

Officially he claimed to have sunk one of the two merchant ships with two hits and to have damaged the other or one of the screen.

'This area's going to be hotted up, so I think we'll beat it. Go to Watch Diving. Keep a good look-out for aircraft. They're sure to send a whole lot out for us.'

The watch took over but, even though it was nearly nine o'clock and we had all been up since the middle of the night, the wardroom light stayed on for the post-mortem on the attack. By the time we had sunk those ships over again it was lunch: soup, cold ham, carrots and raspberries and milk followed by the Coxswain's tot for the Captain, who loathed neat spirit but dutifully lowered his measure after each successful attack. Lunch was interrupted by Gus pressing the klaxon to go deep for an over-inquisitive Arado, but soon all was peace. During my afternoon watch I saw several low-flying seaplanes circling round the area of our attack, but not apparently covering our disengaging course.

We spent that night at a respectable twenty miles off the beach. It allowed everyone on board to enjoy a night's uninterrupted sleep. By next morning the Captain had made up for his lost sleep – he needed plenty to keep him in top condition physically and mentally – and was raring to get at the enemy again. In the wardroom Barry was not so keen.

'I plan to come through this war. You can go to the well only so often . . . then, pft!' He snuffed out an imaginary candle. 'One good strike per patrol should be enough for any man. Where's he going to hit the coast today, Gus?'

'Between Cap Dramont and Antibes.'

'Shallow and mined, I suppose?'

'Of course.'

It was another calm day with haze reducing visibility. However, the lofty bluffs above Agay eventually came in sight, and the boat went in close under them to ambush the next lot that might appear from Genoa – or, better still, from Toulon on their way eastwards to the fighting fronts.

The Captain was still at the periscope fixing our position for the day's patrol when he sighted something coming along from the south-west and ordered us to Diving Stations. My guess was that it would most likely be an A/S sweep going along the coast to try and pick up the submarine responsible for yesterday's outrage still less than twenty miles away. This looked like being the case when a UJ-boat was identified, leading a motley collection of small craft in line abreast.

'Let's get out of here. It's liable to be unhealthy.'

So he ordered the boat to steer off-shore, keeping a periscope watch. The H.S.D. was now reporting three sources of pinging and an assorted variety of propeller noises.

'Yes. There's a UJ-boat in the centre, a couple of R-boats or chasseurs either side of him and two masts of what look like E-boats coming along on the wing. Also two more masts behind . . . wait a minute . . . start the attack. All tubes to four feet – port thirty.'

He had identified two ammunition coasters, identical to the pair we sank off Cape Noli, riding snugly behind that formidable screen of escorts.

'High prows . . . marked sheer down to a squat after-superstructure with a pepper-pot funnel. Those are the ones. Give them eight knots.'

'Vessel transmitting on Red 90 in contact, sir,' Bird reported.

'Well he's not doing much about it.'

Putting the periscope down, the Captain waited for further reports. The UJ-boat was still in contact, obstinately echoing off our hull, which right then must have seemed the size of an iceberg to them. At the next look the UJ-boat was still not hauling out of formation to attack us. Perhaps they decided it was a false echo, for they continued sweeping round without locking on. The Captain let the leaders of the screen pass, then turned sharply in between a large R-boat and a French chasseur to fire the full salvo aimed at both coasters at a range of just under one thousand yards.

Right on time came the first bang, followed at the correct intervals by two more, but the periscope was not up to see them hit. We were at eighty feet scampering out of it. Subdued cheering in the boat had barely died away when Bird reported the other fish hitting the beach, barely a mile beyond the target.

'There goes my tot again,' the Coxswain moaned as he nicked another two notches on the flare-rack.

Retaliation came quickly, as was to be expected after a close-range attack inside the screen. The UJ-boat laid down a pattern of five, close enough to be unpleasant, and quickly added five more for good measure. Again the shattering percussion, the violent whipping of the hull, but no damage other than a few lamps popping out of their sockets.

Light diesel H.E. of the R-boats followed us out to sea and dropped a few desultory charges. Then all was unexpectedly quiet. The boat crept up to the surface and the Captain sneaked a quick look before taking us down to ninety feet.

'Both coasters have gone. Some of the small stuff is stopped around there . . . picking up survivors. That noisy basket of a UJ-boat is stopped beam on. Range that . . . thirty-two minutes on sixty feet. The others are just milling around.'

'Range is 2200 yards, sir.'

And that was that. Less than half an hour after sighting the UJ-boat through the haze we were safely out of it, making out to seaward at ever-increasing speed.

That night a signal was pushed out to base.

'All torpedoes expended. Three hits convoy one large one medium supply ship off Camarat 30th. Two ammunition coasters sunk off Agay 31st. Arriving Maddalena 0830 1st.'

Our passage home was so quick that the Signalman was still stitching the four new bars on our Jolly Roger as we entered the boom an hour ahead of time. Even at that hour the whole base turned out to cheer us alongside and the Captain as he stepped off the casing on to the jetty. Even the miserable Commander (S) smiled. PQ sat on the General's charger and returned our salute. That was some kind of a first.

★ 10 ★

PATROL POOLS

Our berthing in the pens brought the whole Flotilla together in harbour. Deadly Smedley of *Universal*, always a dangerous customer to find sharing one's stand-off, grabbed me by the arm.

'This way, chum. Breakfast's ready down in our boat.'

Seated in their wardroom behind drawn curtains, I greeted D'Arcy, the other member of the trio which Commander (S) referred to as his problem children, propping his head up between his hands. He turned a rheumy eye on me.

'Wotcher, cock, breakfast? Say when.'

Four fingers of Haig was pushed across the table.

'Skol. Now what are all those bars doing on your Jolly Roger?'

After a brief account of our patrol, it seemed that *Universal* had bagged a six-thousand-ton tanker off Spezia, whilst *Uproar* got in the shot which pulled the Flotilla over the million-ton mark. They gunned a large tanker in Oneglia harbour and claimed it as damaged.

I pressed for details.

'They closed this harbour and saw a seven-thousand, five-hundred-ton tanker there, so they upped and smote it with thirty rounds of three-inch.'

'Well, well. Seven-thousand, five-hundred . . . there wasn't a nought added somewhere by any chance? Our old man will be interested to hear about that. But enough of this shop. I think I'd better get along up to base.'

'No hurry. None of the offices are open yet.' He waved a thumb at the clock – 8.35 am. 'Stay a while and get a red nose.'

Presently a sudden need for fresh air overcame me. I got up on my feet – at the third attempt.

'See you later, boys. I must place my orders with Torps for eight new Mark VIII two stars. This time I'm going to hold out for a volume discount.'

Up to the base for the rounds of the offices. First to the Torpedo office to reassure Torps that all his fish ran straight and six of them made the right sort of noise on hitting ships; then to Guns to tell him we needed no ammunition; on to see Eric Douglas, the Paymaster Sub who handled confidential books. He sat in his pyjamas at his desk counting out a pile of lira.

'How's it going, Eric?'

'Not so bad,' he answered in his Scots accent. 'I'm just making up the pay for the wop galley-hands. Seventy-two, three, four.' He put a pile of notes to one side. 'Let's see now, that's Guiseppi Angelino. I hear you had a good trip – nice going.'

I threw a heap of superseded cypher forms down on his desk.

'Did you say you were making out pay for those Italian kids who peel spuds in our galley? Why, they're mostly ten-year-olds.'

'Yes, on the AMGOT scale. The average pay packet works out around two twelve six.'

'Can you fix me up with a job washing dishes in the Italian barracks?'

Eric smiled as he made out the receipt notes for our cyphers.

'Cheer up. The grub's better now. We're getting fresh meat up from Sardinia once a week, and the beer ration is now a fact . . . once a week on Sunday mornings. Where are you going?'

'To collect my bottle of beer.'

I went across the courtyard and banged on the door of the wine steward's office.

'Paul, I want my bottle of beer.'

The old Maltese steward grinned as he polished glasses for the lunchtime session.

'No beer, senor'.

'But there's a ration. One bottle per man per week.'

'Yes, sir.' He pointed at a pile of crates full of empties.

'Well, where's mine?'

'Sub-Lieutenant Douglas said it would be all right for him to drink yours last Sunday, sir. He said you would probably get sunk, and it would be an awful pity to waste a bottle.'

Eric Douglas's cabin door was locked when I got back, so I went along to the staff office. There Barry was picking up the threads from the other spare C.O., Paddy Gowan, who was already talking about coming out with us on our next patrol.

'This place is driving me to drink – as if there was anything to drink here except that rot-gut vino. Oh, by the way, Barry, thank you for your beer ration on Sunday. I thought of you as I lowered the second bottle.'

25 J.O.C. with Admiral Felix B. Stump, USN, Commander US Atlantic Fleet during operation "Mainbrace".

26 Flag Officer Submarine (Vice-Admiral Sir Wilfrid Woods) and Chief of Staff (Captain R.L. Alexander) on an official visit to the USA, conducted by J.O.C. (in the centre).

27 Commander Toby Weston, handing over to J.O.C. at COMSUBLANT, May, 1955.

28 USS *Albacore*, the shape of things to come. Short, fat and 35 knots under water, 1956.

Charles wandered over to where the large 'Incident' chart of the Western Mediterranean hung and plotted our recent successes. The area around Cap Camarat was black with asterisks of ships sunk by the Flotilla.

'Good heavens,' Paddy said suddenly, 'look at the time.' He rushed out through the door on to the pavement in front of the Base, followed by the two of us.

'What's up?'

'Ssh.'

Round the corner of the building came a horse-drawn open carriage, rumbling ponderously along the rocky street. A Carabinieri on duty at the cross-road sprang to attention and saluted. As the carriage rattled slowly past us, the two young ladies lying back in its seat smiled and twirled their parasols.

Paddy murmured that they were a little late this morning and walked back into the staff office.

Barry nudged me and pointed at him.

'That's how Maddalena gets you if you're ashore here for long.'

'Who are they? The local C-in-C's daughters?'

'No, they are from the ratings' brothel and have to report at the hospital every morning at this time . . . just to make sure they haven't caught a cold overnight.'

'I hope they do the same for the staff at our place,' I commented.

That was the slightly less squalid one set aside at different hours each day for the Officers and Chiefs and Petty Officers. We had a grand opening ceremony after a Mess guest night. Only the padre and Commander (S) remained behind when we swept down-town for the ceremonial – an exhibeesh put on by one of the Third Hands, who had drawn the short straw over dinner. The pathetic girls were mostly driven to it to sustain their families, although some contrived to give the impression of enjoying it.

One achieved star rating by being hired for a whole week by an American who somehow got authority to take her over to Sardinia. On her return she appeared in the Italian Officers' Club at a reception for some of our collaborators. Conchita Banana, as she was known, boasted having learnt to speak English. Asked if she had enjoyed her trip to Olbia, she replied: 'Si, very sophisticated. Everybody pissed.'

She was then introduced to our most pompous senior officer, who shook hands and said, 'Delighted to meet you, Signorina Banana.'

'O.K. baby,' she replied in a Texas drawl, at the same time

expending the balance of her total command of Shakespeare's language: 'I suck your bollocks'.

Madame had a few switch-hitters amongst her clientele at her establishment, as two of us discovered when we went to call on her in search of a nightcap. The front door was locked but there was an open lighted window at first floor level, with an easy drainpipe. The first thing to catch my eye at window-sill level was an Italian Cavalry Colonel's uniform neatly hung over a chair. Its owner, still booted and spurred, was grunting away on top of a youth on the bed.

At lunchtime there was a boisterous crowd jostling round the bar, trying to work up an appetite on vino. Having the whole Flotilla in harbour at once had a significance which did not go unnoticed.

'I suppose that lot out there has nothing to do with it?' Deadly pointed his glass though the window, where about a dozen L.S.T.s packed with transport could be seen riding at anchor.

'What do you mean?'

'Maybe there's a landing coming off somewhere and they want us out of harm's way.'

Gowan drew me aside.

'I couldn't help overhearing Deadly then. Just tell him to drop the whole subject. Any bloody fool can see something's in the wind, and there's a tremendous security blitz on. Spread the word around your boat that careless talk costs lives . . . and adverse court-martial verdicts.'

No one spoke for a moment; we were all thinking over the various possibilities. Maybe the Second Front was going to be opened on the South Coast of France. Or it might just be a feint. Whatever it was, it was not a minute too soon. The one o'clock news which broke in on our thoughts made it seem that Kesselring could fight an indefinite delaying action along the Cassino line.

'Those poor bloody pongos,' someone said, 'they're taking an awful pasting. And I bet everybody at home thinks they're basking in the sun eating oranges.'

Outside it was blowing a gale, a bitter easterly wind whipping sand and sleet horizontally along the streets, as it did four days a week on that little island in the weather funnel of the Bonifacio Straits.

'Up in those hills around Cassino it must be cold enough to freeze the balls off a brass monkey.'

'Sounded pretty warm to me,' Barry said, 'two thousand tons of bombs on one monastery. They can have it. Anyway I can't see how the pongos manage to get so enthused over their messy warfare . . . all that blood and muck. Why, they think about practically nothing but cutting people's throats and blowing their brains out. Have you ever seen the gleam in a Gurkha's eyes as he sharpens his kukri? Anybody would think he was going to carve the Sunday joint, not disembowel some unsuspecting Jerry sentry.'

'It's something to do with sexual sublimation,' Eric suggested. 'If you boys want lunch, it's now or never.'

Barry had unwittingly put his finger on the reason why we were all there; why it was that submarines will never be short of volunteers. For those who don't fancy being wounded or maimed, it is the surest way, provided one has confidence in the Captain. He alone can size up the opposition through the periscope. For all the others on board there is no difference between a real attack and an exercise off Campbeltown . . . until after our torpedoes hit. Once submerged, there is no act of individual bravery or cowardice expected of anyone except the man at the periscope. The crew simply hope that the Captain will get them out of any trouble he gets them into.

The next week passed following the usual pattern of life in harbour between patrols. It took three days' hard work to get all the outstanding jobs in the boat cleared up and two new salvos of torpedoes struck down the forehatch. Then it was party time. A few took long walks across to Caprera to make sure Garibaldi's tomb had not been moved. For others there were fierce uncompromising battles on the rocky baked mud football pitch every afternoon, ending with a queue at the sick bay for anti-tetanus shots for those with lacerated knees and elbows.

But one by one the boats got their sailing orders. *Ultimatum* and *Ultor* sailed together for Algiers, for a week's patrol leave. The next day the armada of tank landing craft started pulling out of the harbour. It wasn't until we were at sea ourselves on the way to our old Gulf of Fréjus billet that the Captain cleared the matter up.

'*Ultimatum* and *Ultor* aren't going for patrol leave. They have gone to beach-mark for an army landing near Rome. We're going to wait for U-boats coming out to attack our ships off the beachhead.'

This time we had Paddy Gowan on board as a passenger. He made his position clear:

'With me on board you can count on bad weather, no targets and at least one good depth-charging. Its just monotonous for me; every time I go to sea its the same old sequence of events . . . a gale . . . a plastering . . . and nothing to show for it at the end.'

At least the troops did not share his pessimism. We had just launched our own Patrol Pools. These consisted of a sheet of twenty-five questions which were answered at a shilling a column. The questions ranged from number one, 'Shall we fire torpedoes?' to number twenty-five, 'Will we sight any sailing vessels on this patrol?' I had scanned through the heap of completed question forms and found that the average answer to the question 'How many torpedoes will we fire?' was six and the average number of hits anticipated five. Of thirty-eight forms submitted, only two expected a blank patrol, such was their confidence in the Captain's winning streak. One of them was Paddy's.

At breakfast on the fifth day of a frustrating blank patrol the P.O. Telegraphist handed us his summary of the midnight news from Rugby. The Allies had landed at Anzio, which our chart showed as a tiny fishing port near Rome.

The rest of the patrol was spent in the Fréjus area, hoping for the Germans to send out something on its way to oppose the landings at Anzio. But, although U-boats must have been passing close by us at night to judge from the number of HM Ships which were being torpedoed off the beachhead, we never saw or heard any. If only we'd had an efficient radar set, but Charlie couldn't get anything but rain squalls and false echoes on his beginner's outfit.

After ten days we were ordered back into the Toulon Bay for another U-boat, which S.10 evidently had black market information on. This time we ran into Paddy's promised gale. The weather had not been good throughout the patrol; there had been a steady force five wind whipping up a steep choppy sea all the time. This time it blew up to a real Gulf of Lions gale. Although the size of the swell could not be compared with a North Atlantic blow, the strength of the wind and the confused nature of the sea during our night on the surface was as uncomfortable as any time I have ever spent at sea. Cold water came solidly down through the hatch into the birdbath, a small canvas swimming pool, with the ballast pump running continuously to keep it from bursting its sides.

Dawn next morning found us floundering in Toulon Bay, vainly struggling to keep a periscope look-out for our target. One minute we would be up at fifteen feet with our standards awash; the next we would be plunging down to forty feet. It was hopeless trying to keep close patrol there, so we withdrew and dived deep to get out of the weather. Even at 140 feet we were rolling eight degrees either side in the ground swell. The trip back to Maddalena gave us the only pleasure we got out of the whole patrol: our guest Jonah was sea-sick. But he got the last laugh: as we went alongside *Paccinotti* he cheered up.

'Thanks for the ride, sir, I win thirty-eight shillings.'

'How the heck?'

'I scored twenty-three points and win the Patrol Pool.'

And he had. He failed to score a maximum by two points. He had put 'Yes' to 'Shall we be depth-charged?' and 'Shall we be bombed from the air?'

★ 11 ★

JUMPED OFF FRÉJUS

The only other boats in harbour were *Ultor* and *Unseen* who were sharing the pens with what appeared to be an Italian UJ-boat.

'What's that thing, Nobby?' I asked *Unseen*'s navigator.

'Just the Italian navy helping us out. See that thing on her smoke-stack?' He pointed to the little silhouette painted on her funnel of a sinking submarine with '15.2.42' printed underneath. 'That was *Tempest* they sank off Taranto, and another as well. Now we lie alongside her. What a war!'

One day we received secret instructions to be prepared for attacks by swimmers. At nights sentries were doubled up, listening for the tell-tale bubbling of a swimmer's oxygen set. Fused stun charges were stacked on the casing.

The next night I was sleeping on board as Duty Officer when I was woken at 0200 with a hand message telling me to assume the first degree of readiness for attacks by swimmers. Up top it was a still night, with lamps sweeping the mirror surface of the harbour for bubbles. For the next hour sailors wearily dragged the bight of a heavy wire along the ship's bottom to scrape off any limpets which might already have been attached to the hull. Then a message from down below reported a loud steady Asdic transmission. It stopped, only to ping again for a few seconds every ten minutes. Fantastic solutions sprang to mind; swimmers with a portable Asdic set; an enemy midget submarine in the harbour, pinging its way up to our pens. The looming shape of the Italian *Circe* in the next pen prompted another theory, quickly confirmed – that the transmissions were coming from her. They were beamed straight down the harbour. A better beacon for anyone swimming with a bag of limpet mines towards us it would be hard to conceive.

The Italian Captain's explanation was, of course, that his Asdics were transmitting in self-defence to give warning of anything moving underwater. There the matter rested, but our Captain insisted on *Untiring* being moved immediately to another berth away from *Circe*.

Although there were frequent alarms, our wires never scraped any sticky-bombs off the keel. When we let off our two-pound charges they never brought to the surface an unconscious rubber-clad body.

All these thoughts were forgotten when we sailed again for patrol. *Upstart* passed us in the Straits on her way in, evidently from a blank patrol.

Thirty-six hours later we were on the surface in our favourite hunting-ground off Cap Dramont. Barry sat in the wardroom sorting out the Patrol Pools entries. This time blank forms had sold like hot cakes around the base, until our total pool was worth fifteen pounds. The Captain was open to offers to conduct our patrol to produce a winning line.

'Huh,' Barry said, 'the padre says we fire eight fish, get no hits, collect a bollocking, stay at sea nineteen days and have no U.K. mail waiting for us on our return.'

'Don't worry, the bishop doesn't represent the average view. Exactly three hundred columns filled in, and only seventeen predict us a blank patrol.'

'Bad cess to them,' the Captain said as he rose to answer a call from the Control Room. 'This will prove them wrong.'

It was a report from the listener on watch, who had heard enemy pinging in the direction of Antibes. More than likely it would be an offensive sweep, as we had no word from S.10 of any expected shipping movement. Somewhere out there in the dark – as black as the Earl of Hell's riding boots, as the Captain put it – an enemy force was carrying out a routine sweep of the coast.

When I went on the watch an hour later, the enemy pinging was getting louder. By now they would be between Agay and Cap Dramont. The Captain was on the bridge with Barry, both searching round for the source of the transmissions.

A light flickered ashore. 'Probably a badly blacked-out room somewhere up on the Cap . . . or a motor car passing behind trees.'

Then it came on again. This time it was unmistakable. It was making Morse; Cap Dramont signal station calling up someone out at sea. With startling suddenness the answering light jumped across the water from very close to us. Its beam neatly illuminated the masts and funnels of a large merchantman not two miles away.

Barely had we gone to Diving Stations to begin an attack when the enemy revealed themselves again, this time by two aircraft recognition flares which floated out of the sky . . . two lingering claret blobs, sufficient to show a merchantship with four destroyers in close screen. All was pitch black once more, but the Captain had seen all he needed. Apart from one nasty moment when the escorting aircraft zoomed right over the top of us at fifty feet, the attack was pressed home without the slightest difficulty. It was the Captain's first surface night attack, and it turned out to be a text-book undetected night interception. The sinister outline of a destroyer passed four hundred yards ahead, leaving a clear shot at the target, which we could identify through binoculars – a fat, laden, four-island merchant vessel, with a squat funnel and a cruiser stern.

On firing, the wheel was put hard over and we raced away on the surface. The boat was hardly round when an orange flash shot up into the sky. A long rumbling explosion reached us a few seconds later, followed by another sheet of flame as a second torpedo hit. The light from this gave us a momentary glimpse of the ship heeling over to port with smoke pouring out of the midships superstructure. Barry broke the silence.

'Jesus, I saw that first one hit through my glasses. I swear I saw a longitudinal bulkhead poised on top of that streak of flame. What a beauty!' He moved towards the conning-tower hatch.

'Where are you off to? I'm not diving. Johnnie, get below and re-load as soon as possible.'

Even as my head went down the conning-tower I could see a beam of strong light overhead – a destroyer's searchlight sweeping round. In the Control Room the Outside E.R.A. had his hands on the vent levers and everything was at a split second's notice for diving.

'Relax, everybody, we're not diving.'

They thought I was joking, till the Captain rang down emergency full speed ahead. As I was going through the fore-ends door there was the rippling crack of a salvo of depth charges. The matelots all grinned and flung the loading gear into position. For the next twenty minutes there was a continual series of large patterns being dropped somewhere astern of us. But we were getting out of it at our flat-out twelve knots and each pattern sounded fainter than the last. It never occurred to me that four German destroyers quarrying the sea with high explosive whilst we slipped away on the surface could be such a tonic for morale. Charlie appeared in the Torpedo Stowage Compartment disguised as a hula dancer and put on a one-man floor show for the benefit of the chaps sweating on the hauling-in tackle. Cups of tea and sandwiches came from nowhere and tins of fruit stolen from the Coxswain's store were passed round. The salvo was re-loaded in under the hour, helped by working in fresh air and pumped-up exuberance.

The Captain decided that the area was unhealthy, so we headed eastward at full speed for the remaining hours of darkness, intending to dive in the morning off Oneglia on the Italian border.

'We'll have a quiet day . . . there.'

The Captain pencil-marked a spot a good five miles off the beach.

'There's hardly likely to be anything moving but trouble tomorrow, so we'll keep out of it.'

Sunrise turned out to be one of those hazy days of indeterminate visibility. Through the periscope all the peaks and capes ashore looked alike, making it impossible to fix the boat's position with certainty. With so many minefields believed to be all along that part of the coast, it was imperative that a reliable periscope fix should be obtained, so course was ordered to close the beach for a fix.

We were still making our way towards the shore when the officer of the watch reported a formation of bombers – identified as B-17s – coming up from the south. This was a rare sight, as Allied air activity along the coastline in our patrol areas had hitherto been confined to occasional reconnaissance flights by a Wellington. But this was different. It was a formation on a mission somewhere nearby. Perhaps at last they were going to cut those railway viaducts over which day-long eastbound ammunition trains passed before our eyes.

Fascinated, the Captain watched them.

'About twenty-five of them, three shallow vees . . . long vapour trails, just like the Battle of Britain. There's some flak going up around Oneglia . . . that stuff's miles off target. They're pretty high – I'd say ten thousand easily. Just pass the word though the boat we'll get some loud bangs any minute now if any of their bombs go in the drink.'

We did, dozens of them, as loud and sharp as if they had landed alongside. They were probably only 500-pounders and they were certainly falling over three miles away.

'They're unloading the stuff on Oneglia itself,' the Captain said from the periscope. 'There are four huge spouts of water in the harbour. Can't see what they've hit yet. What a sight. Here, have a look.'

I saw a mist of smoke over the masts of shipping in the harbour, with beads of tracer criss-crossing upwards. A largish fire was burning in the town itself. One by one, most of the crew had a quick look, till the Captain took over again to spot any ditching aircraft. But the B-17s sailed serenely on, still in perfect formation.

'That seems to be all.' He swung the periscope for an all-round look. 'Hullo, here's the next wave.'

He watched another formation go in and put their bombs fair and square on the town with more underwater detonations.

'You know, you'd think they would have told us about this. We could at least stand by to pick up any survivors. Hey, there's something moving in the harbour, a couple of masts and a tall thin funnel.'

Slowly he watched it clear the breakwater and turn beam-on to us, a small old-fashioned tramp steamer of some 1,500 tons.

'There's all manner of stuff coming out of the harbour. It looks mostly small stuff . . . nothing else worth a fish. I suppose they're getting out before the next wave of B-17s come over. Our man is going up into a bay to the west of the harbour. There's one poor devil in harbour with no steam up. I bet the crew have beaten it ashore.'

From the chart it could be seen that the tramp steamer was going up to anchor in shoal water, but there was a clear run for our torpedoes in a minimum depth of five fathoms.

'We'll give him two kippers . . . depth six feet. He's stopped now.'

The tubes' crew were elated to get off another salvo within twelve hours of the last. No tedious 'P' routines due next morning; no more reloads left on the racks.

The range was cutting down quickly. At three thousand yards the Captain could distinguish more clearly the armada of craft which were clearing out of harbour for the safety of the open sea.

'There are a couple of drifters over there. A tug with everyone on the upper deck wearing tin hats. And here's one motor boat batting straight out to sea as if the Devil himself was chasing him. The target is still stopped. Call it three hundred feet long and flush deck. Single red stack and a privy over the stern – stand by . . . Fire one, starboard five. First aimed at the foremast. Midships . . . steady. Fire two! Point of aim, the mainmast.'

'Both torpedoes running, sir. One on the red oh two, one right ahead.'

The fish hitting in shallow water made disappointing bangs, but they were nonetheless effective. The first brought down his foremast and blew a hole in his side up to the gunwale. After the second hit the Captain watched her settle slowly on an even keel. It lay with its decks awash and smoke billowing out of the after hold.

'Damn thing's not sunk. I suppose it's too shallow,' he grunted. 'Matter of fact, it doesn't look a total loss to me. What do you think Barry?' What he did not add was that, if we could fire one more, it would justify returning early to Maddalena. The crew realized this full well and jumped for joy when Barry took a look and pronounced that the vessel was still a salvageable proposition.

The next torpedo achieved the unique distinction of hitting the target on the bridge superstructure. The force of its explosion blew the funnel over the side and reduced the upperworks to scrap. All that remained to be seen sticking up above the water when it came to my turn for a quick look was the mainmast with its derricks slung drunkenly over one side. She must have been loading cargo when the raid began. A Nazi ensign fluttered obstinately from her gaff.

We were heading out to sea at full speed, grouper down, trying to get clear before the Germans could bring their A/S striking forces to bear on the area. They had bases for UJ-boats at Savona, Nice and various other secondary ports in between.

'With luck we might have an hour,' the Captain decided. 'That is, *if* they don't happen to have any ships already at sea and *if* there aren't any UJs in Oneglia harbour which didn't come out during the air-raid.'

'In an hour at this speed we'll be there . . .' Gus spanned the dividers five miles to the southward.

'Just where they'll start looking. Right, we'll surface.'

'That's funny,' I heard the Coxswain whisper to the fore planesman, 'I thought I heard the skipper say we were going to surface.'

He did.

'I want two officers permanently on the bridge. Johnnie, you take the port side aircraft look-out; Gus, you take starboard. One rating each side to keep surface look-out. Remain at Diving Stations.'

The blinding midday sun which hit me as I went up through the hatch dazzled everything into a blur for an instant. Then a quick look round at the situation: we were close enough to the harbour to see people running along the breakwater, making for the nearest shelter maybe. The red roofs of houses and little white village churches dotted the mountainside running down from the impressive background of snow-tipped peaks. The nearest moving thing to us was the little motor boat, still scudding out to sea, about half a mile away. Thank God, there were no aircraft about. Our generators urged us along at full speed, carving a beautifully clean symmetrical wake, as if cut on marble. The sheer beauty of the scene made one forget that we were gambling on our small silhouette to give us just long enough to put a safe distance between the boat and the beach. The enemy were doubly alerted, standing to for another wave of bombers and after seeing our torpedo tracks before that ship exploded. Heavy anti-aircraft guns and coastal defence batteries were all fully manned, but they never gave the slightest sign of spotting us. The only people who did were those in the little motor boat, which had turned round abruptly and shot back towards the harbour.

'Aircraft, green one three oh, sir,' Gus sang out, 'two flying from left to right, angle of sight five degrees.'

But they flew right along the coast and were lost to sight in the mist over Monaco. Probably they had been sent to repel the American raid. Thirty-six hours later we were in our old berth in the pens at Maddalena. The best news to meet us was that we were due for docking at Malta.

★ 12 ★

UJ-BOATS – A SPLIT DECISION

The fortnight in dock at Malta seemed like leave in London. To have the choice of half-a-dozen cinemas; to see shops stocked with goods; to dress for dinner in the Mess; to go to the Saturday evening dances at the Union Club, where it was rumoured real live white women were sometimes to be found; to be able to cable U.K. and get a reply in two days; to go on board ships of the Mediterranean Fleet and meet old friends – all these things had been denied to us at Maddalena. The base at Lazaretto had been reinforced by boats from the Eastern Mediterranean, who found Malta austere and boring after their ski-ing chalets in the Lebanese Alps and the night-life of Beirut. However, they were already clearing away the rubble of bomb damage and rebuilding the old base as a permanent home for submarines.

Our first night in harbour coincided with the official opening of the new wardroom and farewell to *Dzik* and *Sokol*, two Polish boats who were sailing back to U.K. after spectacularly successful commissions with twenty-seven ships sunk between them. Just before they were due to go on board and head out to sea there was a lull in the mess as the B.B.C. news came on. The first item said that Churchill and Roosevelt had agreed to Russia annexing the eastern portion of Poland, which included Lvov. The Poles could not understand. We had entered the War to guarantee Poland's frontiers, hadn't we? We were winning the War, weren't we? Now, long before any talk of a peace treaty, their home was to be handed over to the Russians. Their officers could not understand; and I, for one, could not look them in the eye. These Poles had braved the mines of the Skagerrak in 1939 rather than submit to invaders from east or west; they had left all behind them and fought like tigers. For three years there had always been a Polish boat in the Tenth Flotilla, matching the equal of our best. Now they were going back to look for their families in occupied territory in Eastern Europe. I pressed another drink on Oscar, who was in tears.

Ashore, Malta had changed very little. After the invasion of Italy the island had suddenly changed from being a strategic springboard with the hopes of the whole world centred on it to being a secure backwater, existing on a weekly convoy and daily doses of self-approbation in the *Times of Malta*. The 'Gut' was packed nightly with sailors spending their pay on watery Cisk beer at two shillings a pint. The Cliff elevator swayed its way precariously up from the Grand Harbour landing-steps; every time I travelled in it I found someone at my elbow telling how once, during the heavy raids, the cage had crashed a hundred feet to the bottom. Dghaisamen jostled and screamed at each other for a fare across to Dockyard Creek. Scraggy ponies of unbelievable endurance still pulled one up the streets of Valletta. Travelling in these carriages, one got the impression that all roads in Malta go uphill. Indian merchants had strengthened their hold over the souvenir and gift trades.

'No, not exactly real silk, sir, but very good artificial. Wears much better and lasts longer. Like nylon. Fully-fashioned. For you, sir, only seventeen and sixpence a pair.'

Then there was a bitter rugger match on the rock-hard ground at Marsa, hitherto forbidden to submariners due to the risk of injury from the shrapnel which was still all over the ground. The R.A.F. proved to fifteen of us that beer is not always best, particularly if taken in large quantities just before the game.

A memorable crew party ended with the wardroom flunkie and I exchanging uniforms. I went for a run ashore down the Gut with the fore-endmen. Whilst the A.B. made it undetected to the bar of the Union Club in Valletta, I thought it had gone far enough when I returned and found him turned in on my bunk ashore, out for the count, with my mosquito net partly burnt by the dead cigar in his hand.

It was par for the course to solve the problem of getting back to Lazaretto from Valletta by pinching a gharry. Two of us left the Union Club after midnight and found an untended carriage. We hadn't gone far before a hue-and-cry developed in our wake and we had to whip the poor old pony into overdrive. We also took a snap decision not to risk the long trip round to Manoel Island, but to take the shortest route home. Abandoning the carriage at the foot of the cliffs, we were already halfway across the narrow channel to Lazaretto when we heard the owner reach his bewildered pony. Somehow we slipped ashore at the submarine base without being intercepted by a sentry. We sat tight on the general signal from F.O. Malta next morning asking for those responsible to own up.

These sort of escapades would never have occurred if there had been suitable female company available. The first batch of Wrens had just returned to the island after the siege had been lifted, but they were scooped up by fat cats on the Staff and Coastal Forces officers, all of whom seemed to have fully-licenced luxury flats in Sliema. Anyway, they had not been in circulation long enough to suggest some other pattern of off-duty behaviour than that enjoyed by an Extra 'A' rugger XV in Croydon after an away match. In accordance with the tribal mores of many Mediterranean countries, intercourse, social or otherwise, was firmly discouraged with the heavily chaperoned daughters of local families on the social register, unless an early date at the altar was on the menu.

There was just one attractive English-speaking blonde left behind when all the others were evacuated. She had arrived on the island in 1939 as a cabaret artiste and stayed to run her own dimly-lit little bar in Valletta. She had been betrothed to two submarine officers in turn, neither of whom returned from patrol. When we got there one of the Polish submariners had her doorkey, so she kept firmly to her side of the bar.

Conventions at the other end of the scale in Malta would have interested any student of human anthropology.

'How many kids have you got, Tony?' was a suitable opening gambit with any dockyard matey.

'Fifteen, signor, but I don't know how many are mine and how many are God's.'

It wasn't until I read Morris West's novels about the degenerate priesthood in remote parts of Southern Italy that I realized there might have been some truth in the story that a Maltese labourer returning from work dare not enter his own home if a rolled-up black umbrella was parked outside the front door.

On our last night in Malta there was a touring variety show from England. After much bargaining with a man who knew a man who had drawn a ticket for the show in the Command ballot for seats, I floated on the cloud of nostalgia created by Leslie Henson, Hermione Baddeley and their team.

By the time we sailed, we had forgotten all about the war and the misery of being at sea in bad weather, which we encountered between Sicily and Sardinia. The patrol orders handed to the Captain on arrival at Maddalena brought us up with a round turn . . . the Toulon billet – that nasty little hornets' nest of UJ-boats, where we might have to spend days acting as a target for A/S exercises. To reduce our chances of a successful strike still further, our self-confessed Jonah, Gowan, came as a passenger. He was as cheerful as ever:

'Here's my pools entry . . . no hits and a good old-fashioned hammering.'

His pessimism seemed well-founded after we had spent several days dodging the familiar pattern of patrolling UJ-boats criss-crossing the Bay.

During the forenoon of the fifth day the Captain seemed to be taking more than usual interest in the pair of UJ-boats as they pinged their way round us. He even carried out a dummy attack on them, at a respectful distance outside their Asdic range. As they passed us he checked his estimations.

'Mast-head height of sixty-five, target speed nine. That seems to be right. I reckon we would have hit one of them at least. Still, one's enough. The other would have been distinctly angry. Up a little.'

The panel watchkeeper inched the periscope up and the Captain had another good look at the two UJ-boats.

'Nasty looking customers. They seem to have three throwers either side and four racks aft. I'd say that was an 88-millimetre on their fo'c'sle. Two twin Bofors, and small stuff sticking out all over the place like a pin-cushion.'

I calculated the size of pattern they would drop with that outfit. Probably three flung out either side and four pairs dropped astern – at least a fourteen-charge pattern. I hoped the Captain would not get bored with constantly having to go deep and run off-track from their advancing sweep, not so bored, anyway, that he would finally turn round and have a crack at them. They would not trouble us again for another two hours, the time it took them to complete a lap. Over lunch, the Captain was describing them to Paddy.

'Eight hundred tons each. One of them is a converted coaster, but the other I'd say was specially built for the job. Quite like one of our *Flower* class. They certainly pack a hell of a wallop, though.'

'They must have seen my pools entry,' Paddy said happily. 'I expect we'll get a taste of it if this goes on much longer.'

When the two hunting craft came round again during the afternoon, the Captain stayed at the periscope to watch them pass. The range closed to about three thousand yards, with us getting further out on their bow, all according to plan, when suddenly the Captain stiffened.

'Diving Stations. They've both altered towards us. Any change in the characteristics of their pinging, Bird?'

29 Crossing the
International Date
Line at 400ft in USS
Stickleback; J.O.C.
teaching US officer
to play "Rule
Britannia" during
crew party.

30 NATO
underground HQ
Northwood,
C–in–C (J.A.S.
Eccles) and French
liaison officer; on left
J.O.C. and
American member
of staff, 1958.

31 Parade and march-past of all forces, before the Governor of Bermuda, Major-General Sir Julian Gascoigne. J.O.C. behind him.

32 HMS *Ark Royal* leading the Aircraft Carrier Squadron with ship's company about to cheer Her Majesty in the Royal Yacht. Astern of *Britannia* is HMS *Apollo* flying the flag of C-in-C Home Fleet off Invergordon, May, 1957.

33 HMS
Bermuda
children's
party in
Hamburg
with the ship's
capstan as
carousel.

34 HMS
Bermuda at
Malta.

35 Father perplexed by chart.

36 Steins of lager in the Reeperbahn, 1959.

'No, sir. They're just sweeping, using a three-thousand-yard interval.'

'We're seven degrees on the port bow of the nearest one at a range of twenty-eight minutes. What am I off-track?'

I spun the wheels of the fruit-machine and said that the enemy would pass six hundred yards ahead on his present course. That would leave us well inside his Asdic range. Uneasily I remembered those fourteen-charge patterns.

'Set six feet on all tubes. Same target speed as this morning . . . nine knots, wasn't it? Down periscope.'

'Fore-ends,' I said softly over the phones, 'we're attacking two UJ-boats, so don't make any mistake about the depth-setting . . . and keep your fingers crossed.'

'Aye, aye, sir,' the T.G.M. replied and added a message which I did not repeat. 'Tell that mad Irishman not to start anything he can't finish.'

The control room crew were unusually quiet, tensely watching Bird as he swung his pointer to and fro across his Sperry repeater. There was a bad moment when he reported one of the enemy in contact, but it soon lost us again. Gus's plot showed we had run out for a few hundred yards and then turned bows on to the target. The Captain had another look. They were in line abreast, about two cables apart. The nearer one would pass about a thousand yards away.

'I shall fire at them on a 105 track, when they should form a continuous target,' he said.

All was ready for'ard and the boat seemed to be in a good trim. Using rubber-covered wheel spanners, ratings were quietly shutting off various sea-connections for depth-charging. The wardroom flunkey was standing ready with his two-foot-long spanner with which he would forcibly check the tendency of a 'Q' outboard vent to jerk open.

The Captain was taking quick looks through the small attack periscope, kneeling down to the deck so as to show the minimum amount of stick above water. The angle on the bow dial on the fruit-machine was going round with every look . . . sixty-six . . . seventy-eight . . . eighty-two.

'Stand by . . . fire one!'

A kick underfoot as the boat recoiled. The noise of venting air from the firing gear coming faintly over my phones. 'One running, sir,' from Bird.

'Fire two!'

Again the shudder and the hissing noise for'ard. 'Fire three . . . fire.

four. Christ, what a bubble. One hundred feet. Starboard twenty-five. Group up.'

Hardly had our routine avoiding action been initiated when there was a thunderclap explosion, dead on time for our second torpedo at the end of its run.

'That's one of them,' Gus said unnecessarily, 'ten seconds to go for the next one, eight . . . five . . . four . . . three . . . two . . . one . . . now.' Nothing happened.

'Three torpedoes still running, sir,' Bird said sadly.

Gus stopped me at the chart-table.

'The H.S.D.'s just reported the other UJ-boat coming in on the port quarter now, in firm contact. If you've got a rabbit's foot, rub it.'

I squatted on the control room deck and waited. In the awesome silence the flivver of his propellers overhead sounded like an express train going through a country station. Instinctively all heads looked upwards, half expecting to see through the pressure hull and watch depth-charges float down like leaves in an autumn breeze. No doubt about it this time. Split seconds dragged into endless seconds. The signalman had his piece of chalk poised over the small board he used for keeping a tally of depth-charges. The Captain and the H.S.D. quietly removed their headsets.

No language could describe the noise of the salvo of explosions which followed. The deck under our feet bucked madly, a shower of cork and flaked paint came down from the pressure-hull overhead, most of the lights went out, the depth-gauge needles flicked up twenty feet . . . and a solitary cup on the wardroom table jumped out of its saucer and smashed on the deck. The blast had come in two waves: the first like a giant kick in the pants under the port quarter and the second as a savage blow over the starboard bow. The pressure-hull must have been momentarily squeezed, like one of those hyper-speed photos of a golf-club on impact with the ball. A perfect straddle.

A few seconds and it was plain that no serious damage had been done. The boat remained on a level keel, close to her depth; the steering and the planes worked. Smiles all round, and furtive discussion of the number of charges counted. The signalman's board had twenty-one little white ticks on it.

'H.E. decreasing on green six-oh, sir.'

Now the UJ-boat would be lying off to wait for the disturbed water to settled and allow her Asdics to pick us up again. Overhead there would be a coloured smoke-float burning to mark the datum-point of her last attack.

An annoying pain in my ears caused me to look at the barometer.

Sure enough, the sensitive gold needle was creeping away from the black needle (set at atmospheric pressure on diving that morning). The Captain had noticed it too.

'Chief E.R.A., have a quick check round the H.P. air system. There's a bad leak somewhere.'

It was not dangerous, but increasingly uncomfortable as the excess pressure built up to over three inches. A report came in from the engine room that the cast steel top of the lub. oil separator – weighing a couple of hundredweight – had flown off and dented the watertight bulkhead. Several sea-valves had to be nipped up after they had slacked back against the kick of underwater blast. But, otherwise, all was well.

Bird reported the enemy coming in again, and we tensed ourselves for another lot like the last. This time, however, she appeared to lose contact just before reaching us and the subsequent pattern was noticeably less violent. The crack of multiple explosions was almost as bad, but the feeling that the whole main battery was being shot up through the deck-boards and the pressure-hull was buckling was not there. It seemed that the enemy had crossed astern. A few more bulbs had burst, but, once again, everything was well in hand. Only that gold needle on the barometer kept on creeping up, the insistent pain on the ear-drums reminding me that something was wrong somewhere.

When the Chief E.R.A. had finished his look round he reported that the H.P. air system was apparently intact, but he thought he had heard the noise of air escaping in the torpedo stowage compartment. Before anyone could look into it, the enemy came over again, this time dropping a much smaller pattern – five or seven – not so near as the first lot, but still uncomfortably close. Then there was a lull. The H.S.D. said that the UJ-boat's propeller noises had slowed down and then stopped out on our quarter and its Asdics were sweeping. For the first time in twenty minutes they were uncertain.

Meanwhile the TGM had found the source of the air leak for'ard. It was coming out of the rear end of the air-vessel of one of the reload torpedoes in the racks. A flaw in one of those air-vessels could lead to an explosion if compressed air at 3000 lbs/sq.in. suddenly erupted. I whispered the news to the Captain, who ordered the compartment to be cleared.

'Keep your fingers crossed. We'll drain it down when we've shaken this bastard off.'

'In contact, sir. Red one hundred. H.E. increasing . . . transmission interval two thousand.'

The Captain ordered an alteration of course and speeded up, which threw the enemy off his aim, for the next pattern was wide of the mark.

For another hour we zig-zagged steadily out to seaward, varying depths and speeds to upset the UJ-boat's plot of our movement. Her attacks became less vicious and at longer intervals. The signalman's tally showed between eighty and a hundred charges dropped when a series of reports of nothing but sweeping transmissions indicated that it was all over for the time being. We crept up to periscope depth and the Captain snatched a brief look.

'He's stopped astern beam on, frantically flashing to someone. Range about two miles. Can't see much about. Wait. There are a couple of R-boats near him.'

At that moment came three distant bangs.

'R-boats being directed on to us, I expect. There's a puff of smoke from her funnel. She's moving off . . . gathering speed . . . and there go her charges. Down periscope.'

Even at two miles they sounded dangerous, but we were obviously clear away now. The enemy was attacking a false echo, perhaps our wake. Whatever it was, we were gaining valuable time and distance. At the next look, she had turned away and was heading inshore, having unloaded her complete outfit on to us.

The next problem was to relieve the excess pressure, which had by now had the barometer needle hard up against its stop. The Captain's solution was simple.

'Open the lower lid. Stand by to surface. Just plane her up, Number One, and get someone to hold on to me when I open the lid.'

He waited up in the conning tower whilst the boat came up till the bridge deck was awash. Two seamen held on to his legs, a precaution taken ever since one of our captains was blown clean over the side by escaping pressure in a submarine surfacing off Norway in 1940. The shallow gauge needle read eleven . . . ten . . . nine feet.

'Surfaced, sir.'

Swoosh! The upper lid flew open and air roared out like the relief valve on a boiler lifting. The sudden drop in pressure kicked our ear-drums, and all round me I could see matelots champing their jaws to clear their sinuses. Murky vapour was sucked up out of the bilges till the control room was like a main line railway station on a winter's morning. The gold barometer needle moved slowly back and settled on the 1013 mark. The noise of escaping air finally stopped altogether. The patch of strange sunlight on the control room deck was blotted out as the Captain slammed the upper hatch and told Number One to take her down. When he stepped off the ladder his hair was still standing on end and his right trouser-leg rolled up to the knee from standing in the slipstream.

'The R-boats are still pottering around three miles away and there's an Arado bumbling about over towards Cepet. But I don't think they saw us: we'll soon know, anyhow.'

For the next two hours till dark, all hands cleared up the mess and made good minor damage; bits of broken bulbs were picked up and the mess of dirt and chipped cork swept away. A queue formed to get into the wash-place and rinse hair out in hot water; no amount of combing would get rid of the dirt which had showered down from overhead after each pattern. A tot all round put the matelots in high good humour.

We surfaced at dusk and set off at high speed to put as much distance between ourselves and Toulon as possible. The three good torpedoes were loaded and the leaking one drained down and rendered harmless. (On our return to Maddalena the torpedo staff of the base stripped it down and discovered that the end-door of the air-vessel had been partly blown out, so we had narrowly missed a spontaneous explosion which would have sunk us.) Just as we were all settling in for a good night's sleep a telegraphist handed the Captain an 'Immediate' from S.10.

'Proceed with utmost despatch to area SX. German blockade runner expected to arrive Port Vendres a.m. 28th.'

'That gives us just tonight and tomorrow to get there,' the Captain said.

The chart showed Port Vendres just on the French side of the border, at the foot of the Pyrenees where the coastal plain begins. We had known for some time that the Germans had been shipping bauxite from Barcelona. Thence the blockade-runners crawled up the coast inside Spanish territorial waters as far as the border, leaving themselves only a 50-mile dash through French waters to Port Vendres, whence their precious cargoes were sent overland to the Ruhr. The difficulties of attacking this contraband traffic previously had been reckoned overwhelming: the ships used were disguised as neutrals and sailed at times deliberately designed to be confused with the sailings of many safe-conduct ships, which had guaranteed passages to Marseilles with their medical supplies and stores destined for our prisoners-of-war; the sea around the area was shallow and known to be mined. For these and other reasons, none of our boats had yet been sent to operate against this shipping. However, we had on board a series of photographs of the suspected ships. Even with these, there would be a risk of sinking the wrong ship by day. At night safe-conduct ships were bound by international law to show all navigation lights burning at full brilliancy and with their superstructures floodlit.

'There they all are. Mostly typical three-island tramps, with a single drain-pipe funnel and two masts; between 1500 and 3000 tons, speeds ranging from eight to eleven knots. I suppose Lloyds have thousands like them on their books. This one here is a little bit different: the *Jerez*. She has a cruiser stern and a squat funnel. You can bet your bottom dollar they all have *Espagnol* in large letters along their sides and wear beautiful seven-breadth yellow and orange ensigns. Short of listening to their Captain's accent I don't see how we can be sure.'

His pencil drew a line across the chart in the middle of a shaded area marked 'Mined'. 'That eliminates some of the wheat from the chaff, because I doubt if the Hun would dare to run disguised neutrals any further north than Port Vendres. At night we'd better go down near the Spanish frontier, which will get us out of the range of harbour defence stuff and give us sea-room to shadow anything suspicious for a couple of hours.'

At dawn we were fifteen miles off the coast. We stayed up to get the best fix we could from the serrated line of similar peaks of the Pyrenees and then dived and ran in opposite the spot where the plains of the littoral began. We were now in water of less than a hundred feet, amongst minefields marked on the chart. The plan was to steer straight for Port Vendres, thus 'sweeping' a clear path for ourselves to come out again, or for other boats to dive along in the future. By lunchtime a few cranes and a spire rising out of a group of houses at the foot of the mountains were identified as our objective. By two o'clock we were only three miles off, when I sighted the smoke of a ship coming up from the south.

No signal had been received giving the warning of a safe-conduct neutral so it seemed we had hit the jackpot first time. As the ship came nearer it looked more and more like the ones in our photographs; tall single funnel, Spanish flag, two masts. The tubes were brought to the ready, shaping up for a decisive strike from point-blank range.

The Captain was not altogether happy. 'Get the cypher log and check through every report of neutral shipping movement in this area. Get out Talbot Booth's *Book of Merchant Ships* and try to tally up the features. Funnel markings are red, with a black band near the top.'

Gus feverishly thumbed through the pink signals in the log. 'Nothing here, sir. There was one through yesterday and there's a Swiss job due at Marseilles on the 5th. But there's nothing in between those two.'

'I wonder,' the Captain murmured, taking another look. 'It's certainly going into Port Vendres, and what the hell's it doing here without us being notified? Well, give it the plot speed of eight knots, depth six feet and a course parallel to the coast.'

Gus bent over the chart and laid off the enemy's course. A telegraphist came along from aft and put a signal on the table beside him. With a 'don't bother me now' expression, he pushed the signal aside.

'It's important, sir,' the telegraphist whispered.

Gus read it.

'Just a minute, sir . . .'

'Bearing is that . . . red four two. What does that put me on the bow? Give me a D.A.'

'Sir, there's a signal here from Flag Officer, Gib. "Spanish vessel *Santa Rosa* sailed Barcelona p.m. 26th along approved safe-conduct route to Marseilles, due a.m. 29th. Not to be molested on voyage".'

I turned up Talbot Booth's and showed the Captain a picture which confirmed the ship's identity.

'Phew. That was nearly an international incident. Stop the attack. Fall out. Even so, though, she's no business to be going into Port Vendres. Maybe the skipper's got a bit of stuff there.'

The Captain was clearly shaken by our narrow escape from sending a thousand tons of Red Cross supplies to the bottom. He was going to take a lot of convincing before loosing off at any ship in this part of the world.

We went on right close in to the port and saw the masts of a 3000-tonner unloading, but the mouth of the breakwater did not open up enough of the harbour to allow a torpedo shot. On the promontory to the south-east of the town there was a battery of guns and several searchlights, with the mattress aerials of a radar station nearby. Withdrawing to seaward, we spent the last hours of daylight zig-zagging about in an area one mile square to satisfy ourselves that it was clear of mines and safe for future operations.

On the surface, in pitch black darkness with no moon or stars, the boat ambled southwards about three miles off the beach through the opaque night.

I was almost pulled out of my bunk by a rating telling me that the night alarm had gone. Still half asleep, I found myself setting bearings on the fruit-machine. Information was coming down the voice-pipe as fast as a commentary on an ice-hockey match.

'Give it ten knots. Range two thousand five hundred. Get an H.E.

count on the Asdics. Hurry up with the tubes. Hard a'starboard. Start both generators.'

The boat swung round on to a tracking course. The thud of the generators starting added to the general background of orders and reports being passed.

'Target length 300 feet. Course parallel to the coast.'

We were soon bowling along at full speed somewhere on his starboard quarter. For once, Screwball was producing adequate data from the radar and the plot showed us to be stalking the enemy about a mile and a half away. Pretty soon that range opened slightly, and it became clear that we were trying to keep pace with a ship which was doing at least one knot more than our top speed of thirteen knots. I began to think it might be a destroyer, but Gus, who had been on the bridge when it was sighted, put me in the picture.

'A large flush-decked merchantman, batting along without any lights. All we could make out was that it had a cruiser stern.'

So it was the *Jerez*, slightly ahead of schedule.

'Tell the Chief E.R.A. to go on to emergency full ahead,' the Captain ordered, but the answer from the engine room was that we were already doing that. Still the radar ranges continued to open. We were now 4200 yards astern. There would not be the slightest chance of getting in an attack. Port Vendres was ten miles away, or fifty minutes' steaming. To enter the harbour, the enemy would have to alter course to port and slow down. In doing this he might lay himself open to a snap shot – a slender chance, but the only one.

After another three-quarters of an hour, the radar range had gone out to nearly three miles when there was a dramatic change in the situation. The ranges steadied, then started coming down. At the same time the bearings began to draw left. The enemy was altering course and reducing speed to enter harbour. We swung to port and shaped to cut across close inshore by the rocky point with the gun batteries.

At a range of just over a mile we fired and immediately dived. One satisfying wallop was heard almost as soon as the Captain reached the control room. Through the periscope he could see the ship, beautifully illuminated by shore searchlights, sinking on an even keel. When it came for my turn for a look, I could plainly see three lifeboats, one of them on its beam ends, surrounded by heads bobbing up and down in the water. A solitary E-boat came out through the harbour mouth and stopped near the lifeboats. All that remained above water of the *Jerez* and her cargo of bauxite were her masts, barely a cable's distance from the breakwater. We got in our shot not a moment too late.

Afterwards an analysis of the attack showed why it was that neither the E-boat nor the searchlights had probed to seaward after the *Jerez* blew up. The tracks of the two torpedoes which missed were plotted on to the end of their run six miles away. A convenient indentation on the coast-line allowed them to complete their run without going up on the beach. Consequently the enemy would not have heard them explode and may have presumed that their ship had been mined. There had been no attacks by submarines within fifty miles of the area for over two years. As if we had not already had enough for one patrol, we had to beat our way home through a violent gale. One huge sea, more like the Denmark Strait than the Riviera, broke green over the bridge, and tons of water poured down into the control room, bursting the bird-bath, and surged unchecked around the compartment. A cursing, sweating human bucket-chain baled it into the engine-room bilges to be pumped out. When the worst of the damage had been made good and tired members of the watch below were making their way for'ard to turn in, another cascade crashed down the hatch and flattened the sides of the bird-bath again.

The bad weather was quickly forgotten when the storm abated next morning, and we duly made our landfall south of Ajaccio.

★ 13 ★

TO THE ST LEGER WITH
A WEDDING – CAKE

Maddalena was alive with buzzes about expected landing operations. The Second Front, everyone said, was definitely going to be a simultaneous strike across the Channel and into the Riviera. In the mess they were saying that *Untiring* would not do another patrol but was being held in reserve for beach-marking duties.

In due course we received orders to sail on patrol again. Number One hinted that the Captain had secret orders which he was not to read until we were clear of the land. The troops circulated a tale that we would be rendezvousing with a fishing boat off St Tropez and embarking a diplomatic mission to negotiate for the peaceful entry of troops into Southern France, just as *Seraph* has done off Algiers in 1942.

The Captain broke the news that we had been assigned the billet from Cannes to Nice.

'I expect we'll just sit out our fortnight off Antibes, playing uckers. Oh, there is one thing . . .'

This was it. We were all ears for the big news.

'We have now got within one ship of *Ultor*'s record. This time we must level the score.'

In the anticipation of cloak-and-dagger operations, interest in our rivalry with *Ultor* had waned. Thanks to her having been lent to the Aegean flotilla for two months in the Greek islands, where torpedo targets were scarce, we had been able to creep up to within one of her score of ships sunk.

But no opportunity came to stitch the equalizing bar on our flag. It was a blank patrol – fourteen days spent staring at the rocky coast with no sign of anything bigger than sailing boats for targets. There was a breathless moment one night when a destroyer passed within three cables of us at upwards of twenty knots, but it was alone and was gone almost as soon as its pluming bow-wave had rushed at us out of the night. In his determination not to let any legitimate target slip through our area, the Captain patrolled unusually close inshore at nights, never more than two miles off. The only satisfaction we could get out of the whole patrol was being able to say truthfully on our return to base that not so much as a ton of supplies had got through our blockade.

The reason for the lack of targets reaching us came in a signal from *Ultor* – now back with the flotilla – two days later. She had been on patrol to the westward of us and reported having sunk five ships by torpedo, thus putting her score beyond reach, until the next patrol anyway, as the Captain put it.

But I was not to be with him for that trip. There was a job waiting for me as First Lieutenant in the training flotilla at Blyth. At dawn three days later the unpressurized Dakota in which I had hitched a ride home from Gibraltar dropped down through the clouds to make her landfall north of the Scillies from 20° west. Beneath us were the familiar cliffs of Cornwall, somewhere near Trevose Head, fringed with foaming Atlantic rollers. Across the black waters below an endless convoy was sailing in three columns unmolested towards Normandy. It was D-Day plus one.

Somehow, I suppose, *Untiring* fitted into the pattern.

I felt a bit conspicuous walking along Piccadilly into Hatchett's men-only bar at 1100 in white tropical uniform. A glance at our Term's private address book kept there confirmed, not surprisingly, that there was no one around. Everyone else was involved in Operation Overlord. Even Billie the barmaid and mother-confessor to us all had left, fired on the spot for peeing in the till as a mark of disrespect to her boss.

Gieves fitted me up with a complete new uniform off the peg within the hour and sent my whites to the laundry.

'What's this?' I asked, pointing to the bronze oak leaf stitched above the left-hand top pocket. They knew before I did that I had been Mentioned in Despatches in the *London Gazette* a day before. Bobby got his DSO, Digger a DSC, the Coxswain, Chief ERA, the TI, Dickie Bird and the LTO in charge of the motor room got DSMs with Mentions for another three. Sadly, Gus was not on the list, although it was put right for him at the end of the war. The announcement which reached Maddalena did not mention my name, so the Captain fell in before P.Q. and in due course got me three months' extra seniority by way of compensation. At a stroke that put me in competition with the top Lieutenants in the Term ahead, a two-edged compliment.

Next I reported to Flag Officer Submarines' headquarters in a block of flats at Swiss Cottage. Barney Fawkes was by now Chief of Staff there and couldn't wait to let me into the secret of the Mulberry harbours then being assembled off the Normandy beaches. He pushed a pink signal towards me. It was a summary of patrol activity from S.10: 'Two UJ-boats sunk by *Untiring* in position . . .'

It was to be her last strike of consequence. Next came beach-marking off Hyères for the U.S. Rangers' landing, opening up the South of France front, followed by one patrol in the Aegean in which she was nearly sunk after the non-contact pistols in her warheads failed to detonate under a destroyer. So to a low-priority refit in a Dockyard at home before sailing on a seven-year loan to the Greek navy renamed *Zifias*. She now rests on the bottom off Start Point where she was sunk as an A/S target in 1957.

The Jolly Roger with 15 bars on it was nicked by her new Signalman, who was also reputed to have the ship's bell in his kitbag when he walked through the Dockyard gates for the last time.

I went down to Portsmouth during my ten days' leave. Spithead was still jammed with follow-up assault ships and seemingly no one was getting shore leave. I dutifully found the Coxswain's home near Fratton Park and explained to Mrs Willoughby that her husband was in good heart and had just been awarded the DSM.

'You can stuff your DSM,' she replied crisply. 'When's the bugger coming home? He's needed here, not in amongst all those French and Eye-tie bits of stuff.'

That was the end of my pastoral work. Not at all the way Noël Coward would have written the script.

It was time to go to sea again.

So, late in June, 1944, I found myself once again at Blyth, this time as First Lieutenant of HMS *Otway*, a noisy unwieldy hulk built in the mid-twenties for the Royal Australian Navy, who promptly handed her back. She had a complex electrical system quite unlike any other afloat.

'Don't worry about it,' my predecessor said soothingly. 'The last officer to understand it was someone on the China Station. Leave it all to the LTO [Petty Officer in charge of the motor-room]. He's a pensioner, been with the boat ten years and no one dares move him. Now here's something more interesting, which you'll have to allow for when working out the diving trim – the wardroom bathroom.' A panelled door slid open to reveal a full-length tub all boxed in with polished mahogany. I resolved to luxuriate in a steaming bath whilst submerged before moving on to a modern boat, where five officers shared a tiny metal washbasin, without so much as a shower to dissipate the limited supplies of fresh water. It turned out to be the best bath I ever had in my life, even if Michael St John, the Captain, put a big bow-down angle on the boat to slop all the hot water over the edge.

Our duties were not too onerous. Five days a week we embarked groups of trainees at 0830 and trundled about ten miles offshore to find waters deep enough to give them a chance to go through basic submarine drills. The young conscripts took in turns all the tasks they would soon have to carry out at Watch Diving: helmsman, control-room messenger, lookouts and raising or lowering the periscope to order. One day the boat was trimmed a bit heavy and I kept ordering the periscope to be raised a few inches higher. The young trainee seemed to be unduly slow to respond. Furthermore, he was not making the correct responses to orders, but let out stifled moans each time I flicked my fingers upwards to ask for more stick. By the time I got angry he had passed out cold, with his foot crushed in the hydraulic ram of the hoisting press on which he had been sitting. Flesh and blood oozed through his boot. Láter the Admiralty issued a Class A. & A. (alteration and addition to existing machinery) fitting an expanded metal guard around the moving parts.

Not having radar of any kind, only persistent thick fog would prevent our being secured alongside in time for tea and ready for the evening's frolics.

It was a glorious summer, but there was a national shortage of beer, with pub opening hours adjusted accordingly. Our nearest boozer was the Astley Arms, about two miles along the coast road towards Whitley Bay. They had a flagpole on their roof which was visible from the main gate at our base. When they hoisted the Jolly Roger we had just half an hour to get there on battered old bikes before the beer came on, possibly only for an hour. The pub was presided over by a warmhearted, elegant barmaid, reputedly still in love with a Chief Petty Officer who had not returned from patrol off Norway in 1940. When I revisited the Astley Arms twenty years after the war she still had on the shelf the bottle of Black Label he had won in a pub raffle. It is now in the submarine museum at Blockhouse.

High on the priorities for unwinding after an operational commission was the company of pretty girls. I had three Captains in *Otway* in as many months. Two of them got married during their time at Blyth. The third, Mossy Turner, was suspected of being a misogynist or at least dedicated to fighting the war to the exclusion of any outside distractions. Hitherto he had survived in command without conspicuous success. I soon got the feeling that he was, in

141

golfing terms, over-pressing with too fast a swing: he was trying to prove a point even in the old *Otway*, for ever carrying out drills as though in the presence of the enemy. At one time there was talk of us carrying 100-octane avgas in our ballast tanks to supply a forward airfield in Norway, a dicey operation at the best of times, let alone in *Otway* with barely four hours of darkness each night. He recalled me from my honeymoon at the Savoy to prepare for this operation, which was luckily overruled, to his evident disappointment.

In due course he chose me to go as his First Lieutenant in *Trespasser*, then refitting at Devonport before going to the Far East. Within two weeks he was flown out to Trincomalee to take over the old minelayer *Porpoise*, whose Commanding Officer had suggested to the Captain (S) in charge of the Flotilla that it was not a justifiable risk patrolling this massive submarine in flat calm seas with leaking external fuel tanks leaving a tell-tale trail. He was summarily relieved of his command. Mossy took over and was sunk on his first patrol in her. Briefly he had suggested I might care to go with him.

Before we all left Blyth Mossy had earnestly advised me against marrying Sylvia Syson, by common consent the prettiest and most agreeable Wren Officer around. 'You mark my words,' he said as we cycled towards the Astley Arms, 'she's no good for you. She's a lazy girl.'

Even now, nearly half a century later, neither of us can figure out on what he based that judgement. Maybe he thought a married First Lieutenant would not suit his master plan.

The only other hiccup in our wedding plans was when the best man, Hollis Coulthurst, in the 60th Rifles at Fulford and, along with most of his brother officers, an inveterate horseplayer, declined to do the honours if we married on the Saturday chosen in September: it clashed with the substitute St Leger at Newmarket. To my astonishment, my indulgent in-laws agreed to a 48-hour postponement. So Hollis and I set off in a standing-room-only cross-country train for Newmarket. I was lugging a heavy plywood box the size of a portable gramaphone. It contained our wedding present from the Training staff, a traditional two-tier cake with marzipan and all the fixings, into which they had sunk their coupons and their tots.

It was one of those dream days at the races. We backed the Aga Khan's Tehran to win the St Leger, followed by a 100–8 touch in the Dewhurst on a beautiful chestnut called Chamoissaire, winner of the Leger the following year at York, with progeny like Busted and Bustingo proving his worth at stud. Later we became close friends with its owner, Stanhope Joel.

To get to Town that evening posed a logistics problem. Wartime restrictions put a limit on the radius at which taxis could operate, so we had to change to a London cab at Royston. Just before getting there I remembered the cake, which had been checked into the Gentlemen's cloakroom under the Members' stand. So it was back to the course where, miraculously, the plywood box was still in place.

Before we cut the cake in the garden of the Sysons' house in Marnhull there had been another drama. The service was to be conducted by an old hunting parson, complete with a white mane under his broad-brimmed hat, a flowing cloak and a four-storeyed, fully-staffed rectory. The poor of the parish were not exactly neglected, but treated as spiritual panel patients, whereas people like my in-laws, no matter how impoverished, were in his golden book, because the Admiral wore a bowler to church, was presumed to be well-connected and was a conscientious if chivvying churchwarden. The best man and one of the ushers were bidden to lunch with me in the rectory by the Canon. All the stops – or rather corks – were pulled out, with Haut Brion '29 and Graham's '09 appearing from nowhere. Suddenly a flustered verger broke in, saying that the Admiral and his daughter had already appeared at the church door in the black limo driven by the local undertaker and had set off to do a lap of the village, whilst we got into our starting-blocks.

It was a beautiful wedding, with the old ham in tears throughout, putting on a show straight out of Barchester. His wedding present to me, taken off his sideboard during lunch, was a cut-glass water-jug with antique silver trim. Alongside the marriage he blessed, it survives to this day.

The cake was superb.

★ 14 ★

FIRST OF CLASS –
PAINFUL LESSONS

We finally got away from refitting at Devonport Dockyard to shakedown in Scotland in the cold, dark early weeks of 1945. On passing our sea inspection, the boat was painted olive green overall and embarked final stores for the long passage to join the 4th Submarine Flotilla in the Far East. Abruptly a policy decision reached us from on high: only new-construction boats were needed out there, so we were kept on hold for a training role somewhere. The prospect was depressing, since there were still targets in the Far East. I had a private incentive to be in at the kill in the Pacific: my father had been held prisoner by the Japanese in Shanghai for nearly four years.

By now we had more submarine commanding officers than we knew what to do with, so whatever chances I might have had of doing an early qualifying course for command, known as The Perisher, receded. Thus it was some compensation to be appointed to Vickers Armstrong's yard in Barrow-in-Furness as First Lieutenant in HMS *Amphion*, the first of the new 'A' Class. They were designed to have the necessary radius of action and surface speed to operate alongside battle-proved USN Fleet Submarines, by then well on the way to winning the Pacific War. On paper *Amphion* had it all: 17 knots on the surface, 700 feet diving depth, a bow salvo of six torpedoes, with four pointing aft and ten reloads. But her torpedo-control system was still in the bow-and-arrow class and the radar was confined to a first generation air-warning set with which we played electronic Russian roulette. Her captain was the much-decorated, roly-poly Commander Hugh ('Dogberry') Dewhurst who had followed his successful operational tour by spending two years working with the Admiralty Ship Design department to make sure that she matched the specifications he had largely devised for her.

The 'A' boats were very much his baby, which is probably why he

37 Racing off Vancouver Island, 1956.

38 Greeting Stanhope and Gladys Joel aboard *Bermuda*.

was given command of *Amphion* shortly before his 40th birthday, at a time when an age-limit of 35 for officers in operational submarines was enforced. Apart from his vast experience he had a facile, retentive mind and could hold any audience with esoteric facts and figures trotted out in a manner which brooked no argument, not so much as a raised eyebrow. It was a favourite wardroom game to let drop some obscure but trivial scientific tit-bit and wait for it to be played back as his own by Dogberry a few weeks later. 'Did you know that the Chinese built an aircraft before the Wright Brothers?', scored 9 on the wardroom scale. Our Fourth Hand, Dick Crutchley, scored a winner when he got into the repertoire with one about a 3-year-old winning the Epsom Derby over $1^1/2$ miles at a slower speed than Golden Miller had won the Grand National over $4^1/2$ miles and 30 fences at Aintree carrying forty pounds more on its back.

He had a genius for mental arithmetic, based on swingeing approximations, but nonetheless invaluable in by-passing our antiquated torpedo-control system. We always knew he was on dodgy ground when he prefixed his answer to, say, converting the cost of 17 US gallons of fuel bought in Canadian dollars to the equivalent number of Imperial gallons paid for in sterling with: 'Something in the order of . . .', as he twisted his little Vandyke beard.

Vulnerable as a figure of fun and as a latter-day Baron Munchausen he might have been, but he was a generous, understanding Captain who taught us all a great deal. He trusted his subordinates implicitly and never sought to interfere in matters of routine. To the sailors *Amphion* – to this day pronounced by them as '*Am*-fee-*un*' – was known everywhere as 'Mr Doo'urst's boat'. She certainly was.

I joined her in time to celebrate VE-Day by driving Vickers' trains around their yard long after midnight. I took over from Jeff Dickson, a recently repatriated PoW who survived the sinking of the minelaying submarine *Cachalot*, then made his escape by stepping off a train carrying prisoners to Germany at the last station before the Swiss frontier. He grabbed a basket of oranges from an old lady and was selling them to the train's passengers when it pulled out. Jeff walked across the Alps and borrowed his train fare to the Spanish border. Before the war ended he was being dunned for the £150 involved. Outwardly gregarious, he had a notable zest for life. When I shared a room with him in digs at Barrow, I had nightly reminders that his ordeal had left a permanent scar. When he wasn't shouting in his sleep he was grinding his teeth like an old tugboat berthed against an unfendered dock in a rising onshore wind.

After the war nothing worked out for him, so he drove to a remote loch in Scotland and quietly took his own life – a war casualty as surely as if he had gone down with *Cachalot*.

Amphion had already done her torpedo trials when I joined her but still had to work up and carry out a prolonged habitability test cruise code-named 'Cook and Freeze'. This involved a ten-day dived patrol on the edge of the ice NE of Greenland, followed by another ten days submerged near the Equator. The health and welfare of the crew were to be monitored by a Surgeon Lieutenant from the Medical Research Council. Frank Ellis duly appeared the day before our departure from the Holy Loch. Behind his horn-rimmed glasses lay a debonair, unfailingly courteous personality with the sort of enquiring mind needed for his job. Frank said he had a few medical stores waiting on the well-deck of the depot-ship for us to embark. When I saw rows of cardboard boxes the size of tea chests alongside tarpaulin bags like hammocks, I had to check through and reduce the amount to what we could accommodate – or get through the hatch. Two of the largest crates were full of anal thermometers.

'Well, you see,' Frank said, polishing his spectacles, 'I plan to give the entire ship's company a daily checkup, which involves using these on a one-off disposable basis. I reckon I need 2500 of them. Any other way is not accurate enough.'

I persuaded him that no submarine ship's company would readily submit to having their body temperature recorded daily by thermometers shoved up their backsides. We compromised by having six guinea pigs who would get the full probe, whilst the rest of the ship's company would get their health measured once a week by more conventional methods.

So we sailed nor-west past the Mull of Kintyre heading for the Denmark Strait a few days after Hiroshima. Any doubts about whether our journey was really necessary were dispelled over the next few weeks. The patrol off Scoresby Sound in 70°N was unremarkable, but on our way south to Bermuda, where we were under orders to stop only long enough to take on fuel and mail – so as not to bias Frank's physiological observations by the side-effects of both watches having a run ashore – there were two significant events.

On a Sunday forenoon we dived for Prayers in the control room and then went to 750 feet for bathythermograph readings on the edge of the Gulf Stream. At 700 feet there was a loud bang from under the wardroom in the amidships Auxiliary Machinery Space (AMS). We returned to periscope depth. At that point the cook went to the refrigerator room in the AMS to draw out some joints. When he opened the stainless door he was all but swept off his feet by a gush of water. There did not seem to be any ready explanation. One remote possibility was that our deep dive had shown a flaw in the pressure-hull welding, which was in the immediate vicinity.

On the surface we shut off from diving, which meant cottering all the main vents, then allowing some liberties such as opening the gun-tower hatch above the wardroom. The diesel generators drew a cooling draught of fresh air down through it, whilst the crew sunned themselves on the deck under the cloudless sky. The submarine was barrelling along at 16 knots through moderate seas with a rhythmic roll when it happened. *Amphion* rolled as usual to about 15°, paused and then went right on to the point when green seas poured down the gun-tower hatch into the wardroom. She had laid over to 60° when a big solid wave broke into her.

A signal went to the Admiralty about the flooding in the AMS, without mentioning the boat's unladylike behaviour in a sea which had produced the classic 'loll' (when a ship rolls so far, pauses, and then goes a lot further). Within hours we were ordered to stop in Bermuda until Admiralty experts were flown out and had investigated the situation. A further message directed us into Nelson's old Dockyard at Ireland Island where we were ordered to strip out the wardroom furniture in order to lay bare the pressure hull's suspect areas. The local Flag Officer authorized that the officers move to shore accommodation during the experts' examination. The only person unhappy about this arrangement was Frank Ellis, whose medical records could no longer be said to be obtained in conditions comparable to a 60-day war patrol. Once Jack got ashore, all his medical observations were meaningless. Even the anal thermometer was now a redundant tool.

We found a house in Paget called 'Harbour Lights' lent to us by Jean Cookson, a kindhearted delightful estate agent. We moved in our wardroom staff, wines and spirits and proceeded to live like kings. It was our first taste of peacetime after six years, with no blackout and the certainty of uninterrupted nights. The '21' Club added an 'Amphion Special' to its list of cocktails: equal parts orange juice, Cointreau and light rum. It was still being served there after my first Bermuda Race in 1956.

We played golf at Mid-Ocean and Riddle's Bay, swam at Elbow Beach, danced at the Belmont, ate at the Royal Bermuda Yacht Club and were entertained by all the Forty Thieves in turn. They were descendants of the original families washed ashore with Sir George Somers from the wreck of the Virginia Company's ship *Sea Venture* in 1609.

The Admiralty experts drew a blank, lacking the X-ray equipment needed to check pressure-hull welds. Every theory to account for the flooding in the AMS was disposed of in turn.

After three weeks we were sated by over-indulgence. There was only one way to prove whether we had some built-in flaw – go out and dive to 700 feet again. So, making good an invitation given at Government House, we sailed one morning with His Excellency on board and duly slipped down to that depth only two miles off St David's Head. All was well, so we transferred him to his barge, headed south through the calm seas of the Bermuda Triangle to the eastern end of the Venezuelan coast and dived in the chocolate-coloured effluent of the mouth of the Orinoco. That didn't prove much either, so we headed for home 5000 miles away.

Somewhere in the vicinity of the Azores we were caught in a severe sou'westerly gale. Running before its frightening seas we suffered again on several occasions from the hesitation roll we had first experienced in the warm waters of the Gulf Stream. This time the loll left us all but on our beam ends with bridge personnel swept over by green seas, saved by improvised safety harnesses. Finally we had to heave to and let the gale abate.

On our return to Holy Loch we learnt that our sister-ship *Aeneas*, the first to emerge from Cammell Laird's Yard at Birkenhead, had developed this tendency during engine trials in the Irish Sea, to the point where her builders refused to sign the customary certificate that she was stable and safe to sail the open seas. These two incidents sent the Naval Architects back to their slide-rules. The structural modifications then ordered were indicative of the seriousness of their original miscalculations. Two external fuel tanks were found to be situated above main ballast tanks, so that on the surface their weight was above the vertical centre of gravity. The four main ballast tanks which were supposed to be empty on the surface were wrapped around the pressure-hull, meeting in a common duct-keel under the boat. In practice they were never completely empty, so that the residual water at their bottom formed a free surface whose centre-of-effort would slosh over to the leeward side as the boat heeled, giving greater impetus to each big roll.

It was back to Vickers for major structural alterations, which took five months, allowing us time to get to know the Lake District and enjoy our accumulated end-of-war leave.

I spent mine at Rock in Cornwall playing golf and drinking scrumpy with my father, now returned from some barbaric treatment at the hands of his Japanese jailers. I became friendly with Bill Orchard, the mechanic of the Padstow lifeboat, who had several lines of lobster pots offshore and collected gulls' eggs off some of the rocky islets. Heaving in his pots in up to 25 fathoms of water was easy enough for his iron physique after a lifetime at sea, but it left me knackered, blistered and thirsty.

Towards the end of that glorious holiday I made a date with Bill Orchard. By this time we had another Captain in *Amphion* and were under orders to sail for Hong Kong to join the new peacetime submarine flotilla there. He readily fell in with the plan I had made with Bill. I said that if he was waiting outside Padstow in his boat with a sack full of lobsters we would rendezvous with him and exchange them for Scotch and pussers' rum. Heading south from the Clyde, we closed the Cornish coast north of Trevose Head and dived five miles short of our agreed meeting-point. Through the periscope I could see Bill in his boat, looking around towards the horizon. We blew up so close alongside him that our emerging saddle-tanks nearly scooped his boat out of the water. A transfer by heaving-line completed the transaction, and we were dived again heading sou'west within two minutes. There were enough lobsters to feed the wardroom and all the Chiefs and Petty Officers.

To his dying day, 40 years later, Bill Orchard, who became a legend in the lifeboat service, would never reveal the name of the submarine, 'for fear of getting my mate into trouble' as he put it.

Before leaving Vickers the mystery of the bang at 700 feet followed by a flooded refrigerator compartment was solved. We had a new air-conditioning system which drained all the moisture it took out of the atmosphere into a sump in the AMS bilge in an unregulated fashion. What we did not know was that it was finding its way into the cork lining under the thin zinc floor of the refrigerator closet. At 700 feet, with an external pressure of over 300 lbs per square inch, the hull contracted slightly which aggravated the swelling of the cork lining and suddenly popped its floor, after which the whole refrigerator filled with moisture spewed out of the air conditioning system. I fancy the specific gravity of the moisture must have been close to that of seawater, or one of our sleuths would have spotted it between Planters' Punches in Bermuda.

At the end of 1947 Hong Kong had HMS *Adamant* as depot-ship for the first flotilla of 'A' boats which soon assembled there. The Captain (S/M) was Ben Bryant, the swashbuckling, no-nonsense submariner with a DSO and two bars and a DSC won in *Sealion* off Norway and *Safari* in the Mediterranean, who had pronounced *Untiring* fit for operational service. To this day the legend persists that he would have got the Victoria Cross but for the intervention of Admiral Sir Andrew Cunningham, whose admiration for submariners was qualified by their scruffy appearance and informal discipline. He first blocked the recommendation as Commander-in-Chief Mediterranean and a second time when he reached the First Sea Lord's desk in the Admiralty in time to spot that someone had reinstated Ben Bryant's name on to a list of those recommended for the highest award for gallantry. Every submariner knew that he had earned it twice over.

By signing chits for everything, we ran up bills which often exceeded our monthly pay, bowling every evening at the Hong Kong Club, eating and dancing at the Grips or out at Repulse Bay. We revived the Royal Hong Kong Yacht Club on Kellett Island by basing all Service 14ft dinghies and ex-German Star Boats there, went racing at Happy Valley, as often as not to cheer our Commander (S/M) Philip Francis home on a winner, and then won the first round of the rugger 7-a-sides by having our opponents, the Sappers, to lunch on board HMS *Adamant* before the game. Next day's *South China Morning Post* had us in the headlines: 'Stylish Submariners set to win Colony Sevens.' We were unceremoniously thumped by the RAF. I had the embarrassing task of marking their fly-half, Flt. Lieutenant Arthur Dorward, without laying a finger on him. He got the first of his many caps for Scotland two years later.

Occasionally we went to sea and exercised with the 8th Destroyer Flotilla without learning any new lessons on either side. There were a few inconclusive anti-piracy patrols in Mits Bay, but all the junks looked alike. So did those on the southern approaches to Hong Kong where we patrolled to catch some who were lifting the main telegraph cable from Singapore and cutting out long lengths of copper which fetched high prices in Macao. Soon they reappeared for sale in Hong Kong as dog-collars, birds' cages, or wastepaper baskets beautifully woven from fine copper strands. Patrolling the line of the cable was too dicey, since all the junks appeared to be fishing on the same spot. Cable and Wireless technicians ashore soon knew when the cable was being interfered with. Their potentiometers (Wheatstone's Bridge) told them exactly where, so we got a signal on VLF transmitted via Rugby which alerted us. Sure enough there was a junk with a length of telegraph cable held in a bight level with his gunwale. We moved in for the kill and surfaced right alongside, with his fishing nets draped all over our casing and periscope standards. By the time we had cut ourselves clear, the evidence of grappling for the telegraph cable had disappeared and Their Lordships were left with a hefty bill for new fishing nets.

After suffering the first post-war refit in Hong Kong Dockyard we were detached on loan service with the Royal Australian Navy. Based on an antique old depot-ship HMAS *Platypus* at Watson's Bay, our crew soon fell in with the routine of having steak and beer for breakfast two days a week. But many found the time under way to the famous Heads where we met Pacific rollers too short for their sealegs. The Aussies worked us hard Monday to Friday, slipping at 0800 each day and not returning until dusk. They also played hard. The wardroom acquired an old jeep left behind by the British Pacific Fleet. Crossing the Bridge at first light on our way to Watson's Bay from some all-night junket on the North Shore we always met the same milkman and swigged back a few pints of the best milk I ever tasted.

At weekends there were race meetings at Randwick or Warwick Farm and golf on Sundays at Rose Bay. The weeks flicked by until our departure was set for 1800 on a Saturday evening, which made for a tight return from the track, complicated by the fact that a horse called 'Oh Johnnie' paid 100–1 on the tote at Randwich. On the way our faithful old Jeep conked its last, so we abandoned it in the heart of downtown Sydney and took a taxi in time to rejoin the rest of the crew all bemoaning the loss of their last Saturday night in Sydney.

By this time I knew that I would be leaving *Amphion* on our arrival at Hong Kong to go home for my Perisher. The Captain felt it would be useful experience for me to assume command on the 10,000-mile voyage back to HMS *Adamant*, an unexpected compliment which called for an instant, sober review of our passage plans via Norfolk Island, the New Hebrides and Darwin. The first problem arose when I discovered we had sailed a day early, due to the navigator having worked it out with August as a 30-day month.

Somehow 24 hours had to be lost on a 3½ day passage without any of the crew tumbling to why they had been deprived of their last night with some sheila in Bondi. Slowing down would have been a dead giveaway, so I ordered a long detour to the south, ostensibly to take bathythermograph readings over some non-existent submerged volcanic peak.

At Norfolk Island we anchored outside the surf and a canoe brought alongside the Resident and a gentle giant with fingers like leather bananas and a gnarled face creased like a big walnut. After consuming the best part of a bottle of Scotch, he signed his name in our Visitors' book as Benjamin Fletcher Christian, a direct descendant of Bligh's mutineers. His grandfather was almost certainly one of the few survivors of the massacre of all but one of the *Bounty*'s mutineers on Pitcairn Island in 1793. In the middle of the 19th century a visiting HM ship took all those who wanted to leave the island and deposited them on Norfolk Island 5000 miles to the west.

From Norfolk Island we headed north for Malekula in the New Hebrides group. Here we became the centre of attention for a group of wild men hiding in the hills, adherents to some gruesome cult who believed that the war was not over and that one day a USN submarine would arrive to rescue them. At nightfall, fires were lit on the mountainside to the accompaniment of tom-toms and weird high-pitched screams. Some even approached us in dugout canoes, but didn't much like the look of our armed sentry or the 4-inch gun mounting. To them it was manned and ready to blow them out of the water. To us it was an ideal setting for giving the Resident a sun-downer whilst he told us the legend of the rescuing submarine. We had converted the upper-deck ready-use 4-inch magazines into ice boxes in which we kept beer and wines beautifully cool. Thus in practical terms our main gun armament was at extended notice.

Little did we suspect that this peaceful scene would hit the head-lines, nor the manner of its so doing. We called at Darwin only long enough to refuel. All of us went ashore for showers and lunch, leaving on board the navigator, who, apart from having screwed up our departure date from Sydney, was under stoppage of leave for being caught asleep in charge of the bridge watch as we closed Lord Howe Island at 16 knots. 'Don't wake him, sir,' one of the lookouts said, 'he's been having such a beautiful sleep.'

When we sailed there were a few empties on the wardroom table, left over from the Duty Officer having entertained port officials and other freeloaders, including a solitary journalist. As the only reporter on the *Northern Territories Bugle* he was, it later transpired, also a stringer (local correspondent) for the international news agencies and *The Times* of London, probably the *Daily Express* and half a dozen others as well.

Soon after sailing a high priority classified signal arrived which we identified as being addressed to HMS *Amphion* from the Admiralty – clearly not a routine message. Beyond that it was just a string of 4-figure cypher groups which we had no means of unscrambling. The navigator had not drawn the appropriate one-time pads to allow us to crack it. So we had to come clean in plain language saying that we were unable to handle any cypher traffic after a stated date. Their Lordships did not mince matters in the clarifying signal which arrived next day. Could we explain the circumstances under which the Captain of *Amphion* had given a press conference in Darwin telling how we had arrived off Malekula and nipped in the bud an armed rebellion by hostile tribesmen?

On reaching Hong Kong I briefly met the new Captain (S/M) David Ingram who was in high good humour as he congratulated me on being selected for the Perisher. I stayed in the cuddy, drink in hand, whilst the wretched navigator was led in. There was no discussion. The Captain (S/M) said only six words which consigned the accident-prone culprit to a surprisingly successful career in escort forces: 'You are superseded forthwith. Get out.'

I was lucky enough to take passage back to Portsmouth in HMS *Opossum*, a frigate commanded by Pat Norman, one of our most successful wartime submarine captains. We steamed up the English Channel on a still, motionless, November night. To see the lights of Start Point near Dartmouth and the Casquets off Alderney simultaneously on either beam was curiously emotional.

★ 15 ★

THE PERISHER AND FIRST COMMAND

There were only two others on my Submarine Commanding Officers' Qualifying Course – to give the Perisher its proper title. John Blackburn, who had great potential, was to lose his life in his second command, HMS *Affray*, which took down with her not only her ship's company of 65 men but an entire training-class of submarine engineer officers, many of them the sons of serving officers. She had only just come out of an extended time in dockyard hands when she was abruptly ordered to sea, straight into the potentially dangerous procedure of snorting by night in a main shipping lane. It was not in John's nature to question his orders, no matter what misgivings he must have felt. Another Commanding Officer in a boat in a similar state of operational unreadiness flatly refused to sail on the exercise which led to the untimely end of *Affray* and her fine company. Significantly no disciplinary action was taken against him, and he was soon afterwards promoted to Commander. *Affray* lies in 250 feet of water next to the Hurd Deep, fifteen miles north-west of Alderney Harbour. The other candidate on my Perisher had an uneventful subsequent career.

So soon after the end of the war, the Submarine Command did not have to look far for the ideal person to turn a First Lieutenant into a Commanding Officer, a considerably greater step in the extra dimension of submarine warfare than in any other ships. My course was lucky to have two of the very best, with four DSOs and three DSCs between them, and assured of a place in submarine history by their exploits in the Mediterranean. We started on the Meccano-set dry attack teacher at Fort Blockhouse run by mischievous Wrens with the power to make any candidate they fancied look better than he was, literally by pulling strings and vice versa! They probably did not fool our first Teacher, Commander Hugh ('Rufus') Mackenzie, whose ready smile and infectious sense of fun concealed a shrewd observant mind. We now learnt the first of many steps in the choreography of converting data visually observed by the attacker through a World War I monocular periscope into the final solution of the velocity triangle formed by the target's course and speed and that of a 45-knot straight-running Mk VIII** torpedo. The angle to be aimed off at the moment of firing was known as the Director Angle, or D.A. It was arrived at by cranking target data (course and speed from a plot of periscope ranges and bearings) into the fruit-machine − a crude mechanical angle-solver. Unlike German and American submarines, our torpedo control angle-solver did not have its inputs fed in directly from the periscope, nor was a running solution available allowing for the change of bearing generated between successive periscope up-dates. The velocity triangle was frozen each time the periscope was lowered. So if you had to go deep to run in and close the track or to dip under the escort screen, the captain got no reliable steer where to look when the periscope next broke surface, unless sonar was delivering useful data.

Most captains carried an approximate running solution in their heads. Others were disorientated and swung the periscope around frantically in search of the target. This situation was known as being 'lost in the box'. In the rapidly developing closing stages of an attack it often meant the target had slipped past the firing point and the D.A. was missed. One of my most terrifying moments in peacetime was when a captain, who conspicuously lacked any intuitive feel for a developing attack scene, solemnly had the periscope held on the D.A., say Green 22 (22 degrees aim-off on the starboard bow) and fired a deliberately aimed and spread salvo of six dummy torpedoes at an aircraft carrier whose screws were heard throughout the boat thundering over the after ends. It can't have missed us by much, but the captain's claim to have scored 3 'hits' was never disputed.

Apparently Rufus was satisfied with our efforts on the synthetic nursery slopes at Fort Blockhouse, for we then went up to the Clyde and joined the Perisher boat for honing our art in Inchmarnock Water, starting with straight targets at moderate speeds, then graduating to dealing with high-speed Fleet destroyers escorting a zig-zagging convoy, by day and night.

Early on during this phase Rufus left, later going on to greater things as a Vice Admiral in charge of the Polaris Executive which delivered Britain's nuclear ballistic missile submarines dead on time, after the Skybolt fiasco. He was replaced by someone I knew well from La Maddalena, George Hunt, formerly C.O. of *Ultor*, the top-scoring submarine of her day in the Tenth Flotilla. He was a quiet, undemonstrative man who didn't miss a trick. Every one of the hundreds of attacks we carried out under his tutelage was patiently analysed afterwards. His stopwatch checked the duration of each periscope exposure and whether they were too frequent. But, above all, it told him the precise moment to step in and abort an attack by pressing the klaxon to flood 'Q' tank and get the boat below any risk of being rammed by a destroyer. During the later stages of the course the destroyer was allowed to turn towards and make a threatening charge at any periscope sighted or sonar contact. It was then up to the student to break off the attack under peace-time safety rules, or suffer the humiliation of having Teacher do it for him. On the other hand, pulling the plug too soon earned you an equally undesirable mark. With a destroyer turning towards at, say, 500 yards and capable of being on top of you in 30 seconds there wasn't too much time to scratch your arse and ask advice from the attack team.

The final catch was that any student enjoying a run of successful undetected attacks was cut down to size by Teacher ordering the big periscope to be raised and left waving around in the air until the destroyer's lookouts saw it.

I always felt sorry for the C.O. of the submarine in which we stumbled our way towards the required standards. He was ultimately responsible for the safety of his own submarine, yet had to stand aside and watch potentially dangerous situations deliberately contrived by Teacher. At intervals there were consecutive long days and nights intended to stretch the students and see how they reacted when fatigue blurred their judgement. Ironically, it was Teacher who visibly sagged the most. We at least only had to concentrate for one attack in three, the others being played out on the fruit-machine or the plot.

Recently a TV series was built around the Perisher with all kinds of mental hangups, domestic distractions and personality defects holding centre stage. That was never the case, and I doubt if it is today. No candidate is selected for the course unless his qualities of leadership and mental equilibrium have already been proven. The most common cause of failure was for Teacher to realize early on that a student lacked 3-D vision through a periscope, not being able to size up a given situation in full perspective. Or he may lack the mental agility to cope with a rapidly developing situation. Sadly for some very fine officers, the weakness of their periscope eye is not exposed until they get out there in the Perisher boat, after years of faultless service from Fourth Hand to First Lieutenant. So they are reverted to General Service without a stain on their record, or so they are blandly assured by Flag Officer Submarines. In practice they might as well start reading the Appointments column in the *Daily Telegraph* right away.

Our course ended in March 1948, alongside the depot ship off Rothesay when George Hunt took each of us in turn for a stroll along the upper deck. None of us had failed. He predicted a bright future for me in submarines, but twelve years later seemed to have forgotten the conversation when he was Chief of Staff to Flag Officer Submarines and I was newly promoted to Captain. My prospects of a further submarine appointment in the short or medium term were not even bleak. It seems they were non-existent. So I left the Navy.

But then, in the Spring of 1948, I walked tall into HMS *Dolphin*, the submarine base at Fort Blockhouse to take over command of HMS *Truncheon*, an operational 'T'-class and one of the first fitted with a schnorkel – or 'snort' as we called it in those pre-cocaine days – the pipe through which enough air could be drawn at periscope depth to run the diesels and recharge the batteries without surfacing. I was ordered to relieve Lt-Commander Michael Lumby DSO, DSC, who had been sunk off Bastia in *Saracen* after a horrifying ordeal during which he spent more than a day trying to hold trim with his after-ends flooded, whilst two Italian frigates held him in firm contact and subjected him to a prolonged depth-charging. Finally he surfaced and abandoned ship in the nick of time.

Most of my time in *Truncheon* was spent day-running from Portland for the anti-submarine training school, often uncomfortably close to the notorious Race. But we made ceremonial visits to Copenhagen and Oslo, besides taking part in Flag Officer Submarine Summer War exercises in the Minches, after which we got a favourable nod from the boss for having used our snort gear to remain submerged almost throughout, which was a valuable foretaste of the future.

As a training flotilla, there was a high throughput of officers who were appointed under report – that is, for a make-or-break assessment through the second and final opinion of a different Commanding Officer. I had three, one after the other, all of whom were clearly not worth persevering with. Only one of them disputed my decision, in an unhappy acrimonious correspondence drawing attention to my own shortcomings. He shouldn't have worried: he took early retirement from the Navy and became a worldwide best-selling author, churning out novels with submarine backgrounds. Every time I see his paperbacks on show at the bookstall at Waterloo

I derive wry satisfaction that my arbitrary death sentence on his career quickly brought him a comfortable lifestyle with a lasting sense of achievement, which he could never have enjoyed as, say the Motor Transport Officer at Chatham Barracks, where he might have ended in the Navy.

The other two readily agreed with my decision and remain well-disposed towards me. One at least married well and was set up as a gentleman-farmer, high on the guest list to nearby Hunt Balls. Any day now I look to see his name gazetted as a High Sheriff. His last days in the Submarine Service were devoted to writing up the Fair Log which was a month in arrears – and I insisted should be completed. Finally a cabin trunk emerged from the fore-hatch, followed by our ex-navigator, dressed in a marmalade-coloured tweed suit and brocade waistcoat, who stepped into a London taxi waiting for him on the pier at Portland. It was a pity such style had to be lost to the Submarine service.

A visitor with a very different IQ boarded us during a visit to Dartmouth. He fired off a string of technical questions which I soon realized could not be fobbed off by some imprecise or partial response.

'What's that for?' he asked, pointing at a large analogue barometer in the control room with a rotating outer ring showing a green band up to 4 inches below the current atmospheric pressure and a red zone in the area 4″–6″ of vacuum.

'When we are snorting with the diesels running, the upper float-valve shuts off when the snort head dips below the surface. The engine air intakes quickly pull down a vacuum which can be measured on that barometer. As often as not the boat's trim is recovered, the float valve opens and the vacuum settles back.'

'Yes, I see,' he said, moving in for the final thrust, 'but what's the red zone for between 4 inches and 6 inches?'

'We work to different levels of permissable vacuum by day and night. As everyone knows [I thought to myself] a high vacuum impairs one's night vision, so we don't let it go above 4″ in the dark.'

'Balls,' said Sir Henry Tizard, for it was he, Chief Scientific and Defence Research Advisor to the Cabinet.

So I drafted a careful signal to my Captain (S/M), repeated to Flag Officer Submarines, reporting the eminent scientist's views on the relationship between suddenly reduced atmospheric pressure and one's ability to see through the periscope at night. Shortly afterwards the inhibiting criteria were removed by a deadpan Submarine Temporary Memorandum. That incident led me over the rest of my career to question many other sacred cows in our accepted underwater operating doctrines.

Before my time at Portland came to an end, I gave my old father-in-law an outing he never forgot. After being shown round *Truncheon*, we enjoyed the best lunch the messman in the depot-ship HMS *Maidstone* could contrive, with lashings of pink gin. Since he had served on Admiral Brock's staff at Gallipoli, his reminiscences of the Royal Navy 40 years previously are worth preserving. It seems he was serving in a battleship at Portland in the days when post-Captains had arbitrary powers to commit an offender to civil imprisonment without any procedural niceties like a Flag Officer's Warrant approving the punishment. This was convenient at Portland where the prison was overlooking the Fleet anchorage. An old lag was before the Captain as a defaulter for the umpteenth time. The Captain heard the Master-at-Arms read the charge.

'Before I send you up the hill for 28 days, do you have anything to say?'

Along with everyone else on board, the old villain knew that the Captain had a black sheep of a brother doing a stretch in Portland Bill.

'Yes, sir, I have. Just one thing. Is there any message I can deliver to your brother?'

'Certainly. Tell him you got 56 days.'

On another occasion he was serving in HMS *Nelson*, the Fleet flagship, when King George V arrived to inspect her. The diminutive, bearded figure wearing cocked hat, frock coat and sword stood in the sternsheets of the gig which pulled over from the Royal Yacht *Victoria and Albert* with sailors wearing wide-brimmed straw hats. The whole of *Nelson*'s 1200-strong ship's company was manning the side on which the gig approached. After giving three cheers, the Commander ordered them to move inboard and fall in by Divisions for inspection. He then took his place at the head of the starboard quarterdeck ladder just as the Royal gig came alongside. As the King was about to step on the platform which had been plumbed level with the gig's gunwale, the effect of 1200 men moving themselves 50 feet inboard from the ship's side caused the 35,000-ton battleship to heel perceptibly to port. The platform at the foot of the ladder went nearly 3 feet upwards.

The King knew who to blame for this farce. He prided himself on knowing the names of every Commander and above in the Royal Navy. His bellow was heard by most of the flagship's Company:

'Arbuthnot! What do you think I am? A fucking monkey?'

My job at Dartmouth was as a House Officer, second-in-command of the 150-strong group of 18-year-old cadets who had entered directly from public or grammar schools, as I had done eight years previously. My appointment coincided with a relaxation of the rule that House Officers could not have their wives living within 50 miles of the College. Sylvia and our two small daughters, both under 3, moved into a rented cottage at Blackpool near Slapton Sands on a short let.

After a depressing winter in a dripping annexe to a residential hotel which never saw the sun, we finally ended up on the edge of the river on the Kingswear side between the ferry ramp and the moribund Royal Dart Yacht Club. In the summer evenings we had the last of the sunshine, hours after Dartmouth on the west bank had been plunged into early shadow. Each morning at 0630 a cutter under oars manned by cadets who had only been in uniform for a few weeks used to appear alongside and row me up to Sandquay in time for breakfast. They learnt about tidal currents the hard way when it was on the ebb at Springs. If it was foggy, as it often was, I would start ringing a handbell to guide them into sight of my steps, but not before voices carried clear across the still morning air: 'Reckon the old bastard's about here. Pull up, port.'

In formal classroom instruction I taught seamanship and, more importantly, Naval knowledge, supposedly to enable them to conform with the tribal rites and customs of the Fleet they were soon to join. Lesson No. 1 was: if addressed by a senior officer there are only two permissible answers: if it is an order or an opinion, you say, 'Aye, aye, Sir'; or if it is a question to which you had no certain answer, never try a floater, but just bark out, 'I'll find out, sir' and double away. Never do as I heard a USN Ensign reply to the Force Commander when asked for the screen formation: 'Gee, Admiral, BSOM' which is translated 'Beats the shit out of me'. Junior officers should make themselves scarce to the point of invisibility, get into boats first and out of them last; when afloat, salute all officers first thing in the morning, but never afterwards unless making a report, salute the quarterdeck on each occasion of setting foot on it, even if it is a marked-out corner of a shore establishment; never make passes at senior officers' wives no matter how provoked – in short, keep open minds and closed flies. Don't hold a knife like a soupspoon or blow on the consommé to cool it. Always wear a hat ashore, which includes anywhere outside the gates of a shore establishment.

The Chiefs and Petty Officers we had to help in the training were the best available. But even during my time there the quality of our intake each term declined with uncertainties about the Royal Navy's future role. Vacillating policies about the optimum age for starting a naval career led to our having three streams of cadets going through Dartmouth simultaneously: those who joined at 13, a 16-year-old entry intended to attract secondary schoolboys and the old 18-entry. It was the Chief Petty Officers who were most disturbed. Two of our best declined to go forward for commissioned rank and left the Service rather than run the risk of serving under any of 'this shower', as they put it.

The increasing emphasis put even then on technological know-how rather than leadership potential has inevitably left its mark on much of today's Navy. One of the best submarine COs in my time had been a classics scholar at Winchester who could scarcely add up his mess-bill. The Army keep up their standards by having retired officers acting as talent-scouts among the top schools and quietly introducing their candidates at social functions to the Colonel of some elitist regiment. But boys who elect to join the Royal Navy have no certainty of ending up where they want to – as Fleet Air Arm pilots, submariners or destroyer captains, because their choice cannot be stated until they are well down the training pipe-line.

Nonetheless, being on the staff at Dartmouth was the most enjoyable and rewarding time of my career. The officers worked seven days a week from dawn to late at night, but there were 12 weeks' leave a year to look forward to on fixed dates. In November you could plan to go cruising or take part in the following year's Fastnet in August, certain that only the outbreak of World War III could disturb the arrangements – a point rarely mentioned at the televised NUT delegates' conferences today.

There was also the deep satisfaction of seeing what physical and personality changes could be wrought in an 18-year-old after just one 13-week term at Dartmouth. I always felt that if they never went to sea but left the Navy then and there our job was well worthwhile.

Even during term-time there was much fun to be had for the staff, mostly after Lights Out – or Pipe Down as the Navy put it. Much of it centred around pubs like the Floaters ('The Floating Bridge') outside the College gates, but, for real lotus-eating at a time when food was still rationed and English cuisine had not recovered from the spam-and-chips era, we would head for the Fountain Violet (FV), a luxurious country club facing to seaward near Kingswear Castle, set in a high bank of floodlit flowering shrubs.

It was run by Derek and Daphne Sanderson, a most agreeable and attractive couple who set standards of elegance and hospitality which have never been exceeded. I suspect they had taken a leaf out of Rosa Lewis's book at the Cavendish Hotel in London, for impecunious

N.O.s were rarely presented with a bill that approached the real cost of what we had consumed.

Before the evening's business got into full swing, Derek liked to stroll down to the Royal Dart Yacht Club for a few gins-and-Lillet with an old fox-hunting friend called Eric Wilton. I joined them occasionally, once in time to hear Eric describe a bizarre accident which had caused him great pain. It seems he was standing in his shirtsleeves dressing for a day out with the hounds and was adjusting his stock with the aid of a framed mirror on top of his shoulder-high chest-of-drawers.

'I leant forward to get a better view of my stock. In doing so, my knees pushed a drawer shut, which promptly trapped my old man in it. You really can't be too careful.'

One of the attractions of the FV was that the living-in barmaids were always picked more for their looks than their expertise in shaking up a gimlet. Several ultimately married visiting officers. One particularly voluptuous blonde agreed to an assignation with a submarine C.O. who happened to be staying at the Club. The Sandersons would never have approved such goings-on in their home, so it was arranged that the over-excited submariner would wait till after midnight, then tap on a door with white shoes left outside it. He sat on the edge of his bed frothing like a bottle of Bass, looked at his watch and saw that he had half an hour to wait. He awoke at dawn, still fully clothed – on his own bed.

The same blonde had the prize for a motorcar treasure hunt secreted on her person. It was a treasure hunt with a difference. The trail took each of the eight competing cars to six different pubs, in varying sequences. On arrival, they could only get the next clue out of the landlord if they had ordered and drunk a pre-designated drink from a list of six possible. The trouble began when a car pulled up at a pub which was not part of the trail and went through the full list of beer, gin, scotch, vodka, scrumpy and Pimms before challenging the landlord, who gave them a blank stare and sent them packing. Today he might well have called the fuzz. Only half the pack reached the FV within the time limit. A retired Chaplain-General of the RAF then pulled on a pink ribbon which brought a half-bottle of VSOP out from our barmaid's ample cleavage.

Life in the College wardroom had its moments, particularly on Guest Nights if we were entertaining some visiting group, such as touring cricket XIs, the Achilles athletics team or the officers from HMS *Devonshire*, the old County Class cruiser which took on our Cadets for training at sea before they joined the Fleet as Midshipmen.

During my first year the running was made by the Commander,

Vere Wight-Boycott, outwardly an austere bachelor of severe, uncompromising personality, who looked every inch the part when he took the salute as Divisions marched past each morning to the oddly-chosen 'March of the Little Pierrots' played uncertainly by the Pensioners' Band, most of whom had just finished waiting on breakfast in the wardroom. When we dined the Commander out at the end of his time, he finished his after-dinner speech with 'Follow me!' He then leapt into his vintage Riley sports car and shot off up the grass bank, over the playing fields and out into the countryside normally hunted over by the famous Britannia pack of beagles. He was followed by a dozen cars and motor-bikes slithering all over the sunken mud tracks in vain pursuit.

The survivors returned much later to the wardroom to find him still immaculately dressed in his mess kit, chatting to the bar stewards as though he was waiting for the action to begin in earnest.

Next morning sharp at 0900 the House Officers' daily meeting was held in his study right after Divisions. To cut the waffle, he always insisted that we should stand around his table. Several could not remember where they had abandoned their cars in the early hours of that morning. So he marked his route on an Ordnance Survey map and sent two of us out on motorbikes to locate them. Four needed tractors for their recovery.

When he finally left, he remarked sadly that his only permanent achievement had been to draw on his skill as an arboriculturist – unusual in one who had spent his career in destroyers – to plant some new trees around the College park.

He was too modest. Apart from the example he set, drawing a fine distinction between an officer's behaviour on and off duty, no one who ever took part in any College activity, whether playing cricket against the Navy XI, boxing against Pangbourne, perfecting the ceremonial for a Royal Visit or sailing in Cowes Week, would be unaware of his enthusiastic support from the touchlines.

When I returned in 1975 for a celebration to mark the 75th Anniversary of the present College buildings, a wide-ranging programme of events had been planned. There was to be no boxing, for the sport had been outlawed a decade previously and the ring itself sold, presumably to guard against a new regime putting the clock back. Along with half-a-dozen other spectators, none of them Cadets or Midshipmen, I sadly watched the rugger First XV getting walloped by a Colts team from Exeter. It was no longer obligatory to watch or take part in any game. It seems that they sometimes had difficulty raising a cricket team out of 600 under training.

Only on the river had much of lasting value survived.

When I joined in 1950 there was some arcane rule forbidding cadets from ever spending a night in one of the College boats, which included six ex-German Windfall yachts, similar in size to 8-metre cruiser-racers. Three of us persuaded the Commander to let us take a Cadets' crew on a race to Guernsey over the Whit-weekend. The start of the race was in Plymouth on Friday evening, to which the five chosen cadets would be sent by taxi from Dartmouth, so as not to miss any classroom instruction. Three of us elected to sail *Harpy* down to Plymouth, about 40 miles to the westwards. Leaving a wardroom Guest Night at midnight, we sailed then and there, with oilskins pulled on over our mess kit. We had to go to windward in a young gale all the way from Start Point, but made it in good time to give the Cadets an armchair ride to St Peter Port and back. The ban on overnight sailing, and thus ocean-racing, was lifted and yachts from Dartmouth played a prominent part in RORC events thereafter.

It also marked the formation of the most exclusive yacht club of them all – the L.Y.S., which stands for Let's-sail-now Yacht Squadron. Membership is confined to those who have set sail after midnight and headed offshore in Force 7 or above, wearing dinner jackets. Its inaugural dinner was our Silver Wedding party at the Grosvenor House, when all eighteen male guests were qualified.

★ 16 ★

HAIRSHIRT SAILING

In 1948 I started sailing seriously – by which I mean ocean-racing followed by all those relaxed passages homewards after finishing up in Spain, Bermuda or Brittany. It all began with 'Uncle' Rouse taking me on the Cowes-Dinard Race in his heavy displacement 35-ft waterline *Golden Dragon* which he had built in Hong Kong to his own design in 1937 on the proceeds of a flutter in gold shares on the Manila Stock Exchange. She was – and still is – a boat to catch the eye, with her graceful sheer line accentuated by deep bulwarks and high-aspect masthead sail plan with a powerful overlapping genoa.

Before the war, John Illingworth had been an Engineer Officer in submarines in Hong Kong, where he first promoted the development of 35ft waterline ocean-racers intended to give very close racing, if not quite a one-design class. He built his own *Maid of Malham*, which was followed by half-a-dozen others, each around 48ft overall.

Golden Dragon was a highly competitive boat on the low rating she got from her heavy displacement, but she suffered through her over-generous owner, by now a retired Hong Kong Government civil engineer, being unable to afford bringing her into racing trim and campaigning her against richer owners.

When I joined her for the Dinard Race she had only just been recommissioned after spending the whole War in a mud berth up the Dart. Her cotton sails and ungalvanized wire sheets and halyards not only had no useful life left in them, but bordered on being dangerous. Her bottom finish was never better than one would expect in a cruising boat at the end of the season. The crew was made up mostly of enthusiastic medical students who could not contribute a penny towards their subsistence afloat or ashore. Throughout it all Uncle sat happily at the heavy tiller with his black Chinese pudding-basin hat on, urging us to drive her harder.

The race itself was a hard, wet thrash to windward all the way, in visibility mostly under a mile. Water cascaded down through the deckhead which had not been properly re-caulked after the seams had opened up each summer since 1940. Our landfall at Le Grand Jardin off Dinard after midnight was complicated by having an uncorrected 1938 chart and nagging uncertainty about which lights had been restored. Uncle placed considerable faith on a leathery old French girlfriend he had embarked for the voyage. Whilst I was in the eyes of the boat conning her in by telling the helmsman to go more to starboard, she was confusing us by commanding '*à bâbord*', which meant the opposite. Anyway it turned out that she was hopelessly confused by shore lights.

Dropping the anchor in a heavy scend off the vedette slip on the Dinard side, we could only see one other boat at anchor. At first light she turned out to be the much larger *Lara*, which owed us a lot of time, although unfortunately not enough for us to take 1st in the fleet. Only four boats out of a considerable fleet finished, mostly not wanting to risk skirting the Minquiers in near-zero visibility with rising wind and seas. So we had the Yacht Club de Dinard and all the local restaurants pretty much to ourselves. Neither was there any difficulty in stepping forward to collect all our prizes, including 1st in Classes II and III. One trophy embodied a gold and silver relief chart of the Channel with semi-precious stones marking all the principal lighthouses. On our return it was impounded by the Customs at Brixham on suspicion that we were trying to smuggle in diamonds. We never visited St Malo on that trip, as it was still awaiting restoration after the USAF had flattened the walled city just four years previously.

The next year I did my first Fastnet Race in *Golden Dragon*. Again there was a long thrash to windward in bad visibility. Just as we caught a glimpse of the Dodman, east of Falmouth, and tacked off to the sou'west, there was a loud crack and the tiller split ominously open fore and aft. We used winch-handles as splints secured by wire lashings, but the heavy strain from countering each wave we bucked into soon persuaded us to give up trying to make it to the Lizard and we turned for Plymouth 30 miles downwind. We anchored off Mashford's Yard in Cremyll and kept our racing flag hoisted. The tiller which let us down was new two days before the race. It was seen to have been fatally weakened by a ham-fisted saw operator cutting well beyond the marked limits of the square hole needed to fit on the rudderhead. Four hours later we set off for the Fastnet Rock 230 miles away, with our split tiller reinforced, brass-bound and through-bolted.

About 60 miles NW of the Longships LV the weather settled in WSW'ly Force 7, right on the nose. There was little prospect of completing the course in time to start the La Rochelle Race from Plymouth, so we hauled down our racing flag and returned once more to Plymouth, where Uncle disappeared, leaving sketchy instructions about victualling. He rejoined us on the starting line in the Club launch with 20 minutes to spare. After a fast sail along the South Brittany coast, it seemed that we had picked the right race. Three miles short of the finish off La Pallice our spinnaker collapsed and we were left wallowing around in a dead calm. There were five masts on the horizon astern of us. They brought a new breeze with them all the way up to us; then we all finished in line abreast. Once again we had been robbed of 1st overall, but only just. In those days the yacht club had its premises in the old underwater dungeons of one of the 14th-century towers guarding the inner harbour, where we secured. On a recent return to La Rochelle, still one of France's loveliest harbours, the tower housed a discotheque serving fast food, whilst the ultra-modern clubhouse is now well away from the old town in a 2500-berth marina.

After the summer of 1949 Uncle could no longer afford to campaign his beloved *Golden Dragon*, so she swung round a mooring in Brixham Harbour for two years, covered in bird-lime, awaiting a purchaser. In August, 1952, I put together a crew of submariners to show that she was still a potential winner. We rounded Berry Head on our way to Santander, once again in a full gale dead on the nose. About 30 miles south-west of Start Point the tiller sheared clean away at the rudder head. The best we could do was to reduce to a spitfire jib on the inner headstay and run right off using a dinghy paddle lashed to a big shifting spanner to grip the square lug on the rudderhead and restrain it from flapping freely from side to side. We headed for Dartmouth, knowing we could enlist the aid of the College engineering workshops to make repairs.

When we switched the engine on a terrifying vibration and knocking noise under the counter suggested that the propeller was terminally damaged. Later we found that the P-bracket supporting the outer end of the shaft had sheared off, creating a noisy and dangerous situation. There were other problems not unconnected with the fact that it was my birthday. As soon as we were outside the three-mile limit off Start Point on our way to Santander we had broken the Customs' seals on our Duty Free supplies, stocked to the limit permitted for a three weeks' cruise to Spain but not intended for consumption in an English port within 24 hours of sailing. To avoid the embarrassment of reporting to the Customs, we hit upon a plan to join in the feeder race from Ryde to Belle Ile where we would be joined for the *Semaine Nautique de Belle Ile* by the Santander fleet racing back northwards across the Bay of Biscay. A phone call to the RORC secured our entry, so we set every sail we had to reach Ryde just in time for the start of the race.

It was a small fleet of high quality, including the new Laurent Giles-designed *Lutine* and our old foe *Maid of Malham*. At dusk we were splitting tacks off St Catherine's, leading the fleet with *Lutine*. By 3 in the morning we were at anchor off Swanage, having split our main from luff to leech in a full gale and observed one of the covering boards lifting as the shrouds took the strain. This was first noticed by an off-watch crew reporting that he could see the moon through the side of the boat.

Nothing daunted, we hand-stitched the main and reinforced the repair by heavy canvas tabling. Then we drilled and bolted some plates over the weakened coveing board and set sail for Ushant.

It was the night that Lynmouth in North Devon was all but wiped off the map by its river from the moors bursting its banks during the terrible storm.

Rounding Ushant in thick fog, we closed a French trawler to check our position. He was busy hauling in his nets but threw in the information that we could expect 40 knots of wind in ten minutes. We got it, but were soon round the Ar Men buoy and surfing towards Belle Ile. Only one other boat finished that 330-mile race, *Sylphide*, a new RNSA 24-footer who came in nearly a day behind us but saved her time. However, *The Times* duly reported that we had won Classes I and II, and Uncle got a telegram in his digs in Brixham making him an unconditional offer for the boat, close to his asking price.

So all ended well for the indomitable Uncle. And all ended well for *Golden Dragon*. Her new owners could afford to bring her into contention with newer post-war boats, putting in metal spars, wheel steering, new sails, ringing and winches. She raced mainly on the East Coast where she was all but unbeatable.

One day a year or two earlier in the Fountain Violet, I met a cherubic figure with pebble pince-nez and a Guards tie to go with his clipped white moustache. He reminded me of Mr Pastry, the eccentric TV character created by Richard Hearne; that is, until he spoke, when he came across more in the manner of an Old Etonian E nest Hemingway. All I knew of Gerald Potter up to that point was that he had introduced the Dragon Class to the Solent before the War and turned his hand to ocean-racing in his mid-forties after demobilization. He first teamed up with Blondie Hasler in the

30-square metre *Tre-Sang*, then raced a converted 8-metre called *Zadig* which had only guardrails and a light cabin-top fitted over her open cockpit to distinguish her from any other day-racing yacht. Recently he had launched *Fandango*, a 33'6" waterline ocean racer which he commissioned from Laurent Giles. She was to have the same underwater body as the revolutionary *Myth of Malham*, in which John Illingworth had already won two Fastnets, but with overhangs to give her prettier ends and a seven-eighths rig. Those aesthetic concessions cost him 4 feet of rating against *Myth*, so not unnaturally *Fandango* was yet to be in the money when I met her owner that evening.

His long-suffering American wife, Ginny, who ran her lovely home overlooking Torbay as a 5-star watering-hole for passing ocean-racing friends of Gerald's, took up the story:

'I couldn't believe my ears. Out of the corner of my eye I saw this young Lieutenant talking to Gerald and heard him suggesting that maybe *Fandango* wasn't winning because she wasn't being sailed right. In the stupefying silence that followed, I wished the ground could have opened up.'

Nevertheless, I was signed on to navigate for Gerald in the Plymouth-Santander race. There was nothing to test us in the light and variable conditions encountered on the way across the Bay of Biscay but from the moment of rounding Cabo Major and sailing up the river to anchor off the applauding crowd gathered on the balcony of the Real Club Maritimo de Santander the crew was put to the rack. The trouble was that in trying to adjust to the local custom of sitting down to lunch at 3.30 p.m. and dinner at 11 at night we failed to break our own habit of opening the bar at 1100 and again at six in the evening. Modeste Peron, one of Gerald's local friends, had been Mayor of the town when the Republicans captured it during the Civil War. Most of the opposition who surrendered were tossed over the cliffs. Just as the Mayor was about to get the heave-ho, the local Commissar intervened to save his life. It seems that Señor Peron had been a generous tipper at the best restaurant in town, where the Commissar had been a waiter.

We went to the bull-fights and even played golf on the course where one day young Ballesteros would learn to caddy. Gerald's first drive was sliced and broke a window in the Clubhouse to gales of laughter from the gallery. Before playing our third shots to the green, a fore-caddie had to run ahead and clear the putting surface of a dozen old ladies squatting down and weeding the grass with tweezers.

Mercifully the race northwards across the Bay to Belle Ile was a fast fetch. This time we finished in the money. Our first morning in harbour we awoke to hear the bagpipes coming from *St Barbara*, the Gunners' boat, interrupted by the public address system warming up for the start of their version of Cowes Week. '*Allo, allo,*' the voice boomed out, '*à la troisieme toc, il y a exactement dix heures*', repeated five times and then, to mark the instant of ten o'clock, the loudspeaker broadcast '. . . *toc* . . . *toc* . . . (pause) . . . *hic.*' You could smell the garlic right across the harbour.

At night most of the RORC fleet patronized Le Risqué Tout, a chic nightclub on a beach made for skinny-dipping and jazz by a quintet on tour from Le Hot Club de France.

It was on our way home, beating to windward up to Concarneau that I first realised that *Fandango* might still be a winner. Given the right man on the tiller, which she had as long as Gerald stayed awake, and a strong crew, she demonstrated immense power to windward in choppy seas.

So I looked forward to the 1951 Fastnet Race in her with mild expectations of being able to beat our handicap if we got enough windward work.

Soon after breakfast at Cowes, when we were on board all set to go, the start was postponed by six hours. At this point it was gusting 68 knots at Calshot and all keelboat class racing for boats smaller than Dragons had been cancelled for the day. Sailing a shortened course, one of the Dragons drove under and sank right off the Prince Consort buoy. Her crew was rescued but the boat was never seen again, probably broken up by the swirling boulders which divers in the Solent dread.

To kill time, we invited ourselves on board *Old Fox*, a small sister of *Bloodhound*, which lay in the Roads. She was owned by a timber merchant from Derbyshire, who kept a crew of three old layabouts from Brixham in comfortable style, with subsidised accommodation ashore, lavish tips and regular cases of beer. In return he wanted two spells of a fortnight's social racing in her, one in Cowes and another during the Torbay fortnight. They repaid him by going fishing in the winter when they should have been refitting *Old Fox* up to standard and by showing a notable lack of enthusiasm for going on the foredeck. Once Gerald was at the wheel when she rounded a weather mark with the Round the Island Race seemingly in her grasp. The spinnaker was called for, but the paid hands said they had to dry out and have a cup of tea below first. Her rivals stormed by under spinnakers.

But they did manage to produce the Dom Perignon, which we drank in *Old Fox*'s saloon. Soon we had further evidence of the quality of the crew's refit during the previous winter. The rain came through the deckhead so strongly that we had to wear oilskins and sou'westers as we drank our champagne down below.

Late in the afternoon the Fastnet fleet was sent away into the teeth of a sou'westerly gale with a spring ebb tide under them. The seas in the Needles Channel were frightening. Their real menace was reserved for me. I was sitting on the rose-patterned porcelain heads in the forepeak when *Fandango* flew off a wave and fell into a deep hole. Luckily I was hanging on to an overhead handgrip, for suddenly I was swinging in mid-air, suspended inches over the jagged porcelain stump of the 'suite', as they call it.

Clear of the Needles, Gerald drove the boat to windward most of the night. Off Start Point the wind moderated and we had an easier point of sailing, laying the Lizard without problems. Somewhere beyond the Eddystone it was noticed that the leeward upper spreader was hanging free. Examination showed it to be beyond repair, even by jury rig. If we could stay on one tack all the way out to the Rock and back, all would be well, but the first tack on the wind would send the mast over the side. We turned back for Brixham.

Over an hour later we encountered *Bloodhound* heading for the sou'west, obviously leading the fleet. We had been over 15 miles ahead of her boat for boat.

Then Gerald sold *Fandango* without any regrets and bought one of the early Nicholson 36s, *Oberon*, in which he won more than his share of races.

Meanwhile I was stuck in Scotland or at sea for the next five years, so only sailed the occasional race in the RORC club boat *Griffin II* (ex-*Yeoman III*, winner of the 1951 Fastnet). I collected a number of offshore prizes in her before taking her on the 1957 Fastnet, still remembered as one of the bumpiest rides in the history of the sport. It was also the deciding race in the inaugural match for the Admiral's Cup between teams of three boats from Britain (*Myth of Malham*, *Jocasta* and *Uomie*) and the USA (*Carina II* and *White Mist*). We were never considered for the British team, which was just as well when we saw the perfect sails and immaculate preparation of the American boats.

The first lull after a succession of gale force winds and bone-shaking seas came north of Round Island, when the wind fell to an uncertain Force 3, yet a big lumpy swell remained which needed maximum drive from the sail-plan to keep the boat moving.

Our mainsail was an ill-fitting cotton reject cut down from *Mary Bower*, an even older boat. It set like one you might see on a model yacht being pushed off the side of a kids' paddling pond. As for our headsails, I recall describing one as looking like a used french letter. From miles to leeward a white-sailed American yawl appeared, crossing tacks and passing two miles ahead until she disappeared out of sight to windward, whilst we flopped up and down in the same hole, waiting for the wind to return.

When it did, we had a rousing sail home, running wing-and-wing from the Fastnet to the Bishop with the mainsail stowed in favour of the 150% genoa sheeted through a block at the end of the boom which was squared off. I'm not sure where *Griffin II* is today, but if you ever see her in a foreign port look for a spot on the portside of her foredeck not far from the mast. Short strips of teak decking have been used to patch up a hole in her deck no bigger than a blotting pad. That marks the moment when the inboard end of the spinnaker pole became unhooked from the mast-fitting under full load. It punched its way clean through the foredeck and stood there quivering like an assegai. Down below it had plunged into the mattress of the port berth in the forepeak, passing right between the legs of its sleeping occupant – the bachelor heir to a peerage, who happily went on to beget four children. But it was a close thing.

In the middle of the night we cleared the Bishop Rock with 98 miles to go. A port bow light had converged on us from seaward and ranged up alongside, also on a close reach at hull speed. She was still there at first light, when we identified her as *Figaro*, Bill Snaith's beautiful Sparkman and Stephens yawl. They worked on her sail plan all the way down the home stretch, with her mizzen and mizzen staysail tried first up and then down, but we remained locked together.

She crossed the breakwater line a minute ahead of us and rounded up. I called for three cheers, to which they responded with *éclat* and a wave of her skipper's double Corona. It was their first visit to Plymouth, so they secured alongside us in Millbay docks and were soon filling our saloon and emptying our Scotch bottles. Thus a whole new circle of translatlantic sailors entered my life, for her crew was a *Who's Who* of US ocean-racing. Besides the unforgettable Bill Snaith and his paid hand Dick Grossmiller, there was Ed Raymond, the sailmaker, Bobby Symonette, the 5.5 Olympic medallist from Nassau, Bucky Reardon and others, with all of whom I later sailed when we won the 1963 Southern Ocean Racing conference off Florida in the next *Figaro*.

Next outboard was *Carina II*, outright winner of the Fastnet Race with her weatherbeaten hard-driving owner, Dick Nye, on his way to setting an unbeatable record offshore by winning the Bermuda and Transatlantic Races three times.

★ 17 ★

PORT BANNATYNE

After less than eighteen months at Dartmouth I was told that I had to go back to sea in command for a spell before taking over the Rothesay Attack Teacher, the modest shore-based synthetic submarine trainer at Port Bannatyne in Bute. It was used not only to provide training for the Perisher but specialized in a course for C.O.s requalifying for command after a tour away from submarines.

The submarine to which I was sent to get my feet wet again was one I'd already spent nearly three years in as First Lieutenant, HMS *Amphion*. The Squadron Commander (S/M) seemed to take a perverse pleasure in arranging programmes to separate Captains from their wives. As soon as he heard that Sylvia was on her way to Rothesay, in anticipation of a long spell ashore at Port Bannatyne, *Amphion* was ordered to Londonderry to spend most of the long, dark winter operating out of the Foyle for the benefit of the Joint Anti-Submarine School based in Derry. There was no hint of the black days to come there.

That was in 1950. But when I went back again later in 1953, and even 1957, everything seemed peaceful enough, with the wives working in the shirt factories while their husbands drew the dole and waited for the betting shops and pubs to open.

Life as Officer Commanding the Rothesay Attack Teacher (OCRAT) had much to be said for it. One lived ashore, in my case in a squalid little terraced house within sight of the Attack Teacher. The depot-ship HMS *Montclare* was out of sight at anchor off Rothesay Pier, but available for Sunday evening movies and other entertainments. Our little girls enjoyed Scottish primary education, unequalled anywhere. The locals were agreeable and friendly, from the gregarious Lord Bute through all the golfers on the precipitous 9-hole golf course, with its stunning views of The Cobbler one way and Arran to the south, to the farmer from Ettrick Bay. He drove his smart pony and trap 3¹/2 miles into town each day to sell buttermilk from a polished churn and was later seen sprawled unconscious over the driver's seat as the piebald pony clip-clopped him all the way home without a hand on the reins. Our local was the Royal Hotel in Port Bannatyne, a tiny waterfront pub which made its money from Glaswegian day-trippers evading the outdated Sunday licensing laws then prevailing in Scotland which allowed bona-fide travellers to drink themselves senseless outside a 12-mile radius from home.

Apart from the pleasure of so many old friends passing through as requalifiers, the work lay at the heart of what little long-term tactical thinking was encouraged from operational submariners.

I took over from Dicky Tibbatts, probably the brightest and most refreshing thinker at his level in the Submarine Service. He had been wartime First Lieutenant to the legendary Lt-Commander Arthur ('Baldy') Hezlet who got six hits on the Japanese heavy cruiser *Ashigara* in the last salvo fired in anger at a major enemy warship. Hezlet's restless agile mind, for ever questioning entrenched ways of doing it wrong, rubbed off on Dicky. He produced a penetrating analysis entitled 'A Quick All-Round Look' showing how far our submarines had lagged behind those of almost any other major navy's in not having effective torpedo control systems. The Captain (S/M) was the much decorated L.W.A. Bennington, an ex-lower deck officer who had got where he was with a mix of unflinching bravery and simple, uncomplicated tactical methods.

Ben endorsed Tibbatts' important treatise and forwarded it to Flag Officer Submarines at Fort Blockhouse. The Chief of Staff at the time was incapable of grasping its significance and predictably saw it as close to a seditious attack on the submarine high command. Ben was ordered to Blockhouse in sword and medals, where he was on the receiving end of a searing rocket, told to withdraw the Tibbatts paper and destroy all copies.

When the nuclear submarine *Conqueror* sank the cruiser *Belgrano* during the Falklands War in 1982, her torpedoes were still the same ones we went to war with in 1939.

During Tibbatts' time, the Submarine Command had received a new wartime directive: priority was henceforth to be given to detecting and sinking dived enemy submarines. This would have to be by passive means, using listening hydrophones, since active sonar would immediately alert the enemy. We had no realistic prospect of homing torpedoes or even workable wire-guided ones, so Tibbatts came up with a beautifully simple choreography from which the attacking submarine might arrive at a fire-control solution without blasting off on power on the sonar.

It depended on getting bearing lines at equal time intervals, first with zero own-movement – by pointing straight at the target – followed by another set of bearings with maximum own-movement achieved by altering the attacking submarine through 90°. If the enemy obliged by remaining on a steady course, a unique solution for his course and speed could then be found by overlaying a rule marked off to the right scale at equal time intervals. With magnetic pistols in our warheads we had wide latitude in estimating the enemy's depth.

Taking over where Dicky left off, I devised a vertical perspex plot marked off in co-ordinates of time against true bearings. On one side stood a rating with a headset from the sonar operator putting a blob with a grease pencil for each hard bearing reported. On the other side of the perspex plot an officer faired off all the raw data into a smooth line from which he could then read off for the navigator on the main plot the bearings at predetermined exact intervals. This became established doctrine and my perspex plot was still to be seen as standard equipment in all our control rooms for years. No doubt it is now all done by computers and microchips handling vastly superior raw data from sonars specially developed for the purpose.

To get the rest of the Squadron indoctrinated, we set up regular Saturday forenoon exercises for every boat in harbour. At the Attack Teacher we would run a U-boat target down the track, calling out degraded bearings at random intervals and sending them over the air on VHF to the half-dozen boats participating. At seven bells I would repair on board *Montclare* for a Horse's Neck with the actual chart under my arm to match against those developed in the control-rooms of the submarines alongside. We also used VHF voice to run duplicate bridge tournaments, but got dropped on from a great height for using Channel 16, the international distress frequency, when other available frequencies were not delivering.

I determined only to teach methods which could be readily grasped by a totally exhausted C.O. who was no Senior Wrangler in the first place. My favourite requalifier was John Stevens who had sunk a lot of ships in the Mediterranean in his aptly-named *Unruffled*. After listening to esoteric mathematical formulae involving rate of change of bearing and the various criteria determining the optimum spread and number of fish to be fired in a salvo of torpedoes under any given set of circumstances, to say nothing of calculating the Director Angle (DA) or aim-off, he declared:

'A U-class only has four up the spout. So I say, if the target's worth firing at, give her the lot and, anyway, the DA is always 10°.' (For a 7-knot merchantman that is a fair approximation).

So I threw away all the graphs and most of the slide-rules and concentrated on developing basic skills within the scope of existing equipment and those in charge of it. High on my priorities were the mental aids for attacking without instruments. Over the eyepiece of the Attack Teacher periscope I had a brass plate fixed with the words inscribed: 'Remember, the DA is always 10°'.

After much correspondence in a docket as fat as a telephone directory, the Admiralty at Bath announced the completion of the prototype of the next generation of Torpedo Control Computer, a successor to the all-cogs-and-shafts manually-cranked fruit-machine. It arrived in a plain van accompanied by the egg-head civil servant who had been responsible for its lengthy development. With luck he could now promise the Royal Navy something comparable to that fitted in U-boats and USN submarines before the War.

Most of the time wasted in our conversation that morning was because none of us could believe that this showroom model had been produced without its designer having grasped the basic need to generate and utilise the target's rate of change of bearing. So it went back to Bath the very next day. I never forgot the name of the man entrusted with this project. It was the same as a ventriloquist's dummy on a long-running TV show. When I left submarines five years later there was still no sign of a torpedo-control system embodying the original specifications which had been overlooked by the design team at Bath.

Another unproductive Admiralty research and development activity was the RN Torpedo Establishment at Greenock. It had magnificent workshops, all kinds of laboratories staffed by enthusiasts, with superb test-firing facilities on its doorstep. I was told that during its lifetime it never actually produced a new torpedo that functioned as intended, although doubtless it laid the groundwork for several that were later produced by private enterprise.

Each July it fell to the Attack Teacher's team to analyse the results of all the dummy torpedo attacks carried out during Flag Officer Submarine's Summer War. Up to thirty submarines took part in a series of set-piece encounters spread over ten days, leaving us over 300 separate attack-forms to analyse. It was six weeks' hard grind, working from early morning until just before The Royal closed, without the benefit even of a hand-held calculator.

The only satisfaction I ever derived from doing these analyses, which no one who mattered read beyond their Summary and Conclusions, was in being able to identify as the Man of the Series a senior

39 HMS *Totem* reunion, Garrick Club, 1982. *Left to right*: Gladys Cooper,
J.O.C. and First Sea Lord (Sir John (now Lord) Fieldhouse).

40 Sylvia at Titty Hill Farm with Sambo.

Lt-Commander who had been summarily relieved of his command for bringing his submarine back from Inchmarnock Water through the narrow gap at Tighnabruaich separating the island of Bute from the mainland. Actually it was no more hazardous than entering a dockyard basin at Devonport across the current in the Hamoaze River. Our target destroyers used it regularly to save an hour's extra passage through the Great Cumbrae, but one had misjudged it recently, or even taken the wrong channel, and wiped off a screw. But the same Commander (S/M) who had sent me to Derry to leave my family unaccompanied on their arrival had it in for Douglas Lambert, the C.O. concerned, so had him summarily relieved of his command and put him into the spare crew. On the eve of the Summer War one boat lost her captain sick. Lambert was the only one available to take over. My special mention of his flawless performance in the analysis came far too late to save his career, which had soon run its course.

Before my second Summer War analysis, my old friend Philip Wood had been appointed as my relief. I was earmarked to move to Chatham Dockyard, standing by the final stages of the conversion of the 1944 vintage HMS *Totem* to an operational submarine capable of 17 knots submerged, similar to the USN *Guppy* Class.

On completion, we were scheduled to join the Third Squadron at Rothesay.

Before going to Chatham I was temporarily assigned to the staff of the American C-in-C Atlantic for Operation 'Mainbrace', the major NATO autumn exercise off Norway. I reported on board the flagship USS *Wisconsin* and made my first acquaintance of Admiral Felix B. (for Budwell) Stump, a man of forbidding presence and few, carefully chosen words. In many ways he resembled the much-loved Admiral 'Jas' Eccles, under whom I later served as Operations Officer in our own Home Fleet. Jas never got beyond being C-in-C Home Fleet because, as he put it to me when I bade him farewell, he was not a member of the club – meaning the Mountbatten set. Likewise Admiral Stump never got to be Chief of Naval Operations, probably because the wartime destroyer hero Arleigh Burke was chosen from a long way down the Flag List, but he had the rare distinction of having already served as C-in-C in the Atlantic before moving west to the top job in the Pacific, where I met him again.

Although only a Lieutenant-Commander, I messed with the Admiral in his quarters in the battleship, exchanging grunts and other views on his nightly Western movies. I was only there to interpret the procedures if a NATO submarine got into difficulties. On our first day at sea a newsreel cameraman shot us on the wings of the flag bridge. Following directions, what passed between us was that he said: 'One, two, three . . .' to which I nodded sagely and replied: 'January, February, March . . .' and so on. My father saw that newsreel in Hong Kong before we reached Oslo at the end of the exercise. The voice-over commentator said that the C-in-C was discussing battle dispositions with the Royal Navy's liaison officer.

On such occasions there is always some newshound determined to make a story out of nothing. So, in the absence of any collisions or aircraft ditching, Clay Blair, filing for *Time-Life*, came up with the hoary old one about our aircraft carriers and aviators being incompatible to the point of being an embarrassment to the USN Striking Fleet, which would be more effective without our carriers in the formation. It seems that the Admiral had ordered that any anti-British stories being filed for transmission to the States should be shown to him forthwith. Admiral Stump said he would not stop the copy going, but advised Clay Blair that Henry Luce was an old friend and could easily be reached by linked telephone call in a matter of minutes.

In Oslo Sound the King of Norway and all the top brass of NATO assembled on *Wisconsin* for fruit juice, cake and New Orleans jazz by their Bluejackets' band, before piling into barges to make the short trip over to HMS *Vanguard*, where the Royal Marines band played Gilbert and Sullivan under her ceremonial striped awning and everyone got stuck into the hard stuff.

We had three fleet carriers in 'Mainbrace'. Admiral Stump was extravagant in his public praise of the Fleet Air Arm throughout the unpleasant weather and short days which prevailed. How *Time-Life* finally reported the exercise I do not recall.

★ 18 ★

HMS *TOTEM* –
A SLIPPERY CUSTOMER

Joining *Totem* meant moving into an overcrowded hut in Chatham Dockyard, full of drawings, unanswered correspondence and dirty teacups. The boat already had the major surgery of her conversion completed. The hull had been sawn in half to accommodate a fourth battery section of 112 cells and an extra main motor on each shaft. Used Group Up, or in series, the extra battery (or 'box' as it was called) could throw 480 volts into the motor-room. The extra main motor with its own clutch gave us the flexibility of diesel-electric drive without the agonizing wait of uncoupling the main engines before the motors could be run each time the diesels were stopped. In the control room there was a new instrument featuring two independently swinging arms over a scale looking like isobars on a weather map. One arm represented the voltage being drawn from the main batteries at any given moment; the other the amperage drain. Where the two arms crossed, the scale underneath indicated how much time remained before the battery was flattened. Starting with fully charged batteries, ringing down Full Ahead Group Up soon had the log indicating 17 knots submerged, but the electronic watchdog's arms crossed over at 1 hour, 20 minutes. However, there were some encouraging intermediate figures not far below 100% power: we could have 12 knots for 4 hours or 9 knots for 12 hours. At long last all our periscopes and masts were stainless steel, making a periscope lookout possible through the big stick whilst snorkelling at her maximum speed underwater on the diesels of 9 knots. The old brass periscopes whipped around and gave the captain blurred vision and a headache at half that speed.

To get the speed all external surfaces had to be faired off, the gun and external torpedo tubes ditched and all the masts enclosed in a narrow fin – or 'sail' as the Americans call it. There were two snags in our case: the bridge which just had room for two officers and two lookouts was enclosed in a small cab not far above the level of the forecasing and barely tenable in any seaway; the streamlining of the fin was broken by an inverted tub-shaped protrusion at its top, intended to house the antenna of a sophisticated new radar which was yet to be delivered.

As soon as I reached a depot ship away from the prying eyes of the Admiralty I had it cut away and replaced with perfectly faired plating. Next day we found we had nearly an extra knot underwater. The radar never reached the fleet in my time.

I was never consulted about the officers or key ratings appointed to make *Totem* tick, but I was confident that the drafting authorities would not palm off too many duds on me, for she was about the best submarine we had at the time. In the event I could not have hoped for better, although I had never met any of them previously. The Engineer who had conscientiously supervised the conversion from its beginning eighteen months previously was Bill Ray, a Lt-Commander with the unusual distinction of a DSC and a DSM, the latter won as a wartime Chief Engine Room Artificer. He was relieved by Geoff Cornish soon after we left Chatham.

The other officers joined soon after I did, led by the First Lieutenant, a quiet, mild-mannered chubby lad, who announced himself as John Fieldhouse. He was soon known as 'Snorkers', a heavily antonymous soubriquet inspired by the unspeakable Bennett, the Australian First Lieutenant of *Compass Rose* in *The Cruel Sea* with whom he shared only one characteristic – a love of sausages. He quickly proved himself to be without equal, on personal or professional grounds. Robin Heath and Greg Courtier followed as Third and Fourth Hand. Finally we unexpectedly had an Electrical Officer appointed, one of the first in the Submarine Service. Before he joined, I was tipped off by Captain (S/M) that he had an offhand not to say condescending manner with some senior officers, as one or two had already reported. If I found him insupportable, a telephone call to Blockhouse would have a relief on his way to Chatham on the next train.

He reported at 0900, immaculately turned out and in even tones said he was Lieutenant Lucy joining as Electrical Officer. I had a hangover and was in no mood to pass the time of day with anyone. Switching on the heavy sarcasm, I remarked: 'We've managed in submarines for half a century without specialist Electrical officers. The First Lieutenant has always been responsible. When something goes wrong he just gives it a kick and it re-starts. What do you have to offer that's so unique?' 'Ah yes, sir,' he replied, 'but I went to University for three years to learn *where* to kick it.'

That did it. Peter Lucy and I have remained close friends to this day. But I could readily think of one or two submarine C.O.s who would not have fallen for that line of patter and would instead have picked up the phone to Blockhouse.

When we were finally ready to go, I invited George Ingle, my old housemaster at school, to come down and bless the ship at a private commissioning ceremony alongside a basin in the Dockyard. This simple enough ceremony landed me in front of the Admiral Superintendent the next day for a tirade of abuse, couched in language I had not heard since one of the Mids in my gunroom in *Repulse* had been sick on the stokers' messdeck on his way to keep his watch on her bridge. It seems that George, then Bishop of Fulham, should not have set foot in the diocese without the prior permission of the Chaplain-General of the Fleet, the Bishop of Rochester and the Archbishop of Canterbury. When I told him later, George was as surprised as I was, being unaware of the protocol involved.

One further change in key personnel had to be made when we touched down at Blockhouse on our way to join the Third Flotilla in the Clyde. For some reason which I have forgotten, the Coxswain had to be replaced. According to Bob Hall, my old Coxswain in *Truncheon*, he was walking through Blockhouse well pleased with having just engineered for himself the cushy number of Drafting Coxswain at HMS *Dolphin* when I met him and asked what he was up to.

'Right,' I said, 'you've got till 0800 tomorrow to get to your office, find a relief as Drafting Coxswain, appoint yourself Coxswain in *Totem* and report on board ready to sail.'

He was so taken aback by this treatment that he complied, much to our benefit. It is hard to underrate the value of a Coxswain of his calibre in any submarine. Bob was a less rumbustious character than the legendary Guts Willoughby but his own way of running the submarine was equally effective. A stoker who persistently disturbed the peace by returning on board aggressively drunk he had put down one of the periscope wells and left him in there with a tarpaulin across its top and a sentry to keep him quiet, without disturbing the Officer of the Day.

One day we sailed from Tunis at an early hour, homeward bound, full of cheap cognac and champagne. As a matter of routine we dived for trim and went to 250 feet to take a bathythermograph reading. One of Bob's lesser duties was to take the card off the machine and fix the stylus tracing showing the gradient of seawater temperatures plotted against depths. When we resumed Patrol Routine he handed it to me before filing it. On this occasion I glanced at the card to find on it a profile sketch of a hen with the words 'A Good Layer' printed alongside.

Towards the end of our work-up in the Clyde each ship in the Fleet was allocated a port in which it would be in attendance in time to celebrate the Queen's Coronation, to say nothing of Roger Bannister cracking the 4-minute mile and Hillary and Tensing planting the Union flag on top of Everest. We drew Oban as our harbour in which to lead the general rejoicing. The opening event was a Reception given for the officers by the Royal Highland Yacht Club. This most exclusive of clubs may not have had a clubhouse nor any yachts in sight, but it had the Lord-Lieutenant as its ex-officio Commodore, who did the honours in the vaulted assembly room of the local Station Hotel, surrounded by weatherbeaten lairds and their proud consorts who looked as though they had left their broomsticks in the carpark. All but one, that is, who was stunningly beautiful. In the middle of the carousal our self-appointed liaison officer tapped me on the shoulder and suggested that I warned my lads off crowding the lady. It seems that the local studs had been trying to make her for years, but she was unswervingly faithful to her own laird.

Two nights later, on the eve of the Coronation, we were her guests in a nearby castle. Winston Churchill spoke on the radio before we were due to pile into Land Rovers and head for a nearby hilltop to put a torch to one of the chain of beacons all round the kingdom. The scene in the big hall was memorable. In front of a blazing log fire Winston's emotional voice had us close to tears – except for the retrievers and the Laird, all of whom slept soundly as we left our port and trooped out into the night. Two weeks later Peter asked for a long weekend and spent it in Paris with the Laird's wife who later became his own.

The day of the Coronation started equally promisingly, with all the officers and chiefs invited to the manager's flat in the distillery to take seed cake with his family and to sample a few bottles of Old Oban single malt whisky which had been bottled on the day of King George V's Coronation over forty years earlier. Since we had already spliced the mainbrace on board in response to a general signal from the Admiralty, the Chiefs were chasing down a quarter of a pint of pusser's rum with this unrepeatable malt nectar from the Highlands.

I had no need to worry. I shared a limo with the Provost out to the local playing fields and stood on a dais awaiting the appearance of the march past of all three Services, with nurses, firemen and cadets bringing up the rear. It was an impressive sight, with my ship's company leading the whole parade of close to a thousand men and women in uniform, marching to massed pipe bands recruited from all over Argyll. In charge out in front with drawn sword was our First Lieutenant, looking lonely and a bit apprehensive in case the parade took a wrong turn behind him without being noticed. After marching past, he brought the parade to a halt facing the dais and advanced to make his report to the Provost. No one had tipped him off that the Provost was a deaf as a post, so his response to repeated offers to inspect the parade met with no more than a nod of his purple face and a happy mutter of 'Aye, they're lovely'. So, John Fieldhouse, showing an early glimpse of the presence of mind which would later stand him in good stead as C-in-C Fleet during the Falklands campaign, noticed my hand signal, brought his sword back to the Present, made an aside about protocol being satisfied and dismissed the whole parade so that the Games could proceed.

We held our own in the tug-of-war against the Glasgow Police by having an unnoticed ninth person on the rope, but were made to look foolish in the shinty match against the Highlands champions.

The next event on the Coronation programme was the Spithead Review. I led a line of eight submarines south from the Clyde, happy in the prospect of seeing the opening night of *Guys and Dolls* at Drury Lane with Sylvia and my father. Steaming down the Irish Sea I went over the orders for the Review in detail and spotted that there would be no shore leave for any of us until after the night for which I had tickets to the show. The Chief Tel said that he would book an R/T call to my father in London via Land's End radio. Our effective range for linking into this service was 40 miles. There was a long traffic list and we were far down the queue of those booking ship-shore calls. I slowed the formation down to six knots, but we were well past Land's End heading eastwards still awaiting a slot on the air. At 35 miles beyond the shore station I was desperate and turned to the Signalman: 'Make: Stop Engines. Hands to bathe.'

Passing ships must have wondered what eight submarines were doing lying stationary off the Lizard, surrounded by black dots in the water. Half an hour later the Chief Tel called me to his office and handed me the microphone. My father's voice could have been in the control-room.

The Review was memorable mainly for the fact that Gerald Potter and a few sailing friends from Devon turned up in a converted Brixham trawler and anchored close enough for us to exchange frequent visits. All the ships' illuminations were switched off late at night by signal from the flagship, but one of our guests found the master switch in *Totem's* control room and switched ours on around 0200. No one noticed.

After the Review we made a ceremonial visit to Oslo and ran out the rest of the summer cruise either based on Londonderry or Rothesay. During Flag Officer Submarines war exercises we remained submerged throughout, which bore heavily on those who smoked, with the 'No Smoking' sign enforced all the time we were running on motors submerged so as to reduce atmospheric pollution as measured in the build-up of carbon-monoxide content. On two consecutive days we did 20-hour spells on the motors, taking careful atmospheric measurements, first through a normal 'No Smoking' dive, followed by one in which the astonished ship's company were invited to chain-smoke throughout. There was no appreciable difference in the atmospheric degeneration at the end of either day. From that day to this our submariners have smoked without restriction whenever submerged, except during the closing stages of a battery charge. At that time I happened to be a non-smoker myself.

During July there were hints that we were to have an independent programme in the early autumn, possibly taking a swing around the White Sea or even going under the ice. By the 1980's surveillance of NATO naval units by Soviet submarines or aircraft was taken for granted. Electronic spy-ships passed happily through our fleet formations, whilst their maritime aircraft 'buzzed them without hindrance. But in the early 'fifties, following hard on the heels of the Berlin airlift and at a time of explosive growth of Soviet sea power, sterner attitudes prevailed. I recall a confidential memorandum on the subject circulated to the Fleet at the time which reminded Escort Force Commanders that there were no prohibitions on firing depth charge patterns to test them at any time. Exactly what similar orders had gone out to the Red Navy remained a matter for conjecture, but no one fancied being the first to find out, as Gary Powers did on his U2 flight over Mother Russia.

Whatever plans the top brass had for our deployment in September were suddenly cancelled, due, I later learnt, to scientific advice to the Prime Minister which gave us little or no chance of going anywhere near Soviet naval forces and remaining undetected. The same argument prevailed against using our fishing fleet for any sort of surveillances.

So we were abruptly switched for attachment to the Mediterranean Fleet to show our paces to their Commander-in-Chief, Dickie Mountbatten. Before we sailed to join them in Malta, Peter Lucy and I made a significant visit to the Admiralty Signal and Radar Establishment on the top of Portsdown Hill. We already had a 3-cm (X-band) search receiver on one of our line of masts, but we were wide open to detection by 10 cms (S-band) radars, especially the superb AN/APS 20 set fitted on USN Neptune maritime aircraft; so we wanted to find out what the prospects were for getting S-band intercept cover.

The civilian scientist in charge of the project was a friend, who had already been our guest on other signal trials. After a good lunch in a nearby pub he showed us the modest little horn that housed a prototype lash-up of the S-band receiver antenna. An hour later we drove out of the main gates with one in my raincoat pocket, against a chit I'd signed for its temporary loan. On our way back to Rothesay after summer leave at Chatham we called at Blockhouse long enough to get the periscope workshop to remove our big search periscope and attach a pressure-tight snout under the top glass, big enough to house the S-band horn, which was then wired up to a headset worn by the periscope watchkeeper. Since intercept gear should in theory always detect an outward radar emission before it has the strength to make the return journey and alert the radar operator as an echo on his CR tube, we enjoyed a clear range advantage. The fact that we had our own unauthorized S-band intercept gear fitted and at sea in an operational submarine we managed to keep secret from all but a handful of the top brass.

We certainly ran rings round various destroyer flotilla captains who dominated night exercises by ordering X-band silence, then easily detecting and putting down snorkelling submarines by using their S-band radars. In this manner we were never once caught napping by surface or air forces, and my 'luck' became a byword.

On passage for Malta, I signalled the Captain (S/M) asking for a routine air search exercise with a shorebased RAF maritime aircraft in an area so far west of Malta that only a Neptune had the range to join in. The boom of his S-band search-radar nearly blew my head off, but gave ample warning to stop snorkelling before he picked us up. On first detection we could get a fair indication of his bearing by slewing the periscope round, noting left and right cut-offs. Anywhere within seven miles he blanketed us with an all-round signal. No questions were asked about these exercises, probably because the Commander (S/M) in Malta was Bobby Boyd who had long ago given up trying to reason out why I did anything.

Soon after our arrival we were despatched to join the Fleet Regatta in Navarin Bay on the west coast of Greece. The first night there I was bidden to dine informally on board the C-in-C's 'yacht', HMS *Surprise*, a lavishly converted wartime frigate. Over dinner and during intervals in the movie afterwards Mountbatten was taking notes, obviously intended for when he addressed my ship's company after inspecting her at 1000 the next morning. I had the names and potted biographical data of two of my crew who had previously served with the C-in-C. 'When the C-in-C comes on board tomorrow,' the Flag Lieutenant whispered, 'have these two fallen in clear of the rest of your ship's company.'

When I rejoined my own wardroom the officers were still up, waiting for news of the morrow. A few jars later someone had the witty idea of switching our two old Mountbatten shipmates. The green barge touched alongside on the dot of time and the great man fell straight into nostalgic reminiscences with Chief Petty Officer Black about service on the China Station before the war together in HMS *Wishart*, ending by asking how his wife and kids were. There were two snags: Black was a confirmed bachelor, who had briefly served with him in *Illustrious*, whilst the real man from *Wishart* was next in line. My own ship's company were in on this rather childish prank and under pain of death not even to smile.

Long after we had both left the Navy I used to see a lot of Dickie, who was always generous and charming, if a shade too ready with his anecdotes about members of the Royal family to whom he was related. In the course of time I felt I knew Uncle Nicky and Cousin Ena as if they were my own family and not just the Tsar of Russia and the Queen of Spain. Sometimes it was on the tip of my tongue to confess to that switch we pulled on him at Navarin Bay, which could only be justified by the gratifying effect it had on my crew's morale. However, luckily I stopped short, realizing that being the good-natured butt of prep-school practical jokes was not Mountbatten's strong point. Nevertheless, his 'break-ranks-and-gather-round-me' style of leadership, backed by an uncanny insight of the personalities who made up each unit, seemed to go down well with the troops under his command in South-East Asia, as it did for Monty throughout the War.

During our three months in his Fleet he and his staff were unfailingly helpful. One by one they mostly did a day at sea with us. In the adverse sonar conditions prevailing after a long hot summer, we had no difficulty making his top destroyers look lead-footed. Once, with Flag Officer Destroyers on board, we ended up alone on the ocean, having first penetrated the screen and fired from close range before cranking on a burst of top speed under the layer.

'Send to Captain (D),' said the Admiral, '*Totem* fired a salvo of six at 1000 yards at 0947. By 1005 contact had been broken and the officers were playing bridge in the wardroom. What were you doing? Report on return to Sliema.' We were about as popular as a pork chop in a synagogue among the escort forces when we met them ashore.

After exercising with an RAF Shackleton one day, her pilot produced some pictures taken whilst we were at periscope depth. The whole of our fin, the size of a barn door, was clearly visible. In conformation with the practice at the time, the vertical surfaces of our casing and fin were painted pale Mediterranean Fleet grey which showed up as though it was white. So that evening we painted one side of our fin black, leaving the other in regulation grey. The same aircraft rendezvoused with us and took oblique shots from each side. The difference was startling, so we painted the whole boat matt black, now the accepted livery throughout the Submarine fleet – as of course it had been for U-boats since before the War.

In the control room we had fitted true bearing rings around each periscope, thus putting an end to half a century of always having to convert periscope observations from relative bearings. More controversial was Peter's ad hoc linking of the sonar bearings on to the radar PPI display, which became dual-purpose with a change-over switch. That gave bearings in degrees true or relative, as required.

★ 19 ★

SURVEILLANCE

We were back in Chatham Dockyard for Christmas leave, having had our bows rebuilt after an encounter with a motorized cargo barge halfway up the river from Sheerness when thick fog had suddenly closed in. It was no place to anchor and we certainly could not turn round and go back. So we hugged the starboard side of the channel, going gingerly from one fairway buoy to the next. I decided to watch proceedings on the control-room radar PPI. At first I could see over the fog through the big periscope. The radar did not have sufficient definition at short ranges to paint the low mud banks of the river through the sea clutter, and it certainly did not pick up the other ship which was cutting a bend on the wrong side of the river. We were going full astern when we hit her at walking pace. She had a well-known construction company's name painted on her side.

The local Chief of Staff told me to enjoy my Christmas leave and not worry about the collision. So I went off leaving Robin Heath's newly-joined successor, Jock Clelland, guided by No. 1, to fill in Form 32 (Report on Collisions and Grounding) and not to mention that the Officer of the Watch at the time was the Electrical Officer who did not have a formal watchkeeping certificate simply because the rules did not stretch to allowing him one. Robin was overdue for a First Lieutenant's billet elsewhere.

Stepping out of the Treasury Solicitor's offices at Storey's Gate, I was nearly run down by a truck belonging to the same company as the barge. The matter was settled out of court 80/20 in our favour, and no questions were asked about where the Captain was at the time. Since our friend 'Daddy' Coombes, in charge of the Dockyard Construction Department, had gone to a lot of trouble to lose the cost of the repairs as a routine docking on the assumption that I would be held accountable, he was not best pleased to find that he had inadvertently cut the liability of the barge-owners down to peanuts. H.M. Dockyards are adept at such creative accounting, for example in keeping the Royal Yacht looking the smartest ship afloat without giving left-wing MPs too much ammunition – or so it is widely believed.

On New Year's Eve I was promoted to Commander at the respectably early age of 32. The immediate effect of this was that I ceased to get Submarine Pay, as the scale did not provide for anyone above Lt-Commander at the time. Instead I qualified for table money appropriate for a Commander-in-Command. Peter Lucy, who massaged the wardroom wine accounts, appropriated the full amount of this allowance for openers, pointing out that in my position as the only officer for many years to hold that rank whilst in command of a submarine, I would naturally expect higher standards of hospitality in the wardroom. It was scarcely worth arguing about for, in the ordinary way, I would expect to be relieved within weeks.

Our next operational session included a fascinating challenge. The Home and Mediterranean fleets were to hold joint exercises with the USN Sixth Fleet somewhere between Malta and Gibraltar. Our brief was to act independently as if we were a Soviet submarine and see how much tactical intelligence we could gather. To make it realistic we had to act only on what information we could gather from the publicly accessible sources, such as the Press. No one except the C-in-C Mediterranean would be told of this plan. He had to know, in case we got into difficulties.

The *Hampshire Telegraph* obliged with an outline of the Home Fleet's Spring Cruise programme, giving the dates and venues of the various Combined Fleet sporting fixtures, with finals to be contested in Gibraltar. The *Times of Malta* published the departure date of many of the Med Fleet heavy units, so the likely progression of the enemy armada could readily be figured out. A further assumption could be made: that the big carriers of the USN Sixth Fleet would be unlikely to join ours and start combat exercises until they were well west of the Sicilian Channel. It was likely that the Combined Fleets would maintain a steady speed 12–15 knots along their route.

Our own movements were covered by a 30-day diving signal quoting communications trials within latitudes and longitudes in the general area of the Azores. At Fort Blockhouse we embarked additional surveillance equipment and operating watchkeepers. One of our tasks was to evaluate the degree of security conferred by the use of low-powered tactical voice nets. This whole area of technology has since become commonplace with sophisticated bank-robbers and hi-jackers taking full advantage of intercepting police radio traffic as a matter of course.

Too many shore staff at H.M.S. *Dolphin* were asking questions, so it was imperative that those involved should not be tempted into loose gossip in the relaxed atmosphere of the bars ashore.

That problem was readily solved by chartering the base's 50-square-metre yacht and sailing off for an overnight stop at Old Bosham. The tides were right in each direction, so we slipped back into Haslar Creek an hour before sailing.

Keeping far to seaward, *Totem* ran south, dived by day and on the surface at night, until turning eastwards off Cape St Vincent for the 200-mile breakthrough into the Western Mediterranean. Since all the rivers flowing into the Mediterranean do not nearly replace the surface water lost by evaporation, there is a steady east-going current near the surface bringing cooler water in from the Atlantic. A strong westerly wind with lots of white horses permitted short bursts of snorkelling from Cape Spartel near Tangier across the narrows, hugging the Moroccan coast, as U-boats did in the War. Although there were no major fleet units to be seen, maritime patrol aircraft were clearly searching the approaches to the Straits. I assumed someone had tipped them off to be on the lookout for intruding Soviet submarines.

What I only learnt 30 years after the event was that the submarine *Tireless*, commanded by Philip Wood, had been fully briefed on when *Totem* was likely to transit the Straits and ordered to lie in wait near Europa Point to intercept us. The reason for this trial was that she was fitted with experimental passive sonar using her entire casing as base-length for the antenna, so she took the bottom beam on to our expected line of approach. Presumably I was not told so that we would make the transit without any inspired evasive action and offer ourselves as a realistic target.

Somewhere short of Ceuta I went deep and fast to cross over to the Spanish side close east of the Rock. As usual there were a few merchantmen on passage in the area. *Tireless* heard nothing, being confused by conflicting sources of noise from merchant ships and fishing vessels.

Proceeding eastwards about 5 miles off the then sparsely populated Andalusian coast past Malaga to the vicinity of Almeria there was evidence of USN maritime shore-based Neptune aircraft sweeping ahead of the Combined Fleets, but our S-band intercept gear made evasion simple. Finally we moved towards the Algerian coast near Oran and laid low. Our first encounter with the NATO forces was finding ourselves in the grain of a sweeping A/S force. We began to record UHF voice, take periscope pictures and note their rev-knot ratios. After we had passed under the flotilla-leader, she signalled that she was in contact and conducted a series of co-ordinated attacks on whatever it was she held in her sonar – certainly not us. We recorded the whole hunt and attack phase, including intercepting a voice message hinting at the intruder being nothing to do with the exercise.

Next day we got in amongst the strike carriers, passing through their outer screens to get a close look at the mighty *F.D. Roosevelt* and *Forrestal*, observed their operating procedures and recorded a great deal of tactical voice from ships and aircraft.

At nightfall we hauled off towards the North African coast to recharge whilst snorkelling. Suddenly there was a sharp explosion in the darkened control-room and fluid cascaded in under pressure. At the same instant we lost all telemotor (hydraulic) power which put the hydroplanes out of action and meant that main vents and the crucial snort air intake hull-valve could only be shut by hand. Having done that, I surfaced. Enemy radar transmissions were slowly receding to the westwards, so there was time to take stock of the situation. The breakdown was caused by the alloy bowl of the main hydraulic system filter exploding and spewing all its liquid power out to form a horrible skid-pan on the control room deck. Emergency by-pass arrangements were made and we soon dived again, by now heading west at our best speed to catch up with the main formation. It was a 225-mile chase, mostly carried out snorkelling at 9 knots. Not only did we easily maintain contact with the main force, but reached the eastern approaches to Gibraltar in time to get in among some further exercises there, such as replenishment at sea.

After spending the night off Tetuan, we made a wide clockwise sweep around Algeciras Bay at first light next day, a Saturday. Motoring past Punta Carnero lighthouse marking the western end of Gibraltar Bay we got good periscope pictures of the lighthouse keeper who emerged from his tower, took down his pants and squatted near the water's edge.

Skirting past Algeciras itself, we dodged a few ferries bound for Ceuta or Tangier, whilst noting the berthing arrangements inside the moles at Gibraltar. There was an uninterrupted line of large superstructures showing along the $1^1/2$ miles of breakwater. A lot of chat was recorded, mostly of an administrative nature, but it all added to our library of frequencies and callsigns. We headed south, close outside the detached mole, by now using the periscope circumspectly. At one moment, on putting my eye to it as it broke surface, I found myself looking at the planking of an Admiralty 14-ft sailing dinghy. About thirty of them poured out through the harbour entrance at the start of a race, with us right in the middle. But no one sighted us, or if they did, they did not believe their eyes.

So we slowly withdrew to seaward, once more passing Punta Carnero and on towards Tarifa and Trafalgar. At nightfall we were able to snorkel clear of the area and head for the barn.

The ease with which we had operated undetected in excellent sonar conditions for so long and the detail we brought home surprised many people, but not, of course, Baldy Hezlet, the Chief of Staff who had master-minded the whole operation. For him we had proved that a corresponding probe among Soviet forces was a justifiable risk, unlikely to create an embarrassing international incident. I was debriefed in front of the Admiralty Board. Soon afterwards a summary of the results of the patrol was circulated to Flag and Commanding Officers who had taken part in the Combined Fleet exercises.

The Flag Officer Submarines' Summer War exercises were held off the Shetlands. One of its phases involved us patrolling near the Outer Skerries lighthouse to intercept 'enemy' submarines entering or leaving a nearby bay where one of our depot-ships established a base. The lighthouse itself dominated the area with an excellent view of the approaches to the temporary base. So we launched a folbot with two officers armed with a portable voice radio, several bottles of Scotch and a haversack full of 1¼-pound charges. Peter Lucy and a Midshipman under training, Rodney Carne, who was soon afterwards killed in the Fleet Air Arm, paddled ashore to the lighthouse and 'captured it', persuading the keepers not to report their presence by bribing them with Scotch and fags. For the next two days they kept a lookout over the surrounding area whilst we patrolled undetected dived to seaward. Whenever an enemy submarine appeared, they tossed a signal charge into the water, which was our moment to raise the VHF antenna and listen on a pre-arranged frequency. 'Customer for you, outward bound in position Alpha Lima Four Seven. Course 135 degrees at 16 knots.' Without acknowledgement, we moved in for the kill and maintained a watertight blockade of the enemy base. When we recovered the folbot they came with lobsters obtained by bartering Scotch with the lighthouse keepers.

At the subsequent wash-up, Flag Officer Submarines accepted this ploy as a realistic possibility and I did not get the roasting I expected and probably deserved.

No such games were permissible on our next independent mission, when we batted against serious opposition with some unexpected results. We may well have been detected during a close encounter at one point, and then had anxious moments when our S-band search-receiver was found to be U/S. It was necessary to surface at night and then break the pressure-tight seal on the top window of its housing in the big periscope, a prolonged and, tricky operation during which we were wide open to detection. In the ordinary way this repair would not be contemplated except in a properly equipped periscope workshop ashore. Peter Lucy, who did the job alone, was under no illusions that if we were jumped by unfriendly forces, I might have to dive the boat under him. After our return to Gosport I was unable to get official recognition of his feat for fear of compromising our mission.

At the subsequent debriefing in the Admiralty the First Sea Lord was 'Wee Mac' (Admiral of the Fleet Sir Rhoderick McGrigor). My message was simply that, apart from the raw data which had to be analysed elsewhere in slow time, we had returned with some hard evidence that our naval policy should exploit the opposition's demonstrable weakness in anti-submarine warfare, with priorities adjusted accordingly. Alongside me the Flag Officer Submarines purred.

There was silence among the ranks of the Naval Staff, who were there with all the Sea Lords, broken by an incredulous top planner, addressing his remarks to the Chief of Naval Staff:

'You will appreciate, Sir, that the logical conclusion to this presentation could have far-reaching adverse effects on our Strike Carrier programme and the development of the Buccaneer aircraft.' Quite so. A few months later he resigned and joined Blackburn Aircraft as Chief Executive – to build a new generation of overweight subsonic aircraft in Britain's last effort to play in the Big League of naval air power.

The limited number of those of us who thought about these matters at all wasted no opportunity in pointing out the sheer cost-effectiveness of a missile-firing submarine with a crew of under 100 and a relatively modest logistics tail, against the astronomical numbers in a vulnerable carrier striking force, never mind its supporting auxiliaries and air stations. But it was to no avail. As our national resources declined, so all our priorities were directed at the design and construction of replacements for *Ark Royal* and *Eagle* to give us a semblance of an independent seaborne deterrent and a place at the top table of NATO. It was to be nearly a decade later that our Defence Staff were forced by circumstances for which none of them could claim any credit to make decisions that should have at least been under serious discussion then and there.

I did not know it until someone sent me a cutting from *The Times*, but the last word was said by one of my junior ratings on a train going on leave. Someone in the carriage felt that his detailed description of our recent activities should be reported to the authorities. He was convicted by court-martial of being in breach of the Official Secrets Act.

Soon after I left *Totem* she went into refit and all the officers moved on, most of them upwards. At intervals we have met again to dine on the sufficient pretext of celebrating the steady climb of our old shipmate John Fieldhouse to the topmost post attainable by any Naval Officer, an Admiral of the Fleet and a seat in the Upper House. Twice we dined in the Garrick, then in the Chief of the Defence Staff's luxurious quarters at Greenwich and in 1990 at the Royal Yacht Squadron Castle in Cowes. Six of the officers clocked in for the last dinner with the same wives to whom they were already married when all first met in Chatham Dockyard nearly 40 years previously. On every occasion Bob Hall, the Coxswain, has been present, claiming much of the credit for Snorkers' meteoric career.

At our first reunion dinner in 1982 there was a blank page to fill in on the menu. So I reproduced six confidential reports on the officers, each of them identified only by a key letter. 'Who made First Sea Lord? Who didn't?' was the title. Some thought they were the actual reports they had received from me in 1954.

A. An invaluable member of the team who might pass for a Gunnery Officer manqué, but as such has kept in balance the rest of the wardroom: the dilettante and those who toil in the vineyards. Not surprisingly he is a dependable back in the Hockey XI, especially on a bumpy pitch. Recommended for promotion.
B. An officer of outstanding ability who holds his cards close to his chest and never loses count of the trumps. A shipmate of rare quality and even temperament, with whom it has been the greatest pleasure to serve.
C. An able and promising officer.
D. An officer of great ingenuity and technical ability, self-confident charm and intermittent enthusiasm. We have all enjoyed his occasional visits to the submarine in harbour. His adroit reconciliation of the Wardroom Wine Accounts and indifference to accepted precepts of Naval Storekeeping are a model for all who plan to make their way in life outside the Service.
E. Upright, straightforward and downright. His quiet avuncular manner and appearance are deceptive – indeed, have deceived

many. Behind them lie gilt-edged officer-like qualities and an uncompromising determination to run a taut ship with a soft centre. Should go far.

F. I cannot speak too highly of this officer, who has kept the submarine at the highest level of operational efficiency throughout a long and varied commission. Strongly recommended for higher responsibilities.

Over the port I had to admit that only 'C' was authentic, that being the Captain of HMS *Dolphin's* assessment of me after I had fallen foul of the Admiral Superintendent at Chatham. 'D' was the banker (Peter Lucy), whilst 'A' was intended for Robin Heath who was unlucky not reaching Flag rank after being Chief of Staff to the Polaris Executive. There was much discussion over the last three. Midge Fieldhouse claimed 'F' to have been targeted on her man, but I had to point out that the 'taut ship with the soft centre' was the give-away in 'E' being the future Chief of the Defence Staff. 'F' was for Greg Courtier and 'B' for our unobtrusive plumber, Geoff Cornish.

The old boat came to a sad end, well past what I judged to be her 'sell-by' date. After one more commission she was duly sold to the Israeli Navy, who took her over in June, 1965, and renamed her *Dakar*. After a prolonged refit, incorporating the additional topweight of a wet-and-dry chamber for frogmen to operate from, she sailed for the Eastern Mediterranean in November 1967, considered to be short on work-up and surface stability.

She never made it, due, as any ex-*Totem* matelot will tell you, to having left her totem-pole ashore. It was originally presented by a tribe of Canadian Indians when she was built in 1944, with the solemn warning that she was doomed if it was ever removed. On a visit to Halifax after my time it was stolen, but quickly replaced by another which is in the Submarine Museum at Gosport.

There followed six months' relaxation at the Royal Navy Staff College at Greenwich, a lot of it spent in the watering holes of the West End. The only officers who had to work all hours during the course were the Lieutenant-Commanders in the zone for promotion and the handful of Army officers present. It seems that a good report from the Naval Staff Course got them priority to go to the Army Staff College at Camberley, without which their military careers were put on the back-burner. The naval Commanders, especially those like myself who had their next appointment in their hip pocket, realized they were mostly at Greenwich to fill in a gap between jobs. One of my playmates was Chris Foxley-Norris who was clearly destined to become Chief of the Air Staff, which he duly did. It was apparent that no amount of veiled threats from the pedantic Directing Staff was going to influence his career or his application to duty at Greenwich one way or the other. Dick Tibbatts was also on the course and gave some of the visiting lecturers a hard time by questioning the effectiveness or even relevance of both the carriers and the V-bomber force. At the end of the course I was invited to address them all on *Totem*'s surveillance patrol against the Combined Fleets in the Western Mediterranean.

★ 20 ★

WITH THE US NAVY'S
SUBMARINE FORCE

Towards the end of April, 1955, RMS *Queen Elizabeth* set off down Southampton Water on a voyage to New York. We leant over the rails watching the Isle of Wight recede with our three small girls and their vivacious young nanny. She carried with her a dark secret shared only by an indulgent doctor and a vital piece of paper certifying that she was not pregnant. Without it the Admiralty would not have paid her round-trip fare. She was delivered of a beautiful baby boy a few months later, which had to be adopted at birth, otherwise she could not face her brute of a father back at home.

One of the other passengers in a list of under a hundred, looked after by a crew of 1200, also had dubious qualifications for making the trip. He was going over to get into the same ring as the reigning World Heavyweight Champion, Rocky Marciano. On arrival at New York the reporters and photographers swarmed on board, took one look at our hero, pumped up like a capon, and promptly christened him the Battersea Butterball. Against the odds Don Cockell was not carried out on a stretcher until he had survived eight rounds with the Brockton Bomber.

Unknown to me until I read it in the Cunarder's newspaper, the day of our departure took its place in the history books for a third and altogether more significant reason. A signal had arrived on the desk of the Chief of Naval Operations in the Pentagon from the newest addition to the U.S. Navy: '*Nautilus* under way on nuclear power'.

Officially I was appointed to the British Joint Services Mission as an Assistant Attaché with liaison duties with the Submarine Forces of the United States Navy. Partly due to the popularity of Commander Toby Weston, the man I had come to succeed, I could not have been given a warmer welcome, either in the Submarine Warfare Division in the Pentagon (Op.31) or at the Atlantic Submarine Force headquarters at New London, Connecticut. Right away I met the other reason why I got such a generous welcome – Rear Admiral Frank T. Watkins. Not only was he charming and solicitous, which rubbed off on his staff and indeed throughout his Command, but he had been an unreserved admirer of our Submarine Service ever since he had been on the USN Attaché's staff in London and escaped from his desk to make a number of patrols in our Mediterranean submarines.

This was before America entered the war, so he always reported on board in plain clothes as a naval correspondent, carrying a faked passport in case of being taken prisoner. He had made patrols in *Triumph* with one of our best and much loved C.O.s, 'Sammy' Woods who later became a Commander-in-Chief.

The routine established by Toby Weston was that I should always spend a working week each month in New London at COMSUBLANT's headquarters where they kept a desk with my name on it. The Admiral suggested that I called on him at 0930 every day I was there for a cup of coffee and a chat. During my second week he leant forward and asked quietly: 'Do you mind if I call you John?' There was a lot more than just playing golf and exchanging gossip with him. He was deeply pained by the manner in which Hyman Rickover had usurped some of his Command responsibilities for the nuclear submarines and, especially, the jealous guard he kept against intrusion from British eyes. On 20 June, 1955, Congress ratified the U.S./U.K. Military Atomic Co-Operation Agreement which, at first glance, augured well. It stated, inter alia, that 'the USA may exchange with the UK such atomic information as the USA considers necessary for the development of the UK's defense plans.' Just who was going to exercise the discretion ominously permitted by the wording of the agreement was not at first apparent. The Royal Navy was soon to find out.

All the operational thinking about the future deployment and weapons for the nuclear fleet was passed to me at an early stage by the Admiral himself. He had a special team at his headquarters who were charged with this task. Submarine Development Group 2 (there must have been a SubDevGru 1 in Pearl Harbor but I never came across them) was presided over by Captain Slade Cutter, a national hero, often recognized by taxi drivers, not for his wartime exploits as a skipper in the Pacific but because he kicked the winning field goal in a pre-war Army-Navy match. He had also been North American Collegiate Heavyweight boxing champion and had been tempted to leave Annapolis and chance his luck against Joe Louis.

Slade ensured that I at least gave the appearance of being a working member of his Development Group. He appointed me as a member of his hatchet squad which examined candidates for the annual award of the Force 'E' (for Excellence, meaning the best operational boat in SUBLANT command). This involved going to sea in boats who had reached the quarter-finals at New London, Portsmouth, Norfolk, Charleston and Key West. My job was to cover the navigation side and judge how well it was integrated into the Attack Team.

A few C.O.s hinted at questioning my right to act as an adjudicator. None did after they'd got the message from Slade.

The semi-finalists were assembled at St Thomas in the US Virgin Islands, where our task was to present the Admiral with two from which he would select the champion. We had to transfer between submarines at sea off Charlotte Amalie, usually judging two submarines each day. A barge was provided for moving the five of us from one boat to another. Smoking a large cigar, Slade stepped on to the casing of one of the 'Tang' Class attack boats, lying stopped with its forehatch open.

'Welcome aboard, Captain. What would you like us to do for you? There's coffee and breakfast for you in the wardroom,' reported the C.O.

'Fine. Go to 700 feet,' was all Slade said as he disappeared down the hatch with his stopwatch running.

After a final party, during which the Admiral announced the winner and presented her skipper with the 'E' pendant, we set off to fly home to Groton in a twin-engined Navy version of the Convair 880. Landing at Bermuda, Admiral Watkins stepped out of the aircraft, looked around at the cloudless blue sky and told the pilot that he didn't like the look of the weather. 'Guess Groton will be socked in soon,' he said to the pilot. So the golf bags were unloaded. Two days later we were back in New London.

There was a NATO exercise being held in the Faeroes-Iceland gap, so the Admiral had me flown to join one of his boats at Reykjavik and back from Prestwick after it was all over. I won't forget the 17-hour flight in a militarized DC6 in a hurry.

Keeping abreast of their technical developments was a major task. In those days there were sufficient funds to pursue several major lines of research and trials in parallel, a luxury denied to the Royal Navy. Nowhere was this more apparent than in their plans to deliver the nuclear deterrent. Until a solid propellant with controllable burn-down could be developed, they had to plan on air-breathing missiles. Soon I was at sea in the converted Fleet boat

Tunny which carried a radio-controlled sub-sonic jet-engined missile in a hangar built over the after-casing.

The drill was to surface within 60 miles of the target, open the hangar door, rig up the launch rails and fire off what amounted to a pilotless aircraft. There followed a crash shut-down and dive which seemed to place considerable reliance on electrical door-switch indicators telling the C.O. when everything was secured in the hangar. I seem to remember that par was 4 minutes from first breaking surface until being back at periscope depth with a guidance antenna up to make sure the Regulus bird did not drift off course. In practice a chase-plane picked up the missile and guided it down to a normal touch-down on a nearby Navy airfield. In spite of its obvious vulnerability to detection during launch and flight, the USN pressed on with its development. A second boat was converted which had the rare distinction of firing 1000 Regulus missiles without losing one of them.

During my time they launched *Growler* and *Grayback*, the first purpose-built missile-firing submarines in the history of naval warfare. On paper they were formidable, with all the attributes of a fast underwater attack submarine embodied in a design which included twin missile hangars let into the hull on either side of the fore-ends. They even had Regulus II missiles planned with a strike range of 1000 miles, and inertial guidance. But the fatal flaw of having to surface to launch their birds aroused a good deal of scepticism even among the most dedicated missile adherents.

Another project which I kept a close eye on was SUBROC, a missile which could be fired from submerged out of a standard 21-inch torpedo tube, then skim across the surface homing on to a surface target up to 60 miles away. Alternatively, it could be programmed to plunge into the sea at the end of its flight and destroy a submarine. This weapon would transform the Royal Navy's potential wartime role.

The Aerojet Corporation at Azusa on the outskirts of Los Angeles was one of the defence contractors on my visiting list. During a routine visit I was taken to what looked like a potting-shed outside, but turned out to be an armoured bunker. There on a steel table was a heap of dirt inside a clear vertical tube. It was ignited at the bottom, then fizzled and crackled its way to the top, emitting power at a constant pressure. 'It'll do the same underwater,' my contact assured me.

By this time the USN had its own submarine missile think-tank under Rear Admiral Raborn located away from the Pentagon in the old clapboard Main Navy Building on Constitution Avenue, where our naval staff was also housed. There were other distinguished tenants. Each morning at 0830 a frail old man in uniform was helped into an office below mine. It was Fleet Admiral Ernest J. King, their wartime navy chief, still earning his full pay as a 5-star Admiral. A few doors away was another set of modest offices where I first met Rear Admiral Rickover. Here he not only ran the whole nuclear construction programme with a tiny staff, but conducted his notorious interviews to select all the officers being inducted into the nuclear navy. His technique was to try and throw the potential candidate, chosen from the cream of the Submarine Force, off balance by aggressive questioning intended to provoke an argument. He invited the officer arriving to be interviewed to take a seat opposite him. The chair had six inches sawn off one leg. One failed candidate said he'd rather be interrogated by the KGB after being caught with a roll of film of the Kola Inlet in his briefcase. I went in there to see Joe Seynhorst who had done a major exercise in *Totem* with me the year before and was now a top Rickover aide. Rickover did not even look up when I was introduced. The other officer present was leaning anxiously over a table in the corner with the general demeanour of one having reached the peak of his career when adjusting the level in the coffee machine. So I shook hands monosyllabically with Lieutenant Jimmy Carter and left. When the Royal Navy finally got into the nuclear business years later Rickover insisted that he personally select our candidates for Command and all other key posts. John Fieldhouse told me he was kept cooling his heels in a Washington hotel for three weeks whilst waiting for Rickover to concede to Flag Officer Submarines the right to choose Captains of nuclear submarines in the Royal Navy.

The only other time I met Rickover was at Honolulu airport. I was hitching a ride to San Francisco in a small USN aircraft which had been sent to bring him back after taking his first holiday in seven years – a long weekend on the islands. We were kept waiting two hours in the military VIP lounge due to traffic congestion.

'Well,' he said, 'it's only to be expected: after all this is the second busiest airport in the world after O'Hare in Chicago.' My suggestion that Heathrow was as bad or worse was greeted with a storm of derision. Instead of shutting my trap like many before me, I ploughed on, quoting statistics recently published in the *New York Times*.

It was a long ride to California by turbo-prop with no one else on the aircraft to talk to. The eight hours passed in total silence. I never saw him again but had plenty of time to study the man. It was then that I first noted his physical resemblance and similarity of methods to the Father of the modern Royal Navy – Admiral Jacky Fisher.

We were due a visit from our new First Sea Lord, Admiral Mountbatten, and I was directed to write a brief for him about Rickover. It struck me as being not unlike marking a Romanov's card before meeting Rasputin.

I told Mountbatten how, despite a frustrating and friendless naval career, towards the end of it (sic) Rickover had emerged as the single-minded, single-handed progenitor of the nuclear submarine. From the day Admiral Chester Nimitz signed his famous letter to the Secretary of Defense in December, 1947, stating a firm military requirement for the nuclear-powered submarine, Rickover took off. Here are extracts from the brief I wrote 35 years ago for Mountbatten:

'The story of the building of *Nautilus* reveals a restless, lonely and ruthless man, working around the clock to get the boat to sea, regardless of opposition. It is said that he stoops to quite unethical methods if the end justifies the means – as they always have in his book. For example, he would play off one firm or department against another by attributing quite untrue statements to each other.

'It is difficult to assess Admiral Rickover's true importance today. One must presume that, by virtue of continuing to hold the chief responsibility for the development of naval reactors both in the Bureau of Ships and the AEC, he is now engaged in implementing the USN's recently declared policy to put nuclear propulsion into all ships which will be employed in offensive roles, including CVAs and their escorts.

'But there are many who are eager to point out that his mission was accomplished with the launching of *Nautilus*; and that he will now be discarded as not being whole-heartedly behind nuclear power for surface ships. In any case, they say that he is not a physicist so much as a hard-driving co-ordinator of a specific engineering project, who has made too many enemies in the process for his survival in the Navy.

'Much of this is wishful thinking by his detractors. The USN Submarine Force freely admits that, but for him, *Nautilus* would not be at sea today. They regard him as being more influential than any other serving officer, except perhaps the CNO himself. They accept as a painful necessity his dictatorial methods. Some even explain his boorish manners and insulting conversational gambits simply as devices to make his listeners remember what he has to say.

'One thing is certain: Rickover will pursue his self-appointed course regardless of the opinions of friend or foe, particularly friend.

Even his bitterest enemies cannot deny his single-minded devotion to duty. Nor have they ever attributed to him ambitions for commercial or financial rewards – now or in the future. Nor can he be dismissed outright as a megalomaniac. Whilst he shuns personal publicity of any sort, he has carefully built himself a solid political lobby and the support of the most influential voices in the media and in the highest corridors of power to maintain the priorities he needs for the continuation of his nuclear programme.

'In this respect he bears an uncanny resemblance to the Royal Navy's Jacky Fisher, who became First Sea Lord in 1905 at the age of 64 and proceeded to ram through his revolutionary *Dreadnought* programme, which gave Britain the lead in high-speed, hard-hitting capital ships long before the Great War broke out. Nothing was allowed to stand in his path, even those amongst the highest in the land who mistrusted his methods and feared for sacred naval traditions being dismantled.

'To further his aims, Fisher used the Press and friends in Parliament to a degree hitherto unknown. He wrote anonymous articles in *The Observer*. Friendly journalists got special briefings from him. Soon the public took up his cry: "We want eight, and we won't wait." The resemblance does not end in the two Admirals' drive and ruthlessness, as their portraits show. But to find out what makes Hyman Rickover tick, it is necessary to start by taking account of a lifetime spent in antipathetic surroundings. In the end one has to settle for the fact that he is motivated by a love of the Service which he joined as an expedient and which has repeatedly reminded him how unwelcome he is, rather than by hope of honours, self-aggrandisement or financial reward.'

As Mountbatten flew home after being publicly ostracized by the Nuclear Propulsion Club, he wondered how Rickover could be persuaded to hand over to the British the fruits of his high endeavour. It took nearly two years to bring about a meeting between them. The effort was as far-reaching as it was unexpected. The introvert iconoclast from the Ukraine, who had, by his own efforts, risen to be one of the most powerful men in the Western world, fell under the spell and aura of Queen Victoria's great-grandson. Yet this unlikely friendship overcame much of the undue delay which the development of the British SSN had already suffered.

In March, 1958, Rickover visited Britain. He arrived at the Ministry of Defence while there was a meeting going on of the top-level U.K. Nuclear Advisory Committee to consider a gloomy progress report on the British-designed propulsion system for HMS *Dreadnought*. Suddenly Mountbatten entered the room with his guest from

Washington at his side. He announced that the two of them had just shaken hands on a deal to install a complete Skipjack propulsion unit in our first nuclear submarine.

But it was not until 1961 that Rickover finally met someone in the U.K. defence world whom he considered worthy of his confidence. Sir Solly (now Lord) Zuckerman was the Chief Scientific Adviser to the Ministry of Defence. His qualifications and international stature as a scientist were such that they could not be brushed aside, as were most of our experts who came into the Rickover orbit when the 1956 Agreement finally led to bilateral talks. Their close friendship was to the great benefit of the Royal Navy's ballistic missile programme in its formative stages.

To revert to Washington just before Mountbatten's visit, one day the phone rang on my desk. It was Admiral Raborn from next door, asking me to bring my Admiral and any other interested members of our staff to a presentation he proposed to make to us in one hour's time. So I rounded up my boss (Admiral Sir Geoffrey Barnard) and our Staff Gunnery specialist and filed into Raborn's office.

The object of the pitch he made was to confirm the breakthrough which the Aerojet people had made in demonstrating the feasibility of a solid propellant with controlled burn-down. This had opened the door for a submarine-launched ballistic missile, code-named Polaris, which would now get top priority.

The proposition he wanted the UK staff to take away for urgent consideration was that, if the Brits would take over the development of SUBROC, then we would be joint partners in the Polaris programme at no cost to ourselves. Looking back, it is hard to believe that this offer, no doubt timed in advance of the impending visit to Washington by our new First Sea Lord, was made seven years before we reluctantly had Polaris thrust upon us after the failure of Skybolt.

The CNO was Arleigh Burke, a destroyer hero who saw eye-to-eye with Mountbatten and had invited him over to be the first non-American to go to sea in *Nautilus*. As the RAF Transport Command's Britannia was over-flying Greenland, Rickover used his political clout with leading Senators to invoke his interpretation of the security rules concerning nuclear submarines which put *Nautilus* firmly off-limits to our First Sea Lord. There was consternation as plans were abruptly switched to a day trip to Key West to ride USS *Albacore*, the experimental prototype of the fat, short submarine which was to dominate all USN hull design in the nuclear navy. She developed only 1700 SHP on her single shaft but, thanks to her hull configuration, she could comfortably exceed 30 knots submerged, at that time by far the fastest submarine in the world. She was also highly manoeuvrable with joy-stick hydraulic controls for her hydroplanes and rudder.

Soon after diving we levelled off at 200 feet and motored quietly whilst the CNO was host to a gourmet seafood lunch in her surprisingly commodious wardroom. I thought the silver candlesticks were overdoing it, although I imagine they assumed that our former Viceroy of India never ate against any other setting. Where, I wondered, was the mounted band of the Bengal Lancers? Once the spotless napery had been cleared away *Albacore* went through her paces, doing everything bar looping the loop. Making a 30-knot dive to 600 feet using 35° bow-down angle with the rudder hard a'starboard was beautifully under control, even when we had the two Chiefs of Naval Staff side-by-side on the controls.

The next day Mountbatten went to sea off Norfolk for a Regulus firing, but it was apparent that his plans and hopes for the future still centred on the Carrier Striking Fleet. Admiral Raborn's proposition was listened to in polite silence.

Life on the domestic front was as hectic as it was hilarious. We lived in a comfortable rented house in Chevy Chase chosen for its proximity to a grade school which was held to be superior to those in the ghettoes of the SE suburbs of the District of Columbia. We survived the launch of the Edsel (Ford) and settled for a Studebaker which was years ahead of its time but never caught on in the domestic market of the day. Given Duty Free booze, we could afford to entertain well. For most of our delightful guests it had to be on a Friday night, for they could not contemplate going to church on Sundays with a hangover, let alone report at the Pentagon that way on Mondays. Dinner parties introduced their men to tawny port being circulated in a decanter after their wives had been shepherded out by Sylvia to hit the coffee and cordials, as they described anything from Southern Comfort to Benedictine. 'What's going on in there?' the wives would complain after ten minutes. 'Are they watching a dirty movie?'

Off duty time at New London we spent mostly at the little 18th-century port of Stonington where a brass plaque commemorates the burghers having successfully withstood the bombardment of HMS *Warspite* and others in the war of 1812. I was then invited to navigate a 48ft Allden ketch called *Varuna* on the Bermuda Race. It conflicted with a major submarine exercise being planned by COMSUBLANT at the time, with a few British boats involved. I had a hand in planning the exercise, so arranged for the post-exercise critique (or wash-up) to be held in Bermuda at the end of the race. I was involved in the presentation of the wash-up, so it was as well that we enjoyed a reaching breeze all the way which delivered me on time to pull off a bravura extempore performance without giving a hint that I hadn't been in the Ops Room of the submarine tender, but had threaded our way down the rhumbline from Newport Rhode Island through heavy sea and air anti-submarine searches.

In the middle of our time the Anglo-French invasion of Suez was thwarted by US intervention triggered off by Secretary of State John Foster Dulles whom Winston referred to as 'the piece of cod who passeth all understanding'. It was no concern of ours in Washington, but we received spontaneous messages of support from all quarters. One Admiral rang at 4 am to say that he hoped we wouldn't turn our backs on the enterprise. Later he explained his calling at that hour on the grounds that our telephone was less likely to be tapped at that time.

In the middle of August I received a phone call of a different sort from Op 31 in the Pentagon. Pete Galantin was the hero of bringing back USS *Halibut* after a depth charge had exploded on impact with her 4-inch gun mounted on the casing, damaging her beyond repair. Would I care to go on an unspecified submarine surveillance mission, sailing from Japan?

Three days later I was playing golf at Myonoshita at the foot of Mount Fujiyama. I had arrived the day before, straight from my desk in the Main Navy Building in Washington, and reported to the USN at their base in Yokosuka. I was under orders to go to sea on a prolonged operation in the Guppy Class submarine USS *Stickleback*. The trip carried a high security classification, my uniform was too conspicuous so I was told to get lost until the morning of departure.

The British Naval Attaché was on hand to whisk me away to the hills, where I was joined by my father, who had flown up specially from Hong Kong, and General Hunter Harris, commanding US Air Forces in the area and a hell-raiser after my father's heart – and mine. So much for tight security.

We played golf all day and lived Japanese-style after the massage and paper-and-scissors games with the geishas who cooked our sukiyakis.

The trip in *Stickleback* lasted from late August until early October. One of its objectives was to intercept the annual reinforcements to the Soviet East Asiatic Fleet as they emerged from the Bering Sea after the long voyage from the Kola Inlet. Nowadays it would all be covered by satellite; even then there was little we could add to reports from air reconnaissance, except to check them off in detail and get accurate turn-counts (speed derived from the r.p.m. of their screws). Perhaps we were a back-up for air reconnaissance, or the USN Submarine Force was anxious to prove a point.

Whatever the reason, it was a very long trip, including five weeks consecutively dived, all for not more than three days' action. Time passed with endless cups of coffee and two movies a day. For a memento of my time with them I'd brought with me a half-gallon teapot with a beautiful quilted cosy made by my wife and a few canisters of Earl Grey.

The Americans fell about with laughter, sending up the whole ritual of warming the pot and drinking with a crooked little finger. But, best of all was the Great Weight-Shedding Contest. When I joined, the Captain, Art Newton, was under the gun from the medics to lose 20 pounds. I suspect that confirmation of his promotion to Commander may have depended upon it. As usual, I was carrying a few spare pounds, so volunteered to be a pace-horse.

Each Sunday at 1100 Art and I had to appear in the control-room stark naked for an official weighing by the self-appointed judges; none of your bathroom scales, but using a butcher's steelyard slung under the conning-tower hatch. The whole crew were betting on ounces, never mind the pounds. Rumour had it that one sailor had to sell his car on arrival at Pearl Harbor to settle his bets on the contest. Sergeant Bilko was lurking somewhere.

It was a close-run thing. Art's backers included one of the cooks, who was forever waking me out of a deep sleep, waving a steaming hot fresh pizza under my nose. That was no problem: I still don't like cooked tomatoes in any form. But when we crossed the International Date Line heading for home the submarine went deep for a crew party during the dogwatches. There was much music and many sophisticated side-shows. Some of the fruit juice had been spiked by an ingredient added from the pharmacist mate's locker. But the high point was a magnificent coconut gateau with 'Rule Britannia' and the White Ensign perfectly sculpted into the icing. As I write I can still taste that cake, but I got up like a game 'un to take the last fence just in front, weighing in at landfall having lost $21^1/2$ pounds since my last night in Myonoshita, a mere 8 ounces ahead of Art.

To a man they were great shipmates in a submarine run quietly and smoothly by a crew at least the equal to any I ever served with.

On securing alongside, we were hustled into the debriefing by COMSUBPAC (Commander Submarine Force Pacific). I made some cautious comments suggesting how we might have got more out of the trip if our objective had called for more sophisticated electronic intercept and recording gear, so as to gather raw tactical data which only a submarine could do by playing it pretty close to the horns. This seemed to strike a sympathetic chord, for I was paraded the next day to repeat my views in front of the Commander-in-Chief Pacific himself. It was none other than Admiral Felix B. Stump, formerly C-in-C Atlantic when I had been briefly on liaison duty in his flagship USS *Wisconsin*.

That had been six years previously, but the C-in-C gave me a warm welcome at his headquarters in Pearl Harbor. I said my piece without interruption from the tight-lipped senior aviators on his staff who clearly resented this upstart Limey making a direct pitch on behalf of the USN submariners.

What, if anything, came of it I know not. But USS *Stickleback* was rammed and sunk by a destroyer on her first day of shake-down after her stand-off period. Luckily the whole crew scrambled out in time.

But my teapot and its padded cosy rest in 2000 fathoms.

★ 21 ★

JAS

Our time in Washington was cut short by another sudden appointment, or pierhead jump in naval parlance.

We sailed from New York in the old White Star liner *Britannic* which had survived the Second World War as a troopship and now had her interior restored to its art-deco original. The mahogany-lined lift was operated by the same pot-bellied Able Seaman who had controlled its shuttle service from the lowest cabins to the Boat Deck throughout the thirty years since she had been commissioned.

As we made our way sedately across the North Atlantic to Liverpool, kaleidoscopic memories formed of some uniquely American phenomena which had influenced our daily lives. They focused on three 'Es': Eisenhower getting into the White House; Elvis becoming first choice amongst radio disc-jockeys; and the Edsel car, whose launch made millions for advertising agencies but quickly bankrupted thousands of Ford dealers from coast to coast. Fortunately for us, the word 'environment' had not yet entered their language.

The reason for our hasty return to England was that it was said that I was short-listed to go as Commander of the Royal Yacht *Britannia*, but that happily came to nought when Terry Lewin was chosen. Obviously it didn't do him any harm, for he ended up as Chief of the Defence Staff at the time of the Falklands. Instead I went as Fleet Operations Officer to the Commander-in-Chief, Home Fleet, then flying his flag in the former submarine depot-ship HMS *Maidstone*. As and when necessary, he reluctantly moved ashore wearing his NATO hat as C-in-C Eastern Atlantic to a hole in the ground in Northwood, Middlesex. Significantly it was in the same grounds as the headquarters of AO C-in-C Coastal Command RAF who clung to the status befitting his unique role as being a joint NATO C-in-C (CINCAIREASTLANT). This Gilbert and Sullivan command structure led to them being referred to by the mystified Americans as Tweedledum and Tweedledee.

But NATO affairs had been set aside at the time of my joining in Portsmouth, with all eyes on an impending visit to the Home Fleet by the Queen. This was to be no ordinary visit, for she had decided to spend three days afloat with the Fleet at Invergordon.

The Queen and Prince Philip arrived in the Royal Yacht directly from a state visit to Denmark. As she steamed towards the anchorage she was met by the entire Fleet who approached in two columns on a reciprocal course at 25 knots, wheeled alternately from each column and then turned on a parallel course in single line ahead, overtaking close along the Yacht's starboard side with all ships' companies lining the sides and giving three perfectly timed cheers, with the whites of thousands of cap covers held aloft in unison on the last syllable of each 'Hooray'. Since the assembled Fleet included three aircraft carriers, three cruisers and eighteen destroyers, not counting the submarines and auxiliaries which stayed at anchor, it was a spectacular bit of choreography calling for split-second timing. The C-in-C and his staff were embarked in the 40-knot cruiser-minelayer *Apollo* which fell in close astern of *Britannia* as the twenty-four combat ships went through the hoop, giving us the same view of the pageantry as Her Majesty. Needless to say it was not done without rehearsals at full speed, not wishing to repeat the *Victoria* and *Camperdown* collision off Malta in 1893 when two columns of battleships were ordered to turn together inwards without first ensuring that there was enough searoom between them. The C-in-C who ordered the fatal manoeuvre, Admiral Tryon, lost his life, but survivors testified that he ignored warnings given on his bridge as the two columns lumbered to their inevitable shunt. They were probably too terrified of him to intervene.

Our C-in-C certainly looked as though it didn't pay to contradict him unless you were on sure ground. Admiral Sir John A.S. Eccles (known everywhere as Jas) stood 6'4" tall, a Black Belt judo exponent, Japanese interpreter, former Flag Officer Aircraft Carriers and C-in-C of the Royal Australian Navy. His formidable presence alone commanded immediate respect, but those closest to him recognized what lay behind his staccato orders and aloof manner. Every detail of the Royal visit had to get past his silent scrutiny, with consideration for the comfort and entertainment of his beloved 31-year-old Queen uppermost in mind.

There were commemorative dessert plates specially produced by Minton with an intricate pattern of national emblems, ropework and foul anchors designed by Jas himself. They were used at a banquet in the hangar-deck of one of the aircraft carriers for all the Commanding Officers and above in the Fleet. A week before this event the plates were unpacked from the straw-lined barrels in which they had been delivered. Jas immediately spotted a small deviation from his design, so the whole lot went back to the makers. They reappeared on the afternoon of the great dinner.

It all went without a hitch, ending with a massed fly-past of all squadrons from the Carriers as *Britannia* sailed away. Soon the flagship was alone, heading south off Peterhead on a brilliant sunny evening. The Commander-in-Chief summoned his entire staff to the cuddy – his cabin aft – to splice the mainbrace on orders from the Monarch. It was my first taste of the flip side of his quarterdeck manner. Not only was he a superb host but the wittiest raconteur I ever heard.

It seems that he had two large rare palm trees dug up and stolen from the drive of his home outside Winchester. The police were satisfied that they were the same ones that he later spotted outside the Godbegot Hotel, whose porter was duly arraigned before a circuit judge. No jury could possibly doubt the word of the Commander-in-Chief as he described movingly how he could not possibly put a valuation on the trees. They were part of his heritage, having been cherished by him for years. After the verdict and sentence late in the forenoon the Judge's Marshal sought out Jas and asked if he would wait on His Honour in his chambers. They lingered so long over the vintage port after lunch together that the Court did not sit again that day.

A part of the C-in-C's duties which devolved on me was to ensure that he was given the opportunity to carry out an annual sea inspection of each flagship and flotilla-leader in the Fleet. One Captain(D)'s destroyer was only available for inspection during a visit to Norway. It meant sailing out at 0700 to allow time to steam down the Fjord and out into international waters, where a full programme of exercises with aircraft and a submarine awaited him. The Captain(D) was an old-school salt-horse, not known for his abstinence from any of the good things in life. We awaited C-in-C's verdict as he returned grim-faced on board the flagship after twelve hours at sea. He motioned us down to the cuddy.

'How did it go?'

'On the whole very well. There was just one incident. On our way down the fjord at 0900 I accepted the Captain's offer of a cup of tea; if so, would I prefer China or Indian? When I said Indian without milk, he replied a trifle too quickly that he never drank anything but China tea himself. The Maltese Chief Steward duly appeared with two silver trays each with a teapot and fluted cups. Taking one sip of mine I handed the tray and teapot to Captain (D).

'"I think I have yours, Lee-Barber." We exchanged cups without a word. He did not blink and eye as he sank his brandy and ginger ale and I made do with the tepid Indian.'

He then ordered his Flag Lieutenant to make a signal to Captain (D). All it said was: 'Manoeuvre well executed.' But Johnny Lee-Barber knew well that his ploy had been rumbled.

Jas always supported his staff to the bitter end when they were acting in his name. One of our difficult customers was the Flag Officer Aircraft Carriers who preferred to act as if his command was outside the jurisdiction of the C-in-C's staff unless they were embarked for exercises. He took exception to some part of the programme issued for a forthcoming cruise and sent a signal saying that he would prefer to do it his way. At the time we were on a visit to Rotterdam. The C-in-C sent a signal to the Carrier Admiral ordering him to report on board at 0900 next day.

A long-winded reply timed at 1305 inferred that someone might have had the sense to draw the C-in-C's attention to the fact that the Aircraft Carrier Squadron was then at Gibraltar for independent exercises, so it would be inconvenient for its Flag Officer to wait on C-in-C in Rotterdam.

The C-in-C read through the signal and sent his reply: 'Your 291305A. Make it convenient.' The chastened Rear Admiral was piped over the side on his way back to his own flagship 1000 miles away by 0930 next day.

Whilst in Scandinavian waters later that summer we received an unexpected signal from the Admiralty announcing that USS *Nautilus* would be visiting NW European waters and that she was put at the disposal of the Home Fleet for a week's exercises of our own devising, starting from Plymouth Sound. Our outline plan for Operation 'Rum Tub' was then fired off. It envisaged the nuclear submarine making a long submerged passage west-about Ireland to end up in the NW approaches, after which there would be a wash-up in the Joint Anti-Submarine School at Londonderry. She was to run the gauntlet of other dived submarines, then through a barrier of sono-buoys laid by Shackletons of RAF Coastal Command into the path of the best hunter-killer escort groups we had. From time to time she was to declare her presence by firing a green grenade from deep to simulate a torpedo attack. The last phase broke new ground. It involved USS *Nautilus* acting as part of the screen for our aircraft carrier HMS *Bulwark* who would be attacked by other submarines. Depth separation provided our own safety measure. We wrote into the orders that there should be an RN observer on board *Nautilus* throughout. Thus I became the first non-American to spend more than a few hours at sea in a nuclear submarine.

Before she arrived, having crossed under the North Pole en route, our plans to give *Nautilus* a weekend run ashore in Belfast after the exercise were abruptly countermanded by the Admiralty. Due to the risk of a nuclear accident anywhere near a populated area, *Nautilus* could only anchor over 3 miles away from any city and then with a tug in permanent attendance. The very idea of a Dockyard paddlewheel tug towing the world's first nuclear submarine out to sea after a melt-down in her reactor puzzled us, observing that she secured alongside in New London just like any other submarine and had already berthed in New York.

So we surfaced off the Foyle at the end of 'Rum Tub' and were winched off by helicopter to attend the wash-up. Whilst on board I had to wear a small square brooch called a 'dosimeter' which was to be checked at intervals for any unusual level of radiation to which I had been exposed. By mistake I took mine ashore and was hastened by signal to return it. Before doing so I took it to the sickbay and got them to shoot some X-rays at it. The surgeon in *Nautilus* had the last laugh, when a priority signal was read out at the end of the presentation to several hundred of those who had been involved in 'Rum Tub'. It read:

'Analysis of dosimeter worn by Commander Coote reveals unacceptable levels of radiation exposure. Please arrange one gallon sample of his urine to be shipped to USS *Nautilus* for further checks soonest.'

The most remarkable part of the whole operation was her success as a dived escort for HMS *Bulwark*, a role which she had never before contemplated, let alone rehearsed. She had no difficulty holding her station on the screen and easily detected the only two enemy submarines which came within the range of her sonar.

For once the C-in-C did not ask his staff to draft a report on the operation but wrote his own report to the First Sea Lord, Admiral of the Fleet the Earl Mountbatten. He said:

'. . . we have no counter to the *Nautilus*. This has, of course, been in our minds for some time, but the manner in which our fears were confirmed . . . had a most disturbing, perhaps demoralizing effect. . . . Just as soon as she developed her full capabilities she had the freedom of the seas.

'The impact on the Fleet and Coastal Command is great. We feel that the only answer to a nuclear submarine is another one; and that, if the US programme is any guide, time is not on our side.'

213

He ended by suggesting that I should address the Naval Staff and those then planning our first nuclear submarine, HMS *Dreadnought*, on the lessons learned from 'Rum Tub', but I was never called upon to do so.

Next to the Chief of Staff – a forgettable Rear Admiral who got the job by default – the most important member was the Captain of the Fleet, responsible for administration, discipline and ceremonial. Captain Viscount Kelburn was a signalman of the old school who had risen to his present position after being sent to a Yangtze river gunboat as a Sub-Lieutenant to break off an unsuitable liaison with a married woman, then been Flag Lieutenant to a succession of Commanders-in-Chief. His job on the Home Fleet staff should have started each morning by being on the quarterdeck with the Commander-in-Chief for the ceremonial of hoisting the Colours at 0800 or an hour later in winter. At that moment stiff signals should have been fired off by him addressed to any ships in company who had not conformed with the flagship's movements in switching off anchor lights, unfrapping awnings and generally preened themselves to be above visible reproach. However, at that moment, the Captain of the Fleet was often not to be seen, having left word with his servant to wake him much later with a Horse's Neck. Jas tolerated this because David Kelburn was an urbane, witty companion on whom the Commander-in-Chief could depend to come up trumps on big quasi-diplomatic occasions, such as entertaining the King of Sweden on board or placating the Gaullist French NATO area commanders. All that remained of his family's considerable fortunes was Kelburn Castle near Largs. The rest had been dissipated building cathedrals in the wilds of Scotland. Any visit by the flagship to the Clyde included a golf match at the family seat, a mediaeval castle at Fairlie, and drinks with his father, the diminutive 8th Earl of Glasgow, a retired Captain in the Navy whose harmless outlet away from his strapping wife Hyacinthe was to head south to vote against the admission of Lady peeresses to the House of Lords.

We came across a Nissen hut in the woods which did not contain garden machinery as expected, but three genuine Maori war canoes given to his immediate forebears on their departure after completing their tours as Governor General of New Zealand. Another who was to follow in their footsteps was his cousin by marriage, Bernard Fergusson, the monocled Chindit leader in Burma. At that time he commanded a Highland Infantry Brigade based in Dover. Their summer manoeuvres that year were planned to take place in Norfolk. Over dinner at White's, David and his cousin thought it a good idea to add an amphibious dimension by having some ships of the Home Fleet take part in this exercise to put the soldiers ashore over the beaches where Nelson played as a lad. I duly sent a signal declaring our intentions to the Admiralty, following a pro forma which required at the outset that we declare a two-word code-name for the exercise. 'Jock Strap' seemed screamingly appropriate over the brandy, but the GOC Eastern Command protested at its vulgarity and flippancy. However Operation 'Jock's Trap' got past him and must be on the records somewhere. The Admiralty approved this ad hoc combined operation, so long as it could be accomplished within the Home Fleet's published programme and without any substantial on-cost to our fuel bills. In the event we diverted a cruiser from Rotterdam and sent a destroyer back on its tracks from Hamburg without anyone noticing, except those Norfolk farmers who were able to lodge huge claims in compensation for having their harvests flattened by Jocks swarming roughshod over their fields.

When David became the 9th Earl on the death of his father, we often stayed at Kelburn. By this time he had remarried, most happily to Vanda Becher who shared his sense of humour and all his tastes, including smoking cigars. She did an elegant job of refurbishing the Castle and making it a comfortable home for David, not to mention the American paying-guests they took in to make ends meet. Breakfast followed the traditional routine in Scottish baronial halls: prayers read by the Earl with all the staff kneeling around a side-table, followed by porridge taken standing from wooden bowls whilst the bills from Harrods and Berry Brothers were opened and the agony columns of *The Times* skimmed through. The faithful butler who had served the family since boyhood, interrupted only by war service in a Highland regiment, was apt to be found still on his knees at the table, sound asleep, after having matched his master dram for dram in the pantry into the wee hours.

Another day we were still at breakfast when the butler came in and said that 'the man from London' had arrived. It turned out to be a specialist from Ardente, the hearing-aid people, who had come to adjust the late 8th Earl's appliance to suit the cook.

★ 22 ★

AWAY AT A MEETING

The time came for Jas to leave. At the time the flagship was in dry dock in Portsmouth. Since I had meetings to attend in the Admiralty the next day, I made my way to the cuddy to bid farewell to the great man the evening before. There was a power cut and I found him alone in a darkened cabin. For once he did not hide his feelings:

'If you're not a member of the club, it's better to go,' he said, making his meaning very clear. He did not enjoy his retirement for long. He had a small flat in Petty France, and I sometimes met him dining alone in a nearby steakhouse, clearly sickening for a terminal illness.

The new C-in-C could not be in starker contrast. William Welclose Davis had served Admiral Mountbatten as his Deputy in the Mediterranean Fleet and then as Vice-Chief of the Naval Staff. He had the manner and appearance of an Archdeacon with a lot of mileage on him. His friends said that he had burnt out during his exacting time as VCNS, as which he had day-to-day responsibility for every last detail of running the Royal Navy and planning its future, whilst his Chief, the First Sea Lord, took care of ceremonial and the political in-fighting. The job had killed off stronger men than our new C-in-C.

His arrival coincided with shifting our flag to another, even more spacious, depot ship, HMS *Tyne*. Her Flag Captain was none other than John Stevens, the relaxed submariner immortalized by his dictum in the Rothesay Attack Teacher that 'the DA is always 10 degrees'. We also acquired a new Chief of Staff, Rear Admiral Hector MacLean, a kind and amusing man to serve, always ready with quick sensible decisions after the groundwork had been delegated.

In pre-war days the Home Fleet always cruised to the West Indies during worst months of the winter. So, in mid-January, 1958, we headed sou'westerly, accompanied by the carrier HMS *Bulwark*, a cruiser, flagship of the eight destroyers we could muster, a couple of Royal Fleet Auxiliary tankers (one of them with the C-in-C's wife embarked) and four unseen submarines scheduled to join later. Everywhere we went marked the end of an era. In Kingston, Jamaica, the Governor presided over an establishment scarcely changed since Nelson's day. The Queen was still recognized as Head of State in many of the islands, the English cricket team still had an even chance of winning, most of the big firms had their head offices in London, tourism was geared to the needs of the Brits, the property developers were just beginning to lick their lips, and, English Harbour apart, we saw few yachts. We spent a leisurely time visiting as many of the islands as possible. At each capital city the Royal Marines Band stole the show, Beating Retreat along the main street, timing their show to end with the ceremony of Sunset and all the ships being simultaneously floodlit. None of those outline circuits used by the Americans and lesser navies, with popping lightbulbs and gaps like missing ducks in a shooting gallery, but a beautifully smooth wash of warm light showing every detail of the ship's elevation. The Royal Marine musicians, surely the most hardworking members of the Fleet, would then reappear with mostly stringed instruments, playing for a Reception on the quarterdeck under its striped ceremonial awning.

We were not as practised in such ceremonial as the pre-war Fleet which William Davis had grown up in thirty years earlier, but the nostalgia and the impact on the locals was as strong as ever.

I made the 125-mile journey from Barbados to Bequia along the Trade Winds as part of a race for all the 27ft Admiralty whalers we could muster. Unlike those hanging from davits on destroyers which were in constant use as seaboats, no one could remember when the flagship's was last afloat. We had barely cleared Georgetown harbour when it was apparent that the hot sun had opened up all her strakes. We paid the penalty by bailing all the way across. It didn't seem so bad with the seawater temperature close to 80 degrees. After dusk there was a full moon which caught a silvery glimpse of flying fish coming over the phosphorescence like small missiles, homing in, not by infrared sensors, but on the moonlight illuminating our sails by back-projection.

All the whalers beached on Admiralty Bay at the south end of Bequia, where we had an early barbecue breakfast. The first warning that we had of the Fleet's arrival for the regatta was a helicopter passing overhead with a 2CV Citroen slung underneath it. That was the personal vehicle of Percy Gick, the flamboyant captain of *Bulwark*, no doubt with the postman and the wardroom messman embarked.

The swanning part of the Cruise ended at Bermuda with one last glorious thrash. This centred around a match race for sixteen 14ft dinghies aside between our ships and the Squadron of the Royal Canadian Navy which had come down from Halifax to join us in some serious operational exercises. There was a buffet lunch on the quarterdeck of HMS *Tyne* between morning and afternoon races, at which we were to be joined by the Earl of Selkirk, then First Lord of the Admiralty, and some of his staff. I have a home movie of the event, for which we dressed up my assistant John Gordon-Nixon in a reefer jacket, white trews, wing collar, black tie, lanyard, a painfully tight-fitting old-fashioned yachting cap and pipeclayed telescope. He was introduced to the First Lord as Commodore of the Royal Bermuda Yacht Club. The real Commodore went along with the deception which went right through to the prize-giving on the lawn of the Yacht Club after they had jointly followed the racing in our C-in-C's barge. Geordie Selkirk thanked 'the Commodore' for his wonderful hospitality, whilst Nickers responded with a graceful speech saying how welcome visits by the Royal Navy always were. They were to use the clubhouse as their own whenever they came again. His cover was not blown until he called for champagne all round at 'his' expense. Needless to say, David Kelburn, who'd been at school with the First Lord, was in on the act from the beginning. Mercifully the C-in-C was away for the day on a game-fishing picnic with the Governor.

The final leg of the Cruise was Operation 'Maple Leaf', a joint carrier and anti-submarine exercise carried out along the rhumb-line to Halifax. The operational staff embarked on HMS *Bulwark* who had, amongst others, a top squadron of Sea Vixens, twin-boomed jet interceptors. They had already lost one aircraft during a night catapult launch. I was on the Flag Bridge in the middle of the night to witness a second. The aircraft shot off the end of the catapult evidently with lots of power and simply flew into the sea just ahead of us. It was just awash as the ditched aircraft swept close down our starboard side. I looked down to see the pilot and observer sitting in the cockpit, staring up at me an instant from death. One of them was the Squadron C.O., a fine officer and without equal as a pilot at the time. Later the cause was identified as a malfunctioning cockpit instrument, perhaps the artificial horizon or one indicating rate of climb, causing a highly skilled pilot to fly a perfectly airworthy aircraft into the drink. It was not the first time my thoughts went back to Whale Island parade-ground during the Sub-Lieutenants' courses when I narrowly averted being conscripted as aircrew.

Back in the UK in time for the start of the Flat, the new C-in-C put on his NATO hat and took a small staff with him in HMS *Birmingham* to exchange visits with the governments and naval commanders of three Sub-Area Commands within the Eastern Atlantic. As far as I was concerned, it meant a perplexing meeting conducted with icy politeness by the French Admiral at Brest who was under orders from le Grand Charles himself not to speak or even give the impression of understanding a word of English. So the agenda was dealt with by each side speaking his own language, without the benefit of simultaneous translation. It was all rather pointless, for it was obvious that no joint plans could be safely drawn up because, if and when called upon, the French would do as de Gaulle pleased.

Our next stop was to visit the Commander IBERLANT, a Portuguese Admiral responsible for the seas around his country. His contribution in forces afloat would hardly turn the tide when World War III broke out, but he controlled the all-important airfields in the Azores, straddling our planned Atlantic convoy routes. He also entertained with panache in an 18th century palace perched high on a rock at Sintra, 20 miles west of Lisbon. At one time it was the king's summer palace and had Byron in lodgings nearby. The view was breathtaking, overlooking miles of vineyards from which most of the grapes to make deliciously fresh vinho verde is still shifted in ox-carts or even in pitchers on the heads of young girls. The formal business was soon disposed of, before a long leisurely lunch in the cool, mirrored rooms of the palace. I learnt that their senior officers need never retire, although they were usually allowed to moonlight as businessmen in order to sustain an appropriate life-style. One Admiral present was a senior partner on the Lisbon Stock Exchange. He was 75 years of age.

Next stop was Casablanca, naval base of the MAROCLANT sub-area. Whilst its Commander was a French Admiral, our C-in-C came to pay his respects to King Mahommed V in his palace at Rabat. First we had the Crown Prince Hassan to lunch on board HMS *Birmingham* with the British Ambassador present. Our guest, then just turned 20, turned up in a Bentley Continental exactly 2 hours late, offering neither explanation nor apology. The Ambassador kept us amused with gossip whilst the whole day's crowded programme slid out of control to the right. It seemed that the Crown Prince, with the figure and arrogant style of a matador, had been antipathetic towards all senior naval officers since he did time as a Midshipman in the French Navy and was subjected to the various indignities which they felt were necessary to beat him into shape.

Lunch barely over, we had to drive like maniacs to catch up on the most important event of the visit, as guests of the King to a

Command Performance of verse and song in his palace at Rabat. We were repeatedly told that this treatment was reserved for those to whom His Majesty wished to do special honour. Darkness fell over the ruined palace where we sat on deep cushions sipping mint tea for over three hours whilst the show droned on, no doubt turning on our hosts' carnal fantasies, but atonal and incomprehensible gibberish to us.

It seems that most of the rest of the year was spent briefing and supporting William at successive meetings all over the Western World, long on protocol and ceremonial but short on substance.

After doing the rounds of Washington and Norfolk, Va., we flew back to Gibraltar for a Sunday night stopover in the flagship, which was then in dry dock, before going on to Malta for staff talks there. I had little time in which to be brought up to date in the affairs of the Fleet, so, after the usual buffet and movie, I moved to my cabin with my Assistant to check through outstanding matters. Our office was on the same deck but much further forward, access to it late at night being hindered by sailors' hammocks slung in the flat outside. As was our normal practice, the last thing at night one of us collected the signal traffic from a wooden box by the office door. On this occasion Nickers said he wanted to go ashore to use the heads, which involved going over the forward brow. On his way he was to pick up the late signals. Scarcely quarter of an hour later he was back in my cabin, where we finished off the Jack Daniels I had brought back from the States.

Early next morning the flagship Commander told me that allegations had been made over breakfast by two members of the Boats' Crews mess that a bald-headed member of the staff had interfered with them whilst they were asleep in their hammocks. The Leading Hand of the Mess reported the matter. As Nickers was the only bald-headed member of the Staff except for the Chief of Staff, it was my painful duty to confront him. His denial was categorical, but he accepted that a formal enquiry was inevitable. It fell to me then to relieve him of his passport and turn him over to the Commander.

It should be said that he was the most popular member of the Staff and a dedicated naval officer. His dilettante manner bordered on the effete, but that was his style. He had a great sense of humour and a soothing way with women, especially when he deployed his skills as a gourmet cook in their kitchens. He was at once a favourite guest and the perfect Flag Lieutenant, as he had been on the South Atlantic Station for the last C-in-C we had there. During a summer leave period whilst we were secured alongside in Portsmouth and readily accessible by telephone to the busybodies in the Operations

Division in the Admiralty, I heard him tell our office Yeoman one day to inform any callers that the Fleet Operations Officer was away at a meeting, whilst his Assistant was also not available, being on a course. Since we were both at Goodwood Races, it was literally true.

On my return from Malta a few days later the tumbril had been rolled out, and Nickers awaited court-martial. The President of the Court was Captain John Frewin of HMS *Eagle*, renowned for his incisive, uncompromising mind. The prosecutor was John Stevens, our Flag Captain, whose heart was perhaps not in the matter, since he regarded the accused as a personal friend.

The Chief of Staff had an old golfing partner from Norfolk fly out to lead the defence. He was no ordinary lawyer but one of the top silks of the day, part of the prosecuting team at the Nuremberg trials, then a leading Crown Counsel at the Old Bailey before becoming Common Serjeant in the City of London. Mervyn Griffith-Jones was unmoved by the President's line of enquiry or his unexpected grasp of the law, concentrating instead on the fact that the two accusations did not amount to supporting corroborative evidence, since the events they described were separated by time and distance to an extent which would make a conviction unsafe.

It ended like a sequel to *The Winslow Boy*. The sword in front of the President lay untouched as he pronounced a formal 'Not Guilty' verdict. The C-in-C, in full uniform, greeted Nickers back on board the quarterdeck to congratulate him. As it happens he had already been appointed elsewhere, so we let him go early the next day. He left with a glowing report and every prospect of promotion to Commander, which he duly achieved two years later after he had been further reported on by another Flag Officer.

From then on it was all downhill for the unhappy Nickers. After the Vassall case the appointing authority in the Admiralty let slip that he was regarded as a security risk and could not hold any appointment involving access to classified material, no matter how innocuous. So he was left to rot in a job in a Reserve Group of laid-up ships at Devonport, then took the hint and sought early retirement under one of the Golden Bowler schemes. The man who had added the supplementary sentence of disgrace, which flew in the face of the court-martial verdict, had for long professed to be a close family friend. I suspect he was fearful of what impact that friendship might have on his own career, for which he had high and, I am happy to say, not entirely realized expectations.

Nickers retired to become a professional fund-raiser, which he excelled at, but his thoughts were never far from the Service he so passionately wished to serve. He got a job in Haslemere to act for the Elizabeth Fitzroy Homes for mentally handicapped children. Whilst looking for digs he booked in for a weekend with us. Six months later he left. As far as we were concerned he could have stayed for ever, but he set up home nearby with an old friend who'd already buried two husbands and was desperately in need of cheering up. 'The Poor House' in Buriton was as happy and comfortable a home as either of them ever had, always full of witty, if thirsty, playmates.

The village church was packed to overflowing for his funeral after cancer carried him off swiftly at the age of 60. The names of those attending read appropriately like a guest list for a Reception at Admiralty House.

★ 23 ★

THE PRICE OF PROMOTION

I was then abruptly pitched into another world on being appointed as Executive Officer of the 11,000 ton, 6-inch cruiser HMS *Bermuda*, with a complement of 52 officers and 650 ratings. It was a Navy which I thought had disappeared in 1939, with the emphasis on her smart external appearance not being disturbed by such irrelevances as firing the main armament.

We were to recommission at Devonport. A small advance party of key personnel joined her a few days earlier, making her ready to receive the whole of the rest of the ship's company from the Barracks. The Watch and Quarter Bill was prepared, mess tables and spots for slinging and stowing hammocks allocated and the first set of Daily Orders distributed from the Commander's Office, which was run for me by a handful of officers and men who, unlike me, knew what they were up to.

At 1100 the entire ship's company were fallen in by Divisions on the parade ground and inspected by the Commodore of the Barracks. Men with bleached pale blue collars or caps which had been bashed out of shape had their names added to the Master-at-Arms' first Shit List. Then they shouldered their kitbags and hammocks and marched behind our Royal Marine band the short distance down to the jetty alongside which our new home awaited us. Greeting the crew as they filed on board over the brow was the first pipe (an order preceded by a warning note on the boatswain's call) for 'Up Spirits', followed by 'Hands to Dinner'. Each broadside mess table had all its cutlery and utensils laid out, all drawn new from the Victualling Yard. The cooks had a hot meal ready for issue from the galley of roast beef, two veg, gravy and clacker and duff.

On the jetty it was now peaceful. My new Captain was a Gunnery Officer whom I'd never met, but I knew that he had survived serving under the unforgiving martinet Captain Philip Vian in *Cossack*. We walked along the jetty for some time, whilst he gently pointed out various deficiencies in the ship's external appearance, from slack signal halyards to discrepancies in the elevation of our gun barrels and a wisp of smoke appearing out of one of our funnels. He had just got through a searching catechism about how I proposed to run various evolutions which quickly made me realize that there was going to be plenty of scope for delegating my authority, when there was an unforgettable sight which made the day. As if orchestrated by a ring-master, all the remains of jolly jack's first meal were shot out of a whole row of open scuttles. Looking down into the waters of the Hamoaze we saw hundreds of shiny objects disappearing like shoals of whitebait. That at least provided me with an idea of something to do in the afternoon: order a crash muster of mess utensils on all broadside messes. Sure enough, many of them had tossed all their cutlery overboard rather than wash them up and stow them away. It never happened again, after working parties had marched to the Victualling Yard and back with replacements. Just an early taste of a dirty protest.

Our arrival at Portland gave the staff of Flag Officer Sea Training something to get their teeth into, which they did with evident relish. They were paid to make our lives miserable and they did a fine job. We became proficient in replenishing at sea by night, towing and being towed, sending away the seaboat, shooting down sleeve targets and pulverising battle practice targets which, for some reason decreed by the High Priests of the Gunnery School at Whale Island, were always moving on a steady course at walking pace and engaged by us at point-blank range. On our last day's sea inspection our examiners just about broke us by ordering every conceivable evolution to be carried out simultaneously, leaving the whole upper deck in chaos looking more like a survivor from a wartime convoy battle than a peacetime cruiser flagship. Just as we had a 13,000 ton fleet auxiliary tanker in tow, using cable broken out of our bower anchor chains and dragged all the way aft leaving greasy smears on our holystoned teak quarterdeck, I was handed a sealed envelope.

'Return to harbour forthwith and prepare to receive on board Sheikh Ali ben Ali, Ruler of Rub-a-Dubby, with full ceremonial followed by a reception on the quarterdeck.'

We were 15 miles out to sea, in total disarray, and were supposed to be in our party clothes alongside in just over an hour's time. But somehow it all came together. As the first heaving line snaked on to the jetty, the quarterdeck awning flew up, the Royal Marine guard and band paraded, the Maltese stewards set up their bars and the Captain stood beside me with sword and medals. The

Sea Training staff were easily recognizable in their *Desert Song* flowing robes and roped headgear. The Royal Marines played a heavily accented version of *Colonel Bogey* as their national anthem whilst the Sheikh inspected our Guard. Our tormentors then got their come-uppance by being served soft drinks and sheeps' eyes (hard boiled eggs wrapped in some nauseous membrane) whilst we tucked into a few very well-earned tots of the hard stuff.

At the end of it all, I had to confess that, surprisingly, I had enjoyed it all. So did the officers and men. Perhaps I should have seen more of that side of the Navy. Perhaps, like training for the Field Guns' crews at the Royal Tournament, it had its place even in the nuclear navy.

The Wardroom were a happy lot, although Their Lordships had confused matters by appointing no less than seven executive Lieutenant-Commanders, all deep in the zone for promotion. With the best will in the world we could not hope to get them all promoted, so at least two of them got passed over who might otherwise have caught the selector's eye. Happily David Farquharson, an ex-submariner who had considerable surface-ship time behind him and was now First Lieutenant under me, was one of the first to get his brass hat. The Sergeants' Mess (other Commanders, such as those responsible for the Supply, Engineering, Medical and Electrical departments) were all agreeable, supportive shipmates. We were blessed with the best padre in the Fleet, Richard Knight, an old-school sin-bosun straight out of a Hardy novel who loved his tot. He always arranged one unofficial group run-ashore at each major foreign port for delinquent sailors under long-term stoppage of leave. He never let me down. Off Greenland he organized the best ship's concert I ever attended. Unhappily he was struck down by cancer and died soon afterwards. I drove down to Tavistock for his funeral, but didn't find the church until after it was all over. I confess to weeping alone at his graveside.

We then joined the Fleet and were caught up in a programme of showing the flag and NATO exercises.

The high point of the commission was to embark our Ambassador to Denmark and their Minister responsible for overseas territories to visit the Faeroes and Greenland. The latter involved stops at Godhavn well inside the Arctic Circle, Godthab and Ivigtut, the biggest open-cast bauxite mine in the world, managed by a handful of Danish executives living in Hollywood-style split-level bungalows. We had embarked some special stores for them, books, LP records, films, cigars from Dunhills and various goodies from Fortnum and Mason. They were all unloaded by our crane into one of the mining company's tenders. I watched bemused as one of the cargo slings parted and gently slid a load of cases of Dom Perignon into the deep icy waters of the fjord.

We hastily rustled up all the bubbly we had in our Wardroom wine store, but it was poor consolation for the Danes. Next day a volunteer diver went down and recovered the whole consignment from where it had lain at 120 feet exposed to seawater pressure of over 50lbs per sq.inch in a temperature barely above freezing. I opened a bottle on the quarterdeck. Champagne never tasted so good. The Danes were delighted and insisted we kept a case for the Wardroom.

Next stop, straight from the fog and ice of the Davis Straits, was Bermuda, 2,500 miles south. Our visit was timed to coincide with the 350th anniversary of the shipwrecked survivors who first settled the colony. Mercifully the Gulf Stream was quiet, for we had to heave to and paint ship overall at sea to cover up the depredations of the Arctic. It was all right on the day. The ship looked perfect as we steamed through the Cut with not a hair out of place and the band playing to berth alongside the front in Hamilton.

There we stayed for a week which called for hidden reserves of stamina. The locals pulled out all the stops, for once remembering that an Able Seaman's disposable income would not run to more than half-a-dozen beers a week at Bermuda prices. Stanhope and Gladys Joel opened the batting for the Wardroom by taking over the whole Waterlot Inn in Southampton, with the best of everything, from booze to sun-kissed blondes and seductive music.

One event loomed dark on my horizon. The highlight of the official anniversary was to be a parade and march past of all Service units on the island, led by our band and entire ship's company. Planning for that was handed over to Peter Nichol, our Gunnery Officer and, by definition, O.C. Ceremonial. Late in the day the Captain broke it to me that I was to take charge of the whole parade, and, worse still, lead the march past. Although I had a sword, it had never come out of its scabbard except to cut the cake at my wedding. To ask me to salute the Governor with drawn sword on the march was equivalent to suggesting that I should fly as wing-man with the Red Arrows. So, at 0600 each morning, only about an hour after I had returned on board, Peter used to take me to a secluded beach and teach me the drill, using taped martial music to get each movement timed in step. Somehow, I stumbled through, thinking always of Snorkers' relatively trifling ordeal at the Oban Games on Coronation Day.

At the end of the visit I had planned to fly home to skipper *Griffin*

II in the Fastnet Race as part of the British Admiral's Cup Team. But permission was refused on the grounds that there was a Royal Visit to Canada in progress and we had been detailed by the C-in-C to act as plane-guard in mid-Atlantic whilst the Queen flew home. Just what we were supposed to do if the Royal Flight ditched from 30,000 feet I never discovered, but I hope it was some comfort for the Queen to know that there was a cruiser waiting down below to mark the spot.

As we steamed up-Channel in poor visibility about 10 miles south of the Lizard we came across a familiar yacht. I got on the Aldis and called her. Sure enough it was *Griffin II* with my crew on board, now skippered by Gerald Potter who should have been the RORC's first choice anyway. He sailed a superlative race, beaten only by Sven Hansen's beautiful new Sparkman and Stevens yawl *Anitra*. After the Fastnet, Gerald invited Sven to stop off at Brixham on her way home to Copenhagen. Dinner was a black tie affair at Greenmarch. After midnight Ginny drove them down to the Brixham Yacht Club steps from which three of them embarked in *Anitra* for a nightcap. She resigned herself to a long wait in the car. But life with Gerald was never wholly predictable. Even when the yawl slipped and motored out of the harbour, she thought they would be heading for the Dart. As it was, the next stop was Copenhagen, over 1,000 miles away. They seem to have lived on a diet of hardboiled eggs, ham and cheese, washed down by aquavit. So the 'Let's-sail-now Yacht Squadron' enrolled four new members.

On New Year's Eve, 1959, I was selected for promotion to Captain, the day before our departure to refit at Gibraltar. The promotion did not take effect until June, 1960, the delay having been introduced to enable the Naval Secretary to make orderly arrangements to relieve those Commanders selected and appoint them to Captain's billets.

As we sailed south it did not occur to me to lobby for my next appointment, although it was apparent later that the other newly-selected Captains had wasted no time in beating a path to the Naval Secretary's door. The refit moved slowly towards completion. We played a lot of hockey and often went for weekends to the new Guadalamina Golf hotel, then only one building and with seven holes playable. Sotogrande did not exist, Estepona and Torremolinos were no more than a string of fishermen's cottages along the beach. José Banus had not been dreamed of.

Finally in April I got a letter from the Naval Secretary suggesting that I call on him next time I was in Town. I replied pointing out that I had been in Gibraltar since the first week in January and would not normally be in London until after I handed over to my relief early in May. However, I took the opportunity of stating my preference for command of the Dartmouth Training Squadron or any other frigate squadron. The reply said that all the jobs I fancied had been snapped up by early birds, so how about going on the staff of the NATO Defence College, then based in Paris? David Kelburn had been in the job not long before and enjoyed in hugely, so I accepted. A few weeks later it was all off and I was booked to be Captain of the Dockyard in Singapore which, in spite of the house and servants which went with it, did not sound like the fast lane to the Admiralty Board. I was booked to relieve an officer considerably senior to me who was on the Dry List – not qualified for command at sea. Notwithstanding everything, we resolved to take the job and the challenge it represented, which was not dissimilar to a young high-flyer on the head-office planning staff of Lloyds Bank being sent as manager of their Freetown branch. A date was set. We arranged to let our house and placed our girls into boarding schools.

Then the phone rang. It was the Naval Secretary informing me briskly that my departure from England was to be delayed by six months. It seems that he had just realized that I was relieving an unaccompanied bachelor officer who was permitted that much longer in his appointment, which his Admiral had insisted upon. To fill in the gap I was to do the Senior Officers' War Course at Greenwich, a six months' general indoctrination course intended to focus attention on the world beyond the Navy List and the Queen's Regulations and Admiralty Instructions. I was immediately aware of the serious financial impact of the cost of my new domestic arrangements not being offset by the allowances which went with the job in Singapore.

My eyes and thoughts were already fixed on alternate possibilities. That summer I got leave to take part in the 1960 Newport - Bermuda and Transatlantic Races in Max Aitken's 58-ft sloop *Drumbeat*. After a few wild days at 'Idle Rocks', his home on Point Shares, Bermuda, Max headed for London, leaving Gerald Potter in charge for the race to Sweden. The island's Governor at the time was an old Grenadier friend of Gerald's, General Sir Julian Gascoigne, so we had to conform by attendance at all the official functions in the dress of the day, which was reefer jackets, RORC ties, white straw hats, Bermuda shorts and long white stockings. On Sunday four of us set off in Joe's taxi – on permanent hire throughout our stay – to attend the Yachtsmen's service in the cathedral where the Governor and the Commodore of the Cruising Club of America were to read the lessons. The church was packed to overflowing and it was stiflingly hot. Half-way through the first lesson, which was read by an unspecified member of the congregation, I noticed that none of the hymns advertised seemed to have much relevance to the sea. Joe, our cheerful ex-con, round-the-clock, no-questions-asked driver had delivered us to the wrong church.

Soon after Bermuda dropped out of sight astern on the race to Sweden we were in the Gulf Stream with strong following seas and sou'westerlies gusting up to force 7. On the third night out I was watch captain at the midnight turn of the watch with the wind moderating all the time. I decided to reset the 2.2 oz. bullet-proof spinnaker in place of the boomed-out genoa. I sat on Malcolm Sargent's piano-stool – a launching present for *Drumbeat* from the maestro – steering her easily enough by a bright star over the peak of the opaque triangle of our sail plan. At the time she was a broaching bitch; with her centreboard housed she only had a 4 ft. deep canoe-body to give her any semblance of stability whilst steering down wind. On the stroke of midnight two things happened: I felt a heavy blow on my right shoulder as though taken by a high tackle playing West Country rugger; and the dark triangle of our sails folded sedately away from me, leaving the eastern horizon beautifully illuminated by stars. All hands appeared on deck. None of them was properly night-adapted, having been aroused from deep sleep into white cabin lighting. Some nearly went overboard, reaching for guardrails which were no longer there.

Our new metal mast had folded over at a point seven feet above the deck, leaving its upper sixty feet hanging over the port side with the boom and heavy-duty new terylene mainsail attached. There was still a considerable sea running, and the boat was slamming against the submerged mast, threatening to stave in even our massively-built teak hull. The foot of the main was cut off the boom and was thus free to disappear into Davy Jones's locker, when, two hours and innumerable hacksaw blades later, we finally sawed through the mast and the whole lot slid away from us. An Extraordinary Meeting of the Sorry Max Club, as we called those of us who for various reasons added to the annual cost of campaigning his ocean-racers, called for three cheers and a tot of Duty Free Barbados rum all round from our huge stock at 4 shillings (20 pence new money) a litre.

At first light, a few hours later, we reviewed the scene. The cause of the dismasting was soon apparent. Her single preventer backstay, which carried a radio antenna along its length, had a ceramic insulator let in just above the transom. It was secured by a Talurit splice, whereby the two parts of a wire rope were bonded together by a copper ring slipped over them and squeezed together by a hydraulic press. Unfortunately the point of the critical splice had first been parcelled by light muslin and twine, so that the essential metal-to-metal bonding never took place. The ceramic insulation, which was the size of a promising coconut, had whipped forward under full load, missing the back of my head by inches. What a way to go, I thought, after having survived so many more obvious risks throughout the war. When the *Daily Express* ran the story, mentioning the failure of the Talurit splice, several shifts of miners refused to go down in their cages.

During the day we rigged up a 23 ft. spinnaker pole as a jury mast and then set a small light headsail sideways, led from a point on our weather bow with its clew right aft. We were under control and making about 4 knots, equidistant between Bermuda and Newfoundland, but not far short of 2,000 miles from England. With the Gulf Stream and prevailing sou'westerlies, we could have managed the long way home but for two determining factors: John Rainforth, one of our gorillas and a rugger player of repute, had to go to a wedding in less than 3 weeks' time which he did not fancy missing – his own. The other determining argument was that we knew that *Drumbeat*'s old wooden mast was available at Cowes and that Bowater newsprint freighters made regular journeys to their paper mills in Newfoundland.

It was a further two days before we could persuade a passing ship to recognize that we were trying to communicate with the outside world. A German freighter took a written message for onward transmission to Max and also responded to my request for a chart of St John's which we exchanged for a bottle of Scotch. Heading north, the 700 miles to Newfoundland was a more favourable point of sailing for our dhow-like sailplan and we made it in six days. Entering the narrow harbour in thick fog was slightly complicated by the fact that our new chart turned out to be one for St John's, New Brunswick. Four days later the old mast arrived from London and in less than 36 hours we had it rigged and sailed, carrying a claustrophobic warm front all the way to Brixham, crossing in just under eleven days. We were in time to attend John Rainforth's wedding.

Not long afterwards, Max took me to one side and said that, if I ever felt like making a second career, he would welcome me as a management trainee to Beaverbrook Newspapers, then at the peak of its powers and professional reputation on the 'Sunny Side of the Street'. I was reluctant to throw in my lot with an industry with such a low useful working-life expectation as those on the

Express Group, but he assured me that none of that applied on the management side who tended to stick around too long. He did not mention his father's prejudice against amateurs reaching any position of responsibility in the empire he had created, especially if they were known to be friends of Max's who was permanently and quite unjustly kept under suspicion and surveillance himself.

Before throwing in my hat, I called on the Chief of Staff to the Flag Officer Submarines to see where I stood in his crystal ball. He assured me that there was nothing envisaged for me in the trade I knew something about, which hardly surprised me, because the penalty for early promotion was that I was now the same seniority as half-a-dozen others who had wartime experience in command with decorations to show for it, which I had not achieved.

So I fired off a letter to Their Lordships. I had been tipped off that the case I made had better be a good one, or I would end up as Captain of the Dockyard in Singapore with a note in my file to the effect that my loyalty and dedication to the Service were in question.

So I pleaded poverty, underlined by the recent realization that my mother, who came from a family with a fine record of reaching the finishing straight not far short of a Queen's Telegram, was not yet 70 and would be wholly dependent on me for her support after my father died. My total salary and allowances as a Captain with three children at school was £3,250.

The reply was disarmingly swift and brief. No one wanted to see me or even discuss the matter. Three weeks later I reported to the black glass building in Fleet Street.

Three years later the Royal Navy had the Polaris programme thrust upon it. The First Sea Lord and senior aviator on the Board resigned when the Strike Carrier programme was doomed in consequence. Nobody noticed.

Meanwhile, my old Captain in HMS *Bermuda* was not selected for flag rank which was further evidence of how the higher ranks of the Royal Navy were shrinking, for he had not put a foot wrong during his command. The ship was also relegated to the scrapheap, with better justification.

The change from being in uniform on a Friday and reporting as a management trainee on the following Monday gave me little time to agonize over whether I had made the right decision. Immediately there were many quick to point out the unfulfilled promise of my naval career, a disaster compounded by throwing in my lot with the gutter press. (Early on I found that more copies of the *Daily Express* were delivered to Buckingham Palace than all the other dailies put together).

Naturally I had an uneasy conscience about Sylvia, born and brought up in a naval family, staunchly convinced that my future was brighter than Their Lordships suggested by the alacrity with which they accepted my resignation. We had no option but to look on the bright side: I would never have to sit at a desk in the Admiralty, a barely moving cog in a ponderous machine dominated by civil servants who controlled the circulation of dockets on their tortuous routes to nowhere in particular; she would never have to live in a married quarter in a naval base and play the role of a senior officer's wife with so many boring social obligations.

At the time the *Express* newspaper group was the most influential and exciting of them all. Every talented young journalist in the country set his or her heart on working on the 'Sunny Side of the Street'. Most of them did. Along with the shrewdest City analysts I did not have an inkling of its fatal flaw – Beaverbrook's stubborn failure to cushion against the changing world by diversifying into other fields like ITV and North Sea oil exploration. In the process it can be argued that he dealt his son Max Aitken a well nigh unplayable hand, as he demonstrated in less than a decade after he took sole charge.

My new world suddenly had wider horizons, with stimulating daily contacts with those who made the decisions and the news in all walks of life and to be party to what lay behind the news. Top journalists are invariably good company. They have shrewd facile minds, encyclopaedic memories and single-minded concentration on the current edition until it is sent down to be set in concrete, as they say, meaning that they have to get it right first time in substance and length. Above all, they can sniff a bore or a phoney from ten paces, have a keen sense of the ridiculous and enjoy every minute of life, albeit frequently beset by wigwam problems (trouble on the domestic front). They eat and drink with effortless style, regardless of expense.

When my fifteen-year innings came to its inevitable end, there was little pain as I removed the stiletto from between my shoulder-blades. We settled in West Sussex in a 400-year-old cottage called Titty Hill Farm, soon better known to our many visitors as the Titty Hilton, equally accessible to London Airport, Cowes and Glyndebourne.

Had I not been in the Navy I would never have enjoyed the unquestioning loyalty and enduring friendships of so many ship-mates. Had I let my naval career run its course I would never have joined the Garrick. Nor would I have played video tennis at 2 a.m.

in a Third Avenue bar in New York City with Kiri te Kanawa, flown to Le Touquet with Douglas Bader to play golf with Sean Connery and King Leopold, gone to a 48-hour pop concert in a field in Lincolnshire with Stanley Baker, watched Winston Churchill's funeral with Bill Hearst, the son of Citizen Kane, sat next to Matt Busby as he explained the magic quicksilver talent of George Best at his peak, let alone flattened my birthday cake by sitting on it in Eric Swenson's *Toscana* at the height of the 1979 Fastnet storm.

To name but a few.

INDEX

Ships' names in italics (HMS unless otherwise shown)
References to illustrations also shown in italics

Geisha girls: in Kyoto, 44; in Myonoshita with USAAF General, 206
Gibraltar: seen through periscope, 191–2; during *Bermuda* refit, 227
Gick, Capt "Percy": flamboyant CO of *Bulwark*, 217
Gieves: first uniform, 48; instant uniform on D-day plus 1, 139
Golden Dragon (cutter): 1948 Dinard Race, 165; 1950 Fastnet, 166; 1952 Belle Ile Race, 1967
Good Morning: submarine daily newspaper, 56; Jane strip cartoon, 78
Gordon-Nixon, Lt-Cdr John: Asst Fleet Operations Officer doubles as Commodore, R.Bermuda YC, 218; court-martial, 220–1; funeral, 222
Gowan, Lt Paddy: Spare CO La Maddalena, 112; self-confessed Jonah on board, 115–7; patrol off Port Vendres, 128 et seq
Griffin III (cutter): 1957 Fastnet, 171; photo-finish with *Figaro* and *Carina*, 172; refused chance of 1959 Fastnet – chance meeting in Channel, 227
Griffiths-Jones, Mervyn, QC: defending in Gibraltar court-martial, 221

H.43: a dodgy training submarine, 6; memories of odd behaviour, 13; the navigator's station during attacks, 51
Hall, CPO Bob: Coxswain without equal, 181–2; at wardroom reunions, 194
Hamburg: the Reeperbahn, *36*
Hassan, Crown Prince of Morocco, 219
Haywards Heath: cramming for Navy Special Entry exam, 47
Hazzard, Ldg Cook: most popular man on board, 38
Heath, Lt Robin: Third Hand in *Totem*, 180; promotion, 188; report on, 195
Hezlet, Capt A. R. ("Baldy"), later V-Adm Sir Arthur: legendary CO, 174; planned Mediterranean surveillance operation, 192
Holy Loch: loading shells in 1943, *3*
Hunt, Cdr George: sword dance in USN wardroom, 86; top-scoring CO (see *Ultor*); as Perisher Teacher, 155

Joel, Stanhope and Gladys: their Chamoissaire wins at Newmarket, 142; generous hosts in Bermuda, 226; received on board *Bermuda*, *38*
Jolly Roger: Signalman makes one, 2; after sinking 13 ships, *4*; M. & B. tablet added, 69

Kelburn, Viscount, (Earl of Glasgow): on CinC's staff, 214; Brig Bernard Fergusson and Operation "Jock's Trap", 215; life at Kelburn Castle, 215; fun in Bermuda, 218
King, Lt. RNVR ("Gus"): in *H.43*, 13; joins *Untiring*, 15; as navigator, 53, 57, 71 et seq, 78, 103; Duty Officer on Xmas Day, 87; lookout during surface escape, 123; attack on safe-conduct ship averted, 133; decorated, 139
Knight, Richard: padre of *Bermuda*, 225
Koitschka, Oberleutnant: CO of *U-616*, 65

Lady Augusta (full-rigged ship): commanded by maternal great- grandfather, 41
La Maddalena: *Untiring* entering harbour, *5*; loading torpedoes, *6*; 10th Flotilla base after Malta, 70; billeted in ex-Italian Detention Quarters, 83; lack of fresh food, 84; RN/USN relations, 85–6; Christmas Day, 87. See Brothels.
Larne: base for advanced convoy exercises, 27; unscheduled stop of train to Belfast, 28
Lee-Barber, Capt Johnny: sea inspection by CinC, 211
Legh Light: first exposure off Gibraltar, 54
Lewin, Cdr Terry (later AF Lord Lewin): chosen as Cdr Royal Yacht, 209
Lewin, Capt J. B.: President of Gibraltar court-martial, 221
Lions, Gulf of: a gale to remember, 116
Log, Ottway: cause of *Untamed* disaster, 31; safety interlock afterthought, 34
Luce, Henry R.: shared distinction at China Inland Mission school, 43; friend of USN CinC, 178
Lucy, Lt Peter: Electrical Officer *Totem*, 180; at Oban, 182; acquires S- band search-receiver, 184–5; periscope repair under exposed conditions, 193
Lumby, Lt Cdr Michael: sunk in *Saracen*, 63, 157; hand-over of *Truncheon*, 157

Rickover, R-Adm Hyman, USN: father of nuclear navy, 201; similarities with Jacky Fisher, 202; relations with Mountbatten, 203; trust in Solly Zuckerman, 204
Roberts, Capt P. Q.: NOIC Maddalena and S.10, 84; treatment of Italian General, 85; greets *Untiring* return to harbour on horseback, 110
Rothesay Attack Teacher: 173 et seq; simplifying attack doctrine, 175-6; analysing Summer Wars, 176-7
Rouse, "Uncle": owner of *Golden Dragon*, 165-7
"Rum Tub": first RN exercise with Nautilus, 213

Sahib: lost, 63
St Leger: wedding cake mislaid, 142
St Tropez: patrolling off, 60
Saracen: lost, 63
Scud Hill: submarine officers' accommodation, Gibraltar, 53
Search-receivers: S-band 10-cm cover, 185, 190
Serica (tea-clipper): baby-sitter in Tientsin, 43
Shemara (A/S training yacht): last exercise with *Untamed*, 29
Sicié, Cap: merchantman missed, too close, 62
Simpson, Capt ("Shrimp"): as S.10 in Malta, 69
Sims, P.O.: Torpedo Gunner's Mate (T.I.) conscripted, 16
Smoking; restrictions relaxed whilst dived, 184
Snorkel: early experience in *Truncheon*, 157
Sokol (Polish submarine): news from Yalta, 125
Sphinx, Le: Algiers brothel torched, 66
Splendid: lost, 63
Staff Course: relaxing at Greenwich, 195
Stevens, Capt John: at Rothesay Attack Teacher, 175; Flag Captain to CinC Home Fleet, 216; prosecutor at Gibraltar court-martial, 221
Stickleback (USS): crew party whilst deep, *29*; W. Pacific patrol, 207; dieting contest, 207; sunk, 208
Stonington, CT: bombarded by *Warspite* in 1812, 205
Stump, Adm Felix B. USN: liaison with CinC Atlantic Fleet, 177-8; debriefing at Pearl Harbor, 208
Submarines: CO's responsibilities, 115; losses, 9; external paint, 182; volunteers, 50
Suez: invasion seen from USA, 206
Surveillance missions: advice to Prime Minister, 184; doubts resolved in W. Mediterranean, 189-192; detected during the real thing, 193; Admiralty Board unimpressed, 193; court martial for careless talk, 194; in Western Pacific, 206
Sydney: losing 24 hours on passage to Hong Kong, 151
Syson, Sylvia: marries author, *9*; wedding, 142-3; at Titty Hill Farm, *40*; consequences of my resignation, 232

Tactician: bound for Far East, 26
Talbot, HMS: shore-base of 10th Flotilla, 87
Tantalus: at Holy Loch, 9; at Larne, 26
Tempest: sunk off Taranto by *Circe* (It. frigate), 118
Terrible (Fr. destroyer class): unable to attack, 67
Tizard, Sir Henry: on night vision, 158
Totem: totem pole, *18*; fore-ends, *21*; after collision, *22*; alongside HMS Forth, *23*; Mountbatten inspecting, *24*; reunion at Garrick Club 1982, *39*; appointed in command, 179; operational characteristics, 179; collision in Medway, 188; surveillance missions, 189-93; sold to Israel, renamed *Dakar*, 195; lost at sea without totem pole, 195
Torpedo control: RN inadequacies, 155, 174, 176
Toulon: first patrol, 54
Trespasser: appointed as First Lieutenant, 142; orders for Far East cancelled, 144
Truncheon: first command, *13*; operating from Portland, 157
Turbulent: Cdr "Tubby" Linton lost, 63